SHORT SALES
& LOAN MODIFICATIONS

A Practical Guide For
Real Estate Agents and Investors

Kenneth R. Lawson, J.D.

Copyright © 2009 Kenneth R. Lawson, J.D.
All rights reserved.

ISBN: 1-4392-3737-9
ISBN-13: 9781439237373

Visit www.booksurge.com to order additional copies.

Introduction

Everything I'm going to tell you in this book is true... except when it is not. Now, that line brings a lot of chuckles, but there is more truth in that statement than you might realize, and it is easy to forget that truth. In working short sales, there are many general rules and many exceptions to those rules, so it is important to be flexible enough to adjust for those exceptions.

What should this mean to you? It means that you should go about your business following the concepts, principles, procedures, rules, and steps outlined in this book. There are so many financial entities, that you will find numerous exceptions when these entities exhibit differences in the way they process and approve short sales and loan modifications. You will often find an exception to every concept; an exception to every principle; and an exception when every procedure, rule, and series of steps may need to be adjusted to the circumstances.

Homeowners in financial trouble will respond in certain predictable ways, except when they do not. You already understand this principle in the context of real estate sales. Sellers respond to certain forms of advertising, except when they do not. They will respond to a good listing presentation, except when they do not. They will hire you, except when they will not. When they do list with you, they will be cooperative, except when they are not. If they are cooperative in the beginning, they will stay cooperative throughout the relationship, except when they do not. Even though people will conform to general rules. There are always exceptions for which you must watch and to which you must adjust.

Processing short sales and loan modifications is relatively easy, except when it is not. Once you have your systems in place, everything will proceed smoothly, except when it does not. Your solutions will work, except when they do not. You evaluate the market value of property a certain way, except when you do not. You draft the proposal in a specific format, except when you do not. You always fax the proposal to the lender, except when you do not.

You treat lenders a certain way, except when another methodology is better. You accept the word of the lender, except when it is important to not trust it.

I cannot guarantee that your short sale proposal will always meet with approval. However, I can show you how to work short sales and loan modifications from the perspective of someone who has about 20 years of experience with lending institutions and who has been an advocate for sellers. I will teach you the secrets, the methods, and the procedures, but the most important concept to remember throughout, is to always be alert for the exceptions and adjust accordingly. Never, I repeat NEVER forget this concept.

I cannot guarantee that you will become a millionaire processing short sales and loan modification, but I can teach you how to create a successful business model for short sales. I can show you how to develop business systems that are efficient and profitable. Although it is important for you to adapt any model and the systems to your own style and situation, staying as true to the model and systems as possible is advised. The reason the model is so important is that if you follow the model, it stands to reason that the results of those who developed the model will be yours. If you change the model, then you will also change the results, usually negatively.

As a business coach, I find the most difficult part of coaching is to convince business owners to follow a model for the specific business. A successful model shows the rules and steps that must be followed. If you follow the model, you should heap the rewards of the results.

Although I cannot guarantee your success, I will share with you the models, principles, procedures, steps and simple systems to make a short sale and loan modification business successful.

A lot of people have written books and establish courses for working short sales and loan modifications. Some are excellent, but many of these authors are not the experts they want you to think they are. I have attended a number of short sale seminars taught by real estate brokers and self-proclaimed "experts". I have read a number of the books. The result? I have never attended a seminar that was accurate. Oh, a fair amount of their information was accurate enough, but I discovered a great amount of bad information mixed in with the good.

Why so much inaccurate information? Many of them have been handling short sales for many years, so why would they not know what they are doing? One analogy is that many people think they know the law and how to succeed in court because they received so many speeding tickets. Gaining a lot of experience in court does not make one a lawyer.

I was standing in the back of a crowded courtroom one time and overheard two paralegals discussing their experience and knowledge. They came to the conclusion that because of the knowledge they gained in their respective law firms and through many years of experience, that they were probably 75% an attorney. From the attorneys' perspective, they are possibly 10% of the knowledge skills and experience of an attorney, if that. You see, they don't know what they don't know! They look at the great amount of knowledge they have, so they know what they *do* know, but they don't know what they do *not* know.

Another reason agents often have incorrect understanding of short sales is that many of the people in financial institutions have met so many pushy, controlling agents that they come to despise talking to them. So, they have learned the answers to give agents to put them off or merely tell them what they want to hear. So, the agents gain a lot of experience doing the wrong things, saying the wrong things, and when the bank employees give them a pat answer, the agents believe that their procedures and information are correct.

My approach is to provide you with practical knowledge of handling short sale and loan modification cases, but also to provide you with a successful short sale and loan modification business model through the information in this book, along with the *Short Sale Business Manual* available through my firm. I will provide you with both basic and advanced concepts, along with practical steps and forms to run your business, and to manage short sales and loan modifications. If that is not enough, a coach is available for you to answer questions, resolve specific issues, and guide you toward success.

There are some introductory concepts that you should learn. First, your success will depend upon how well you can keep yourself organized. I have struggled with this over the years. I know *how* to organize, but staying consistent with it is very difficult for me. In the *Short Sale Business Manual*, forms are provided that I use not only for processing short sales, but for keeping myself organized as well. In this book, I will talk about simple, practical methods for staying organized.

It is important for you to honestly evaluate yourself and accurately. Maybe you have a personality that enjoys making and utilizing checklists, filing papers, returning phone calls, setting up files, printing labels, keeping your desk cleared, organizing your day and setting aside time blocks for your various activities, making certain that you don't get carried away talking to people, and putting stuff away. I do not.

However, I do have the responsibility to carry out those activities if I do not have an assistant to do it for me. So, I have learned to develop simple systems to make the activities quicker and easier.

With good, simple, and time-saving systems, even if you slack off and get behind in organizing, you will be able to quickly catch up and get back on track. These time-saving systems mean that you can even assign and train your spouse or child to work the system for you (with appropriate rewards or pay, of course). Virtually everything you do can be simplified into systems that others can do for you, or that you can do very quickly yourself.

Another concept involves how you study and learn what is taught here. When I was in law enforcement, I attended a number of training classes in Interview & Interrogation, Hostage Negotiation, Narcotics Investigations, and other training relevant to my assignments. Most of the students went back to their law enforcement agencies with *some* knowledge of what they studied. They could perform the basics of the training. However, in those three training courses just stated, I was able to perform at a high level of competency. Why? Because I *internalized* the training.

Internalizing requires that you use an organized system of reading, absorbing, understanding, and remembering the details of the training. It is not enough to merely read. What is important is that you read the material at a time and place when you are clear headed, in a study mode, and not distracted.

To gain the skills, it is vital that you be able to absorb the material. Absorbing means that you understand the material in context. Learning and even memorizing the table of contents will make you fully aware of how the information you are learning fits into the entire picture. When you understand the context, it gives you a framework upon which you can hang the details.

When I finished law school, I was required to take the bar exam. That exam was about 3 days long, and required a great amount of not only answering questions, but drafting long essay answers. To study for that exam, I attended a course and was provided with large books containing outlines of all the areas of law.

That was a massive amount of material to learn. Yes, I had studied the law in school, but to remember all of those classes and subject matter is impossible. I had to find a way to absorb all of the details, all of the legal concepts, of all the areas of law.

How did I do it? First, I memorized the entire tables of contents in each of those large law review books. That outline, once memorized, enabled me then to properly structure the details that I needed to learn. Next, I made lists of the details in each outline item, putting them onto flash cards.

It is also important to ensure that you understand what you are reading. Think about what you are learning in the context of the examples given, and also think about how it might apply or not apply to other situations. Remember, everything I say here is true, except when it is not, so it is important to understand when it does not apply.

Fortunately, you do not need to memorize everything in this book, but you should take good enough notes to be able to apply the concepts. The negotiation skills taught in this book require internalizing and a lot of practice to gain the skills and refine them.

The way to internalize this information in this book, as you read make an outline of each chapter, section, and paragraph. As you read, keep a book mark in the table of contents and refer to it often so that you are always fully aware of where you've been in your study, where you are, and where you are headed.

By following the model described in this book, developing simple systems for running your business, and making certain that you internalize the concepts and material contained herein, you are more likely to have the skills and the success in your short sale and loan modification business. "Herein"? The attorney in me comes out occasionally.

Finally, make certain that a short sale and loan modification business is for you. If you are very successful in your real estate business, then you may wish to merely add this as an adjunct business, assigning it to an assistant perhaps. If you are not successful in a regular real estate business, you may perhaps be seeking a niche for which you may be better suited.

If you are a real estate investor, or wanting to be, it is important that you be able to regularly devote at least several mornings each week to this business, Tuesdays through Fridays. Mondays are a particularly heavy call day for financial institutions and it is best to keep these calls to the other business days. You may take the approach either to find homeowners who will sell you the house directly, without a real estate agent, or you could make an offer on a pre-foreclosure home that is already listed by an agent and offer to do the negotiating with the bank.

For either business, you must have a seller who will cooperate. Many people emotionally freeze when they are in financial trouble and do nothing. They are like the flood insurance commercial on TV when the water comes into the house and everyone just ignores it until it's too late. If you think you may be good at motivating homeowners to cooperate and provide all of the massive amounts of documents and information required (not really massive, but it can seem daunting at first), then short sales and loan modifications may be for you.

I sold real estate for a year and a half, and found that my weakness was in finding sellers to list with me. I have a great amount of respect for all of you who can list properties, work open houses effectively, and build a strong sphere of influence with great results in obtaining listings. However, short sales do not normally require a great amount of marketing other than being listed in the MLS or BLC. They do not require open houses. Targeted marketing for listings is much easier for short sales and loan modifications, because you can obtain lists of those homeowners who are behind on their payments. So, finding clients is much easier and can be just the thing for making your profession as a real estate agent or investor rewarding and profitable.

The *Short Sale Business Manual* is designed as a companion to this book and will contain all of the examples, documents, disclosures, agreements, tips and suggestions that are described in this book. The *Short Sale Business Manual* or additional copies of this book can be ordered at www.LawsonGroupMediation.com.

Disclaimer

This book is intended for educational purposes only. Nothing herein is intended to provide legal, accounting, or tax advice. Nothing in this book is intended to represent that any comments about the laws, information, suggestions, recommendations, steps to take, or other material is consistent with the laws of any certain state or the laws of your state. It is also not the intention to assert that any of the recommendations is the correct or appropriate decision to make for your specific fact situation. This book is written to provide general educational and practical information. It is your responsibility to determine the laws of your state and let those laws guide your decisions. You should always seek the advice of a competent attorney licensed in your state for answers to any legal question you may have, and a tax professional for tax questions.

Introduction

Part One – Be a great real estate agent or investor

1. Short Sales and Loan Modifications:
   Get In On The Action 3

2. Marketing For Short Sales 43

3. Alternatives To Foreclosure, part A 57

4. Listing Presentations and Collecting Documents .. 79

5. Understanding Liability 99

6. Agency Responsibilities, Establishing Hardship,
   and Pricing 115

7. Marketing the Property and Managing Offers 139

Part Two – Be a great Negotiator

8. Systems For Effective Organization 157

9. Preparing the Short Sale Proposal 173

10. The Seven Golden Keys To Negotiation 195

11. Communicating and Negotiating With
    Lienholders............................. 247

12. Managing Multiple Cases and Preparing
    For Closing............................. 267

13. Alternatives To Foreclosure, Part B............ 281

14. Summary 289

About The Author

PART ONE – BE A GREAT AGENT OR INVESTOR

CHAPTER 1

Short Sales and Loan Modifications: Get In On The Action

Never before in my lifetime of 59 years have I seen as many home foreclosures as is happening at the time of this writing. A financial recession is putting a lot of people out of work, and home foreclosures have skyrocketed. In addition, the subprime market that permitted some people to own homes who are unable to manage their finances, has greatly increased the numbers of home foreclosures. I recently read that in many cities, pre-foreclosures and bank-owned properties represent ten percent of the inventory, but almost thirty percent of the transactions. Why would any real estate agent or investor *not* want to get in on this market? We will be discussing short sales and loan modifications. Other terms for short sales are *pre-foreclosure* and *short payoff* sales.

A bank-owned property is also called an REO, or Real Estate-Owned by the lender. Upon foreclosure, the property is customarily sold in a public auction and most commonly the lender is the only one who bids, and therefore takes the property. The agent for the lender, Title Company, or Trustee bids in the amount owed. This is a great opportunity for an investor to take the property by bidding in one dollar more than the lender's agent bids, but usually the investor does not have the ability to see inside the property. Sometimes a short sale can be a better bargain, because many short sales transactions are made for a price less than what is owed.

What is a Short Sale?

Any time a homeowner, facing a financial hardship, is unable to afford to make any more payments on the home and, as an alternative to letting it go to foreclosure, sells the property with lienholder consent for less than what is owed to the lienholders, plus the costs of sale (including real estate commissions), that transaction is a *short sale*.

Why would a lienholder allow the property to be sold for less than what is owed? Upon foreclosure, the lienholder gets the property back and then must hold the entire loss on their books as *non-performing assets* until they are able to sell the property. When the lenders sell the property, it is usually far less than what is received in a short sale. In addition, the lender must pay real estate broker commissions, management expenses, maintenance & upkeep, and insurance. Further, the property is usually vacant and vulnerable to vandalism. Also, when foreclosed homeowners lose their property, they are often not motivated to take care of the home and may leave the property in a poor state of repair. Finally, when buyers discover the property is an REO, they usually bid very low for the property. Selling the property in a short sale takes the property off the books as a non-performing asset and mitigates the losses suffered by the lenders.

Why would a homeowner prefer to sell the home in a short sale rather than merely walking away from it? Well, many homeowners do that very thing. Most homes headed for

Short Sales and Loan Modifications: Get In On The Action

foreclosure, end up in foreclosure. These homeowners bury their head in the sand and do nothing. There is something very de-motivating to many people about going into default on their mortgage, so many emotionally freeze. These homeowners who could otherwise find solutions for their financial problems or solutions for avoiding foreclosure, do nothing and merely wait until it is too late for them.

However, some homeowners are very responsible and conscientious about their situation, and seek solutions that may be available to accomplish their objectives. In Chapter Three, we will explore the alternatives to foreclosure and show you how to help the homeowners to decide if that solution is right for them. A short sale is one of those alternatives.

Some homeowners are concerned about their credit score, so a short sale is an alternative that allows them to get out from under the mortgage obligation with the least hit to their score. A foreclosure has the largest negative impact on their credit score and ability to obtain a new home loan in the future, even greater than bankruptcy. As we will explore, a bankruptcy can even be used to prevent a foreclosure and enable a short sale to take place. Under some circumstances, the bankruptcy might even be dismissed after the short sale transaction is complete, and as a result, is substantially the same as if a bankruptcy had never been filed.

A responsible homeowner will be eager to explore the alternatives, understand these options, and make an informed decision themselves about which alternative is right for them. Fortunately for your business, a short sale or loan modification is most often, but not always, the right choice for them to make.

This cooperative homeowner will be quick to express their willingness to cooperate with the process. They will be required to write a hardship letter, obtain financial records, read and sign disclosure forms, produce tax returns, list their home with you, reject any offers from potential buyers who will not cooperate with the short sale process, and respond immediately to requests for additional documentation or information.

The cooperative homeowner will take good care of the home, making it presentable to be shown. They will not decline a showing more than three times and make it available at all reasonable common showing times. They will cause no damage, and in fact will do things that they can afford to do, like deep cleaning, painting, and minor repairs.

For the investor, a cooperative homeowner will do all of the above. The difference is there is no need to show the home to anyone else except you. That is true, except when it is not. They will likely have to permit an appraisal or BPO (broker price opinion) that will require entry to the residence.

Short Sale or Loan Modification?

A short sale is the option when the homeowner wants to get rid of the home and the debt. Usually it is because they can no longer afford the payments. A loan modification is the option when the homeowner cannot afford the payments but could afford a lower payment, and they want to stay in the home.

A loan modification proposal is processed in virtually the same manner as a short sale. Aside from minor differences, the instruction and process is the same, so we will limit our

Short Sales and Loan Modifications: Get In On The Action

discussions to short sales and then show how it is applied to loan modifications in Chapter 13.

Good & Bad Short Sale Prospects

There are some homeowners you should stay away from. Not all pre-foreclosure homeowners make good short sale sellers. You should immediately reject and not waste time with these homeowners.

If they have just filed bankruptcy, get off the phone and make no appointment with them. We will discuss how filing a bankruptcy can be a solution for some short sale problem situations, but if it is not part of a solution involving the short sale, then it is part of the problem and you will be wasting your time.

Once a bankruptcy is filed, the debtor's entire financial estate (all of the income, assets, liabilities, and expenses) is placed in the hands of the trustee. Most bankruptcy lawyers know very little or nothing about short sales, so they are not likely to automatically include the short sale as part of chapter 13 plans or consider it worthwhile in chapter 7 liquidations. Many bankruptcy attorneys do not realize that a foreclosure or deed in lieu of foreclosure that is often accomplished as part of the bankruptcy is worse than the bankruptcy itself on their credit. In addition, the hiring of professionals including real estate agents requires the consent of the trustee and the court.

For investors, a bankrupt homeowner can mean the end of their opportunity to purchase the residence. However, it can also create a new opportunity for you. A bankruptcy petition is a public record, and you can go to the clerk's office and obtain copies of the chapter 7 bankruptcy schedules. A section of the petition is a list of creditors that will list the value of the home and what is owed. You can ask for a copy of just that page on which that creditor is listed, or you can purchase the entire schedule. You should be able to read through the entire petition and schedules to find what you need for both the first mortgage holder and any subsequent lienholders.

In the file, you will find the claims that have been filed by the attorneys for the creditors. The claims filed by lienholders will also tell you who the attorney is representing that creditor. It is common that a creditor's attorney will represent multiple creditors in the same case. The claim will tell you exactly what is owed on the debt plus all accrued costs including attorneys' fees.

The opportunity I am referring to is presented in a Chapter 7 bankruptcy. After filing, a hearing called a Section 341 Meeting of Creditors will be held at the bankruptcy courthouse usually. It is usually an informal meeting where the trustee and creditors' attorneys are seated around a large table. The trustee will go over the case to discover if there are any assets that the trustee is able by law to seize. The trustee personally is paid a percentage of assets that he is able to seize and the balance goes to the benefit of unsecured creditors.

At the Meeting of Creditors, the creditors' attorneys will be asking questions looking for evidence of abuse by the debtor, but more importantly to you, they will be seeking from the trustee the abandonment of the property on which there is a valid lien. Abandonment means that the trustee *abandons* his interest in that asset because the lien is legally sufficient to protect the lienholders' interests. If the trustee says that he will

Short Sales and Loan Modifications: Get In On The Action

abandon his interest, you can contact that creditor's attorney to see if you can purchase the property directly from the creditor. Normally, once abandoned by the trustee, the debtor in bankruptcy will sign a Deed-in-lieu of Foreclosure signing the property over to the creditor. Outside of bankruptcy, the creditor must sell the property in public auction because they have a legal duty to mitigate their damages as much as possible, with any amount received that is less than what is owed, going to the deficiency balance. Any amount received over and above the deficiency balance must be returned to the homeowner. However, in a bankruptcy, the property, if deeded back to the lender, is then owned by the lender and any deficiency balance is discharged in the bankruptcy, including all junior liens.

If the bankruptcy trustee finds that the lienholder's lien is not properly perfected, however, he will seize the property and sell it at a public auction. This often happens in some jurisdictions, and you can find out when the sales will take place and bid on the property. In this case, the creditor's claim amount is irrelevant, because the lien is voided, so the property can be purchased for whatever it will bring at the sale.

Another property to stay away from is when you are only a few to several weeks away from the foreclosure sale. A short sale transaction takes time. Although some lenders may respond and process the short sale almost immediately, some take a great amount of time to assign to a negotiator, obtain approval from any mortgage insurer, and obtain approval from the investor on the secondary market. A loan modification, as we will discuss in Chapter 13 should be limited to when the homeowner is only 2 to 5 payments behind and no NOD filed.

Short Sales & Loan Modifications

In some states, a foreclosure is handled in a judicial process which is basically a lawsuit with the remedy sought being the foreclosure sale by the Sheriff. We call that a *judicial foreclosure state*. In these states, the attorney for the lienholder files a *Complaint* (also called *Petition*). The attorney must wait a specific number of days set by the Rules of Civil Procedure for that state. If the homeowner does not hire an attorney to fight the case, the attorney files a *Motion for a Default Judgment*. This merely means that the defendant did not respond legally, so they are entitled to obtain a judgment by default. A *motion* is a written request that is filed with the court by the attorney. In some states, a motion need not be filed, and since the plaintiff is entitled to the judgment by default, an *Order* is merely submitted to the court for the judge's signature. The Rules of Civil Procedure state a specific number of days until the order is final. When that time period has lapsed, they schedule the Sheriff's Sale to sell the property. In some states, they must first obtain a Writ of Possession which is a court document that grants the plaintiff the legal right to take possession of the property. In other states, the Writ of Possession must be obtained by the purchaser after the sale to remove the owner or tenant if they have not already moved out. Upon obtaining the legal right to claim the property, the sheriff will forcibly remove the occupant from the property.

Sometimes squatters will move into the property, most often drug users. Some states permit police officers to remove them for trespassing. In some locations, however, a legal process must ensue to remove them.

Some states are *Trust Deed* states and have a completely different procedure. Upon default, the homeowner is given a period

Short Sales and Loan Modifications: Get In On The Action

of time to find an alternative to foreclosure that is acceptable to both parties. If none is found, they appoint a trustee to handle the foreclosure process. This is called a *non-judicial state*, because it is not handled through the court system. Instead, the trustee, pursuant to state law, advertises the default of the loan and the sale date in the legal newspaper for that location. On the sale date, the auction is held, the lienholder bids in the amount of the loan plus costs, and if there are no other bidders, takes the property. The new owner then obtains a Writ of Possession from the court if the occupants do not vacate. The trustee can be an attorney, a title company, or even a local bank trust department.

In non-judicial states, foreclosure happens more quickly than in judicial states. Judicial states usually take at least three months for this process to play out, however in some judicial states, it can even take six to eight months to foreclose. In non-judicial states, it is often a mere forty-five days, however, the length of time for public notice and the time required between public notice and the sale is determined by state statute.

Real estate agents know which process is used in your state from their licensing training, so if you are an investor, talk with an agent about the process in your state.

Give great pause if there is little time left to process the short sale. At the time of this writing, it is taking up to 120 days to obtain lender approval, and occasionally longer. A small number of lenders are processing them faster, but in this economic time of large numbers of foreclosures and short sales, their staff is overwhelmed. One lender told me that where they used to process 50 short sales a week, they are now getting 500 or more each day. Add that overwhelming burden to the severe economic hardship many of these financial institutions are experiencing and you can understand that they may not be able to employ a sufficient staff to keep their processing timely.

In a judicial state, it is important to obtain all documents the homeowner has been served or they have received in the mail. If a Judgment of Foreclosure has been obtained, you have very little time to process the short sale. In a non-judicial state, if advertising has commenced, there are only a few weeks left before the sale. Can a sale be postponed? Yes, but many lenders will refuse. Other lenders will only postpone the sale if they review the proposal and find that it is likely to be approved. Still others will only postpone a sale if the investor on the secondary market has reviewed the proposal and given their consent. These processes take time, and it may take some lenders many weeks before they can even review the proposal.

You may ask why they don't just take your proposal off the stack and review it quickly to determine if it's acceptable, so the sale can be postponed. First, if a lender takes a file out of order, it can create liability to someone else ahead of you who may lose their home because they handled your case first, and claim discrimination. So, lenders have learned to use a computerized system to assign cases and the system requires the negotiators and analysts to process cases in the order submitted.

Another reason is that some large lenders route all calls to loss mitigation to a call center so that negotiators and analysts do not have to speak to anyone except the necessary parties to the cases under review. In these cases, there may be no way to reach the negotiator or analyst. Talking to the supervisor, as one so-called short sale expert advises, is ineffective and as we will discuss later, perhaps the worst action to take. Some of the

Short Sales and Loan Modifications: Get In On The Action

call center representatives are willing to send an email to the negotiator or analyst, but that may be as far as you can go.

Now, this discussion is always true except when it is not. Some lenders have analysts or negotiators assigned almost immediately and you can obtain direct phone numbers and fax numbers for them. Some of these companies are very easy to work with, and I am comfortable with taking a case with these lenders when a sale is only a couple weeks away, because the representatives will so willingly reschedule the sale date.

Stay away from sellers who are not cooperative. If in your discussions, you find resistance to producing documents, filling out forms, or providing financial records, this may not be the situation for you. Likewise if they unreasonably resist cleaning, painting, showing or other simple activities that can help sell the home, you may want to consider rejecting the listing or purchase.

If the sellers are investors and not living in the property, this great amount of effort and cleanup may not be necessary. Low income type housing is expected to be in rough condition and it may not be appropriate to put a lot of work into the property.

You should be alert for the subtle clues during an initial telephone contact, during the listing presentation, and when going over the disclosure forms and other information. With experience, if you are not already able, you will learn to detect those homeowners who will reluctantly cooperate at first, but then shut down later. Likewise, you will learn to detect those homeowners who may be a bit resistant at first, but then as trust is built, they become fully cooperative.

Short Sales & Loan Modifications

A cooperative homeowner living in the home should be willing to stay in the home and take care of it. Beware of owners who are urgently looking for an apartment or wanting to move. In many cases, if the homeowner moves out, they may be deemed to have abandoned the property, putting the property at risk of vandalism. This may trigger the lienholder accelerating the foreclosure, and may even cause a lienholder to refuse to approve the short sale. Lenders are comprised of people, and these people can be provoked to not cooperate even though they may lose money by not approving the sale.

I once represented a bankruptcy client whose lender refused to accept a Deed-in-Lieu because the borrower threw a brick through their local office window. The people who work in financial institutions have biases, and if given a reason to not like a customer, they are willing to even lose many thousands of dollars rather than do anything that might benefit a customer who has defaulted.

Recently, I processed a short sale case with a second mortgage. The second mortgage holder would receive ten percent of the principal balance of their account and it would not be in full satisfaction of the debt. They would receive immediate cash on the account and the borrower would still be liable for the debt. The borrower was almost seventy years of age, living on a pension and social security, both of which is exempt from creditor action in his state, and had no assets accessible to the creditor. He is in fact *judgment-proof*. A no-brainer, right? The first mortgage holder approved the short sale, but the second mortgage holder refused because the negotiator stated that she did not want to do anything that would benefit the borrower. Because her refusal appeared on its face to not be in the best

Short Sales and Loan Modifications: Get In On The Action

interest of her company, I attempted to contact her supervisor. He refused to return my call, so I contacted executive management. After an internal investigation, the executive told me that they would not overrule their loss mitigation decision.

The point here is that lenders can be easy to work with or extremely difficult depending upon the particular personalities involved, and depending upon how they view their customer. Having an uncooperative seller ups the odds against your short sale being approved and closing. Difficult or uncooperative people can cause you a lot of stress, are often high maintenance, and if you disregard this advice, you will soon learn the hard way.

Beware also of really nice sellers who are emotionally frozen. Although they are very similar to uncooperative people, these folks seem like great people, will make a lot of promises, but they are just laden down with stress and problems. While never expressing any refusal or resistance to your requests for documents and information, they merely just fail to produce it, or take a long time to do so. They may have often thrown letters and documents away, not kept copies of tax returns, kept no statements from the servicing lender, and may otherwise be very busy. They may fill their lives with distractions but are unable to emotionally face difficult decisions and issues.

The sellers who make great clients are people who are eager to meet with you, will have documents easy to retrieve, who keep everything sent to them by the lenders, who file tax returns on time and keep copies. They are people who respond immediately to requests, who cleaned their home for your visit. They are eager to spend evenings and weekends cleaning, painting, doing yard work, filling out forms. They are people who willingly will allow showings of their homes in early evenings after people get off work or on weekends. They are people who will ask questions and actively participate in the decision-making processes.

Understanding Lienholders

We have discussed what short sales are and which short sale situations to avoid. Now let's discuss who the lienholders are, and how the short sale process works.

First are the lending institutions. When you buy a home, some mortgage lender funds your loan. It could be a local bank, some unknown company that was selected by a mortgage broker, or a mortgage investment group. You likely were required to purchase private mortgage insurance (PMI). You likely signed all of the mortgage documents at the title company.

The document comprising your loan is the *note*. The note is the lender providing you with the funds to buy the home along with your promise to pay the lender back over time, at a specific time period, payment amount, interest rate, and consequences of default.

Along with the note is the security instrument. In mortgage states, you sign the mortgage and this document is how you grant the lender a security interest in the property. The lender must *perfect* this security interest by having it recorded with the Register of Deeds or Recorder for your county. Auto loans require the lender to perfect their security interest by filing a document with the division of motor vehicles for your state and the lender's name noted on the title as lienholder. In real property, however, the mortgage must be perfected by

Short Sales and Loan Modifications: Get In On The Action

filing with the Register of Deeds (or other title such as the County Recorder, etc.) for your county within a specified number of days. Upon default, these states require a judicial procedure to foreclose.

In trust deed states, when you buy a home, besides signing the note (promise to pay), you sign a document placing title to your property in the hands of a *trustee*, who may be a lawyer, a title company, or a bank trust department. The document in these states is called a *deed of trust*. In these states, upon default, the trustee merely must follow state law to provide you with notice of your right to bring the defaulted loan current, and then to publicize the foreclosure sale of your home for a period of weeks, (e.g. three weeks) announcing the trustee sale date.

After the purchase of your home, you make your payments to the lender as agreed. However, this lender no longer has the money they loaned for the purchase. They do not likely have the financial ability to do this too many times before they run out of money, so they sell the *note* on the secondary market. The secondary market is comprised of a number of investment firms with large amounts of capital to spend on loans. Some of the secondary market investors (SMI) may be owners of securities that holds bundles of *notes*. Some of these investors are public institutions, some government owned, and still others are private investment companies. Fannie Mae and Freddie Mac are secondary market investors, and they were set up by the federal government, made public, and recently were taken over again by the government.

The original lender transfers the note to the investor. The endorsed note will be accompanied by a contract spelling out the servicing rights of the original lender, and the rights of the investor. The servicing lender will continue to accept the payments, retaining a portion as their servicing fees, and forward the balance to the investor.

Although you likely were required to purchase private mortgage insurance at closing, sometimes the servicing lender or investor will purchase this insurance later. So, just because a seller may tell you that they do not have private mortgage insurance, or that the time for requiring this insurance has lapsed, does not absolutely mean there is none in existence. Many lenders never cancel the insurance and continue to bill the customer for it long after the expiration date has lapsed for requiring it if the seller does not object. Additionally, the seller would not likely know if the investor purchased it.

The reason this is important is in a short sale, the mortgage insurance (MI) company may have contractual restrictions limiting such things as the total commissions that a real estate broker may receive, or restrictions on seller concessions. In a short sale, not only must you obtain approval from the servicing lender, but you also have to obtain that approval from both the SMI and MI carrier as well. This is one of the reasons that short sales take so long. The servicing lender first forwards the proposal to the MI company, and then the SMI. That is, except when they do not.

Small servicing lenders could be local or regional banks. They may be in areas where foreclosures are rare. In this case, processing short sales is likely much easier and faster. In this case, you want to be sure that you are speaking to and negotiating with a supervisor or manager. If you find yourself speaking with someone who must check everything with the supervisor, you can usually convince them to let you talk directly with him

Short Sales and Loan Modifications: Get In On The Action

or her. If you meet resistance, just ask if they are refusing to allow you to talk to the supervisor. It is rare that they will admit this, and will likely put you on hold and forward your call to that person.

Some of these local or regional institutions may have loan products where the funds were provided by a local or regional investment group. These investment groups may grant to the bank or mortgage company not only servicing rights, but the complete right to approve shorts sales and loan modifications.

I have found in large banks that if you develop a friendly relationship with each person in the call center, that person can do a lot to help you get your case processed and approved. Every time I make a call, I make it my mission to get the person laughing at least once. It is often the case that they will go the extra mile to send a personal email request, or even walk to other floors in the building just to short circuit the long time delay, solve a problem, or to get the case moving. My experience with large institutions is that call center people, if they like you, will do much more for you than will supervisors or managers. Except, that is, when it does not work this way.

The short sale process is relatively straight forward and simple, albeit time-consuming. Upon listing the property, you market it for buyers. When I say market the property, I am simply referring to listing it with the MLS or BLC. Placing it in the online listings may be a good idea as well. However, you should avoid spending money on marketing, advertising, or flyers. More on that later.

You should not contact the lender until you have a buyer. Contrary to many so-called expert opinions, you should not submit the proposal piecemeal fashion. You should have at least one buyer, all of the documents from the buyer and seller that are required, and all the disclosures signed for your protection. You will then draft the proposal. The format is described in Chapter 9 and examples are provided in the *Short Sale Business Manual*, available separately. You will then contact the lender for their specific requirements, and submit the *Authorization & Release*. After that you draft the proposal to match the company's needs and submit the proposal by fax or shipment, depending upon their usual and preferred methods. You may have to wait until an analyst or negotiator is assigned and then work their way through their stack of cases to yours. Meanwhile, you will maintain appropriate communication with the lender so you are at all times aware of what is happening with your case. When the analyst or negotiator gets to your case, you will either make contact with him or her by phone, or that person will call you. The negotiator will order an appraisal, and if there is PMI, the proposal will be submitted to the MI company for their approval, which may take from a few days to about two weeks. If approved by them, the proposal then is submitted to the investor for their approval, again a few days to two weeks time lapse. Upon approval, you will receive a *bank release document*. That may be in the form of either a letter or agreement.

Other Lienholders

There may be other lienholders also. Most commonly they are venders (construction liens aka mechanics liens), former spouses (child and spousal support liens), divorce attorneys who have filed liens for their attorneys' fees awarded by the court, and judgment creditors. To obtain the lien, they must obtain either a Judgment or Order from the court (former spouses, attorneys, creditors), or otherwise follow the procedures outlined by state statute. They must then perfect that lien by filing it with the Register of Deeds or Recorder for your county.

You find out who these other lienholders are by asking a title company to provide you with a *preliminary title report* at the same time you ask for an estimated HUD-1 form. They usually will do this for you without charge, as a customer service in contemplation of your utilizing them for the closing...and you should. The preliminary title report is sometimes provided in the form of a *Title Commitment,* or it can be merely an email to you listing the liens on the property.

Obtaining a release of a lien from a former spouse is often very difficult. If that spouse was represented by an attorney, always call that attorney's office. They may require that you demonstrate there is no equity in the property on which to collect. If they still resist, you may offer them a token payment from the short sale proceeds of about $500–$1,000. The lender will likely not quibble over this amount...except those who do.

Your brokerage may have a *Release of Lien* document. If not, forms are readily available online, and often the spouse's attorney is likely willing to draft it. Upon obtaining the release, take the original document to the title company and ask them the procedure for your state. You may be required to have the original at closing, or you may be required to file that release with the Register of Deeds before the final title work is completed.

Short Sales & Loan Modifications

Convincing a vendor (carpenter, roofing company, plumber, etc.) to release a lien could be easy or it may be very difficult. Some vendors are very emotional people and angry because they were not paid. They may be irrationally adamant in their refusal to release a lien unless they are paid in full. What to do? You could have a lawsuit filed to set aside the lien because of lack of equity, but that is time-consuming and expensive. The easiest way is to learn good negotiating skills to convince them to release the lien absolutely or in exchange for a nominal or full payout to them ($500–$1,000). Chapter 10 will discuss how to develop these skills.

Other lienholders are most commonly second mortgage lenders. Typically, their loan note is fully held by the lending institution that made the loan, although it could be sold on the secondary market to an investment institution. An equity line of credit is a common type of second mortgage, although some are equity-backed credit cards and home improvement loans. Obtaining the release of a second mortgage holder where there is no equity in the home securing their note is usually fairly straight forward and they are often willing to release their lien. However, it is also likely that the second mortgage holders will not be released in full satisfaction of the debt. That means that this lender will be free to pursue collection action against their borrowers for the balance following the sale. They are paid a token amount for the release, usually about 10% of the second mortgage holder's principal balance up to about $3,000, however $5,000 is not unheard of. Some SMIs and MI carriers limit it to $1,000.

Some of these *other* lienholders, however, may resist the short sale vehemently. Some small credit unions, investment lenders, former spouses, etc. may be very angry over the default and may refuse to cooperate with anything that will benefit the borrower from their perspective. There are many people who only want to hurt the borrowers and will gladly lose many thousands of dollars to do so.

Establishing Your Short Sale Business

If you are going to work short sales and loan modifications as a business, you first need to decide if you are creating a new business entity, or merely adding these cases to your existing business structure. Real estate sales brokers and agents who are successful usually have well established groups with assistants, buyers' agents, and sellers' agents. They may have a marketing assistant as well. If you have all of these, then I have little to add. You don't fix success.

However, if your group is not successful, or you are not building a successful real estate practice in this current market, then this discussion may be of some help to you. You may decide that primarily working short sales is a good business opportunity. That makes sense, and as you work with these sellers that few other agents want for clients, they will have family, friends, neighbors and co-workers they can refer to you...and they will!

So, whether you are a real estate sales agent or an investor with time on your hands to work short sales and loan modifications, then you should consider the type of entity to want to establish. A sole proprietorship is acceptable, so long as you keep your business and personal economic life separate. To add protection from personal liability, you may decide to incorporate your business. Make certain, though, that whatever name you choose under which to operate your business, your business name does not conflict with someone else's *service mark*, *trademark*, or *service name*. You can pay an attorney or online service to do this. Alternatively, you could merely use a search engine to check on the name you want and see if the search engine brings up any other businesses with that same name.

Incorporating your business is easy to do and the Secretary of State section of your state's website will often have available forms. Completing the *Articles of Incorporation* is simple. Alternatively, there are online legal forms available to you. You will need at least the *Articles of Incorporation* and *Bylaws* to establish your corporation. If you have questions about how to complete them or want to know what else your state requires, you can call the Secretary of State for your state and they are usually very helpful. Along with establishing your corporation, you need to have an accountant help you to file the election under Subchapter S. This will allow the tax liability to flow through to you personally, rather than taxing the corporation and then again when salary and dividends are paid out to you.

A partnership is just as easy to create, but you should always have a *partnership agreement* to establish your individual areas of responsibility and control, and to agree in advance on how to divide the business in the event you cannot make it. I have had a couple of partnerships in the past, and I have learned that no matter how good I was at determining the character of my partners, going into business will change that relationship and it is fairly rare that it really works out well. A good partnership agreement can be found online or can be custom-drafted by an attorney.

Short Sales and Loan Modifications: Get In On The Action

An entity that has gained a lot of popularity is the limited liability company (LLC). The LLC is just as easy to form as a corporation, and for purposes of reporting requirements, it is like a partnership with corporate protections. You can obtain the basic forms from the Secretary of State (or their website), obtain the forms online, obtain the forms from an office supply store, or have them custom-drafted by an attorney.

It is very important to obtain some professional insurance. E&O insurance is common for real estate agents, and you should check with your carrier to make sure that the particular activities of short sales (i.e. negotiation with third party lienholders) are covered by the insurance. If you are an investor, check with your insurance agent for some umbrella coverage that will cover legal fees should you be sued by a homeowner who claims you are liable for their short sale not getting approved and they lose their home in a foreclosure.

A point to remember here, your liability will be generally lessened through the disclosures and forms that are provided in the *Short Sale Business Manual*. However, it has been said and it is true that anyone can sue anyone for anything. Although the court procedures are designed to reduce or eliminate frivolous lawsuits, our legal system works very poorly in many places, and even if you are able to ultimately prevail, you could incur huge legal expenses to reach that point. So liability insurance is important to take care of potential nuisance suits.

If you create a corporation or LLC, that entity protects your personal assets from the reach of creditors or customers who sue you. That is true, except when it is not! There is a way that judgment creditors of your entity may be able to come after you personally, or against other entities you own. It is called *piercing the corporate veil*, or *disregarding the corporate entity*. Some attorneys only consider corporate formalities, but there are several factors that need to be considered in order to keep this *veil* of protection. Remember, this discussion applies equally to LLCs.

First, the corporate formalities. It is imperative that you maintain all of the records and perform all of the activities expected of corporations & LLCs. Make certain you have bylaws, and that those bylaws spell out the responsibilities of each officer (even if it is only you). Draft a one year business plan stating how you will structure your business, what you will accomplish during the year, the steps you will take to reach your goals, who will perform the business activities, and a reasonable budget for the business. Then have a shareholders meeting (even if there is only one), elect your board of directors, and approve by resolution that business plan.

Next have monthly board meetings. At that board meeting, merely write a resolution that states how you did the previous month, what goals are being met or not, how well you are staying on budget, along with a resolution of what needs to be done the following month to get back on track. The resolution form in the *Short Sale Business Manual* may be used for both shareholder meetings and board meetings.

Many people think that this is all they must do. However, I know from my background representing creditors' rights, there are other factors that should be addressed to provide full protection.

Make certain that you keep your business bank account separate from personal business. Never, I repeat, never use the business account to pay personal items. In the *Short Sale*

Short Sales and Loan Modifications: Get In On The Action

Business Manual there are tips and suggestions for setting up a very simple business record-keeping system. Never comingle personal and business income or expenses!

If you pay yourself a regular salary, make certain that the salary is matched to a reasonable amount for that position as compared with others doing the same thing, and that this salary is reasonably matched to the statement of objectives and steps to take in your business plan. For example, if you decide that you need to list x number of short sales homes in order to generate $xxxx.xx dollars in revenue, you know that your income should be a certain predictable amount. Make certain that your salary is a reasonable amount in the budget. If you generate more money than your budget, pay it not in the form of draws, bonuses, or added salary, but in the form of *dividends* that are paid out quarterly.

Pay dividends. They can be paid quarterly, semi-annually, or annually. Whether they are small or large, the payment of dividends is expected of separate entities.

Keep your overhead reasonably low for the type of business that you have. A home office is best, and can bring you additional tax benefits. An office or desk in your broker's office is suitable. However, if you have an office that is not with your broker, and if you do not have clients or customers coming into that office, then do not have premium rate office expenses when nice but inexpensive will do. A doctor, lawyer, real estate agent may need premium space because it may impact their potential clients' willingness to do business with them. However, a short sale businessman where a premium office is not expected should keep that overhead low.

Maintain appropriate cash reserves and/or lines of credit. It is important to immediately have three months of expenses in cash reserves, or have a relationship with a bank or credit union and they have approved that level of a line of credit. Then continue to build the cash reserves until you have at least six months of expenses on hand and immediately available.

Those are some of the factors to consider. Now, understand the concept. Piercing the corporate veil to pursue the assets of the owner or subsequent entities is accomplished under two legal concepts: *fraud* and *alter ego*. Fraud is establishing the entity solely to avoid creditors. Fraud is held when a court finds that the establishment of the entity is merely a sham and that the business is not really a separate entity but a sole proprietorship or partnership. Alter ego means that you may have a separate entity, but it does not act like a separate entity, it acts like a mirror image of the owner. For example, a separate entity run by experienced business persons would never just pay cash out to shareholders; rather, it would pay dividends according to its business plan. Anything the corporation does that is out of harmony with entities that manage finances to produce the greatest income and value of its shares, but appears to be just benefiting the owner, is at risk of having its corporate veil pierced.

One business, a medical clinic, started out fairly successful. They added a layer of top executives making huge salaries and benefits, including an in-house attorney which a medical clinic would not normally require. The CEO was unqualified for the position but paid himself a high salary greater than his qualifications. They paid other managers salaries that were far above the norm for those positions in their industry. Then they got into a disagreement with one of the doctors, the contract was breached, the doctor sued and obtained a judgment. The company merely closed down that corporation and opened up a new corporation. The second corporation was a sham to avoid their creditors and when the attorneys for the doctor wise up, they will likely prevail in piercing the veil of the subsequent entity and the shareholder personally.

Think of it this way. A corporation or LLC is a separate entity, like another person. All decisions made in the context of the entity must be for the entity's benefit, not the shareholder (owner). For example, suppose you are making a lot of money in your business, and piling up huge cash reserves. Instead of just upping your salary to eat up those revenues, a separate entity would hold off and pay that out in the form of dividends, build up larger cash reserves, or give a small or moderate salary increase at a time consistent with what other corporations do. This is most often accomplished on an anniversary date of the business, at a specific time when you perform an employee evaluation, or if you are the sole employee, through a board meeting resolution. You see, a separate entity or person looks out for its own interests first for the purpose of protecting the value of the corporate shares.

The alter ego theory of law is based upon the concept that the owner established the entity but manages the entity solely for his own personal interests. The factors will show that the entity is for his own personal benefit rather than for the benefit of the entity and the entity's shareholders (which could be bequeathed or sold at any time). Factors showing that the business is his alter ego include improper salary for the qualifications and position, failure to pay dividends, excessive overhead, lack of management policies and procedures, failure to budget, failure to have board meetings and keep board resolutions, failure to have shareholder meetings and keep shareholder resolutions, failure to file tax returns and other legal documents, and the co-mingling of personal and business funds.

Later, we will show you how to easily maintain the financial records that will take up little of your time, but will keep you organized and help you protect your corporate entity.

When you have completed setting up your business entity, you should set up your office to process your activities quickly and efficiently. Your work area should be set up in a quiet place where you can make phone calls without others overhearing confidential information, and organized in a way that you can merely turn your chair to access equipment, files, and supplies.

Your computer should be reliable. It does not have to be expensive, but you should have enough memory to be able to multi-task without it slowing you down. You will need Microsoft Office, and it is available for both Windows and Apple computers. Most title companies utilize Word for their word processing. Office also includes Microsoft Outlook as the email management system, and that system is great for keeping your emails all sorted, along with contacts. Many real estate agents who originally contracted with a popular online database for real estate agents have gone back to Outlook because of its simple but powerful features. In the *Short Sale Business Manual* you can find tips and suggestions for utilizing Outlook to easily and simply manage your emails.

Microsoft Office includes Excel which many title companies use for estimated HUD-1 forms that you will need for

Short Sales and Loan Modifications: Get In On The Action

your proposals, and they may send it to you either in an Excel, Word, or PDF format. You will need to be able to print your documents to PDF format, so that software is a must. There are several publishers who provide software for that purpose. Microsoft Office includes Microsoft Office Document Imaging software to which you can print, to convert large Word or PDF files into smaller file sizes for online faxing and emailing.

You will need a printer and scanner as well. You can purchase all-in-one printer/scanner/fax machines that work great. I prefer an HP model, but I know there are others that work just as well. It is important, however, that you have an automatic document feeder and that the scanning software allows you to scan multiple documents into the same file. Some software only scans and records each page as a separate file, which is not good. You should be able to scan various documents into a Word document. I regularly will scan twenty pages of documents into one Word document.

A fax will be needed for your short sale and loan modification business. You can use a regular fax machine over a standard telephone line. I utilize an online fax service. Watch the prices though, some are more expensive than others. I am generally happy with my service, although I have had a fair amount of problems with failed transmissions and some degradation of the fax quality. I am not certain if the degradation is more than a standard fax, although my suspicions are that it is. Since I utilize a cell phone with unlimited usage for all my calls, having a landline is just an added expense.

I have tried various internet phone services and have generally been displeased with them. I have tried other cell providers too, but I have not found better telephone service than the unlimited usage plan with the best cell provider in my area. It is more expensive than the others, but the reliability has been worth it.

Reliable broadband service is very important. I send and receive a lot of emails, and having fast upload and download speeds makes a great difference. Some providers are down a lot for repairs. The primary broadband provider for your area usually provides the most reliable service, albeit for a price. If all of your incoming and outgoing emails and faxes are via the internet, you are well advised to have the best.

Time Management

There are many books and courses on time management, and it is not our purpose here to compete with authors who know a lot more about time management than do I. Suffice it to say that to run a successful business, you must learn to manage your time effectively.

We will discuss this in more depth later, but for now I suggest you do a search online for time management articles, tips, and suggestions. You could purchase the Franklin Planner, which has very comprehensive software, planner materials, and instruction available. Your local office supply will have various planners and fillers for many aspects of time and project management. In my law practice, a planner was indispensable. There were just too many things to accomplish, activities to attend, documents to draft, research to complete, people to track, time to record, and deadlines to meet.

A short sale and loan modification mediation business, however does not require that level of detail. You could simply use your calendar on your cell phone for appointments and deadlines. A separate form for keeping track of things that need to get done is handy, which you could keep in a binder. For keeping a chronological record of telephone messages, notes, and ideas a spiral bound notebook is helpful and pages will not become lost. Assembling a casebook consisting of a large three-ring binder with Activity Logs and cheat sheets in sections with section dividers organized by property will provide a simple, yet efficient system for managing your cases. Examples and forms for these items are provided in the *Short Sale Business Manual*.

It is important that you schedule the times each day that you are going to work on various activities and to protect the time for that purpose. It is easiest to contact lenders Tuesday through Friday mornings. Avoid calling lenders on Mondays, as this is the busiest time for them and you will discover that you will sit on hold for a lot longer. When you call find out what state they are located in so you know which time zone they are in.

Plan to go to the county clerk's office on specific days at times when that office is not crowded. If you purchase an online resource for homeowners who are defaulting on their loans, it is important to do your marketing activities during set times that you block off for that purpose. Your listing presentations, or interview if you are an investor, will be most commonly in the evening when people are off work.

Bottom line...plan your work and work your plan. Block off time for each type of activity and guard that time faithfully. Simply put, that is time management. The idea is to organize your life so that you can accomplish more, waste less, meet deadlines, and make money. We will discuss this again later in this book.

The people who make the most money are the people who manage their time to accomplish more in the time they have. It is moving from activity to activity quickly, without details *bottle-necking* your activities. Time management is developing simple systems that do not slow you down. It is looking at everything you do in your personal living and in your business, identifying those activities that slow you down, and developing simple systems to maintain efficiency. It is organizing your activities into blocks of time so that you waste less time moving from activity to activity.

For example, you may find that that recording all of your business receipts and expenses is very time-consuming, and it is easier for you to procrastinate and allow the receipts to pile up. If so, an easy system is to take a large three-ring binder, insert 12 monthly dividers, and glue 5 x 9 envelopes onto each side. You can use regular glue stick that you can purchase at an office supply store. When you bring home receipts, merely put them into that month's envelope and write on the face of the envelope a category for the receipt and the amount below it. When you pay a bill online, Simply print a receipt and place that in the envelope as well. You may handwrite the column headings or you can print a form to be glued to the envelope with the categories pre-printed and then merely write the amount below the category title. At tax time, you can then total the columns under each category and enter the totals into a simple spreadsheet. No complicated and time-consuming accounting software for me for this business! This is a simple system that will work for

Short Sales and Loan Modifications: Get In On The Action

you and allow you the time to do many other things...and your tax accountant will be happy!

That example would not work for a law firm, but for a short sale and loan modification business it could be a major timesaver. There are many things that you *could* do on the computer but there are many things that are faster by hand or with a simpler system. A simple bookkeeping system like this may be much easier for your at-home business. For some, this easy system will not match their need for details and complicated systems. Ok, then there is Quickbooks Pro and other financial software available for them.

In the above example, you could keep that receipt binder open on a table top in your office so few steps are necessary to record the expense and insert the receipt. At the end of the year, plan to spend approximately an hour with a calculator totaling the expense columns for each month and inserting the totals into an Excel spreadsheet. At tax time, merely email the spreadsheet file to your tax professional. If you do this though, make certain that you also consider other items that you do not expense out, such as major purchases like furniture and other items you may wish to depreciate over time. Match whatever tax benefits you will seek with simple systems that will take you very little time to utilize.

We will discuss more about systems in the *Short Sale Business Manual*, so that your short sale business will be as efficient as possible.

The Three Reasons Behind Most Businesses Failures

A business *can* fail for many reasons: lack of customers, downturn in the industry, employee theft, competition, sudden increases in wholesale prices, excessive rise in overhead, and a change in demographics affecting your business. However, any of these factors can be overcome or offset with help from three distinct fields of expertise: Finance, Management, and Marketing. Each of these fields of expertise are counter-intuitive, meaning that it is more than just common sense. In fact, many of the basic principles in each category require activities and decisions opposite of what you may intuitively think is the right thing to do.

My first years in law were spent working in a creditors' rights and creditors' rights in bankruptcy practice. I represented banks, mortgage companies, finance companies, investment groups, landlords, hospitals, along with a host of other creditors. Then I opened my own practice and started representing debtors in bankruptcies. When small business owners came to me for a bankruptcy, I discovered that many of them did not need a bankruptcy, but guidance in finance, management, and marketing. I developed an expertise in rescuing businesses from bankruptcy. Now I provide some consulting and coaching to businesses. For some businesses, merely basic level consulting in those three areas are sufficient. For other businesses, having expert consulting or professional services is a must for success.

Principles of finance have been developed into a specific group of usual and customary accounting principles that every business student learns in his first year in college. The principles

Short Sales and Loan Modifications: Get In On The Action

of financial management are very important to the success of the business, because they can guide your financial decision-making to financial success. Without them, you will likely waste a lot of money, get bogged down in financial issues, lose out on tax savings, head for bankruptcy, or at least you will not soar to success as much as you would by following expert financial principles.

As stated, applying good financial sense is counter-intuitive. The problem here is that you don't know what you don't know. That's right, no typo here. I'll say it again, the problem here is that you don't know what you don't know. You know what you *do* know, but you do not know what you *do not* know. In my bankruptcy law practice, when business owners came to me for help because of a failing business, many of them would tell me that they just followed good common sense. Yet when I reviewed their records, almost all of them made very poor financial decisions that helped to bring about their downfall. Their stated reasons for their business failure was almost always incorrect. They all had in common poor decision-making in finance, management, and marketing.

So, what should you do? You could take college courses in accounting and finance, but most of you are not likely to do so. So, alternatively, you should talk to a good tax accountant about setting up the financial structure of your business. In addition – yes there is more to it than that – you should have someone, like your accountant, who you can talk to weekly, biweekly, or monthly to discuss your business, your challenges, your opportunities, and other issues as they arise, and ask that financial expert for guidance. There are also a number of books written by successful business people who can teach you many of the concepts and principles of succeeding in your business. There are also *CFO's for hire* in many communities who offer services to small businesses on an hourly basis. Further, there are often nonprofit corporations who provide such services for free or a small fee. You can contact them through your community Chamber of Commerce. It is no exaggeration to say that every successful business has had a financial expert assist in making that business successful.

Successful management is also counter-intuitive. That means that good management principles could be the exact opposite of what you might think is the correct way, based upon common sense. In a previous example of a medical clinic, the CEO used his department heads as his board of directors. Makes sense, doesn't it? After all, what better way to keep his department heads focused on the best interest of the company and to help make decisions. However, that is only one in a long list of bad management decisions this CEO is making, and his clinic is in trouble. They have been sued by a number of people, and the corporate veil is nonexistent by these management decisions. This owner/CEO does not know what he does not know. When help was offered and he found out what the expert was going to have him do to turn the company around, he rejected the help and fired the expert. He sincerely believed, based upon his own common sense that the expert did not really have the best solutions and he (the owner/CEO) knew more about how to build his company successfully. The amount of losses this clinic has incurred, and continues to incur, are phenomenal.

How do you learn to manage a business properly? Again, there are college courses that teach the tried and true principles of business management, and those who obtain that education

Short Sales and Loan Modifications: Get In On The Action

become much more successful business leaders. Alternatively, there are books you can read that are written by success management wizards. There are coaches and consultants like me who can help you set up your business and make it run efficiently. Business consultants-for-hire are everywhere and available to help you. There is also SCORE which is a group of retired business executives who can provide assistance. They are contacted through the Small Business Administration of the federal government. There are resource centers in many communities that you could contact through the local Chamber of Commerce. Finally, there is a lot of excellent information online. Look first of all at the business section of your state and local websites, along with the websites of other states and cities. I serve on a local resource committee that is focusing on using the local Chamber of Commerce website to link to all of the business resources that are available. We spend our time working on making more resources available to small business people.

Finally, to have a successful business, you need a marketing expert. Again, marketing is counter-intuitive. My brother, who is Senior VP for a large nationwide bank, once stated that effective marketing does not cost anything. Every dollar that you put into marketing, if done properly, brings in more dollars than is spent. You have to know who your target population is, what the demographics are who will actually spend money to your business, and what the most efficient primary methods of marketing are for your business with the resources available to you.

This clinic I used in the example is a good example of horrible marketing. The clinic consists of pediatric specialists in neurology, neuropsychology, therapy, and psycho-social rehabilitation workers, and their patients are all referred by other professionals, such as pediatricians, psychiatrists, family doctors, and family care coordinators. Rather than specifically targeting their market toward these professionals, the clinic paid for advertising at a local movie theater. Good marketing targets the specific target population, in this case, those doctors, psychiatrists, and coordinators. Primary marketing would target only those professionals, not the general population. Secondary marketing, like a movie theater is not prohibited, but when resources are limited, it is imperative to identify the primary target population that will fund your business and use your marketing fund to finely target them with your marketing dollars.

Real estate companies have developed many highly effective marketing approaches. One company teaches its agents to use a system using eight contacts in eight weeks. The concept here is that if a homeowner wants to sell a home, he will likely immediately think of one or two agents to contact. To make that homeowner think of you requires that you first start begin by making eight contacts in each of eight consecutive weeks. A contact is anything that reaches out to the homeowner and makes them think of you. The system teaches that telephone calls are most effective, but cards, letters, little gifts are all acceptable contact activities that will cause them to remember you. That system is followed up by about thirty-three to thirty-six contacts with that homeowner over the course of the year.

The idea here is that a great amount of research, along with a lot of trial and error, has produced general rules for marketing

Short Sales and Loan Modifications: Get In On The Action

that have proven highly effective for different kinds of industries. Relying on your own common sense rather than reaching out to learn these effective marketing rules is foolish. Marketing experts abound and can be hired on an hourly basis, contracted for coaching or consulting, and available for hire on an hourly basis. Additionally, you can find a lot of expert guidance in marketing for your business online.

So if you are a person of good intelligence, and possess a lot of life experience and good common sense, your business will likely fail – unless you obtain expert advice in the three most important areas of finance, management, and marketing.

Summary

In this chapter, we discussed what a short sale is. We spent time outlining the short sale and loan modification opportunities that you should avoid, and the short sale and loan modification opportunities you should seek. We discussed the servicing lenders, secondary market investors (SMI), and the MI carriers who must approve your short sale. We talked about business entities and setting up your short sale business, along with the equipment and software you should purchase. We emphasized the need to make certain that your business entity is operated in a manner that will protect itself and you from liability. Finally, we discussed the critical expertise you should seek in the areas of finance, management, and marketing.

In chapter two, we will discuss marketing for short sales in more depth. With each chapter, you will gain an insight into how a short sale and loan modification business model works efficiently and effectively. We will include practical advice and if you internalize the concepts and methods contained in this book, along with the use of the documents and sample forms in the *Short Sale Business Manual*, no matter how much experience you have had in the past, or do not have, you should improve your ability to succeed in this highly specialized field of real estate sales or investing.

CHAPTER 2

Marketing For Short Sales

This will be the weakest chapter of the book. Oops! Should I admit that I might be anything less than an expert in everything? Remember my most important principle to remember? *Everything is true except when it is not!* A second principle would be that when it comes to such things as short sales, including negotiating, so-called experts *may not know what they don't know!* This is especially true of experienced real estate agents working short sales. A third rule is this: be careful about believing that someone who is an expert in one area is an expert in all areas. *Nobody knows what you may think they know!* This third rule applies to this chapter. I will, however, tell you what I do know about marketing. I have been quite successful in marketing over the years, but I do not qualify as an expert.

I have lived a long professional life and have learned many things about business and law. I guess I could qualify as an accomplished business manager, an expert in some areas of law, a capable business coach and consultant, an accomplished business rescuer, a successful negotiator and mediator, a qualified instructor in negotiation and mediation, and an expert in short sales. However, even though I have learned a lot about finance and marketing, I cannot claim to be an expert in those areas. I know the basic and even a lot of the advanced concepts and principles of marketing or I would not have built a successful law firm or mediation firm. I will share these basic concepts with you in this chapter, and many of you will find some helpful guidelines here, but for others of you with vast amounts of education, training, and experience in sales and marketing, this may be a chapter that makes you feel like you are reading a children's book.

The purpose of this chapter is to summarize some of marketing's basic principles and apply them specifically to a short sale and loan modification business. We will look at ways to locate your target population, and how to market to them. Always remember, though, that in real estate sales, there are marketing experts who possess highly refined skills and they rule!

Basic Marketing Principles

First, there are two *forms* of marketing, primary and secondary, and your basic marketing budget should focus on primary marketing. Primary marketing is focused directly on your target population, while secondary marketing throws money at indirect marketing activities that produces good will and draws some clients. Then there are three *types* of marketing: brand marketing, direct marketing, and media advertising (including internet). The first, brand marketing, is all about getting the word out about your brand. Your brand may be your name as a realtor, your business name, or your national brand affiliation. Brand marketing is all about having people think of your brand whenever the topic of short sale selling or short sale investing comes up.

Brand marketing could be in the form of a dot com name, where you advertise your internet site. Or it could be the name of your real estate brokerage affiliation. Brand marketing is all

Marketing For Short Sales

about getting that brand in front of the public anywhere and everywhere.

In real estate sales or short sale investing, brand marketing is usually *secondary marketing*. It is secondary because your results generally come to you indirectly through referrals from people who think of your brand when they discuss a homeowner's situation. Brand marketing is accomplished through signs on your cars, billboards, pamphlets, letterhead, business cards, advertising, email signature, etc.

The second type of marketing, direct marketing, consists of activities that target your specific population demographic. Direct marketing includes sending letters or other contact methods to homeowners behind on their mortgage payments. Direct marketing could also be used for *secondary marketing* to bankruptcy and divorce lawyers, mortgage brokers, financial counseling centers, church pastors and counselors, credit counseling organizations who may refer their clients directly to you.

Your most productive direct marketing will be *primary marketing* because you are able to single out and market to your target population demographic and only that group. Your marketing budget should first be devoted solely to direct marketing until you those funds are pulling all of the business reasonably possible through this form of marketing. Once you reach the end of your *primary marketing* (run out of people behind on their payments), funds then may be used for *secondary marketing* using a red light, green light approach. We will discuss that shortly.

Media marketing in real estate has moved almost entirely away from such traditional advertising venues such as newspaper, toward direct marketing and internet. Buyer clients are found through social networking, direct advertising to apartment occupants, and internet websites where homes are sold. Seller clients are generally found through networking and an active approach to holding open houses, where neighbors are personally contacted and the open house is turned into an event. There are other ways to effectively work open houses, but outside of the scope of this discussion. Of course, many buyer and seller clients are still obtained from just having your branded *For Sale* sign in someone's yard.

Internet marketing can be very effective if the site is properly built and optimized, especially if you can create a method of viral marketing. There are three ways to make a website work for you. First, you build your site and market your domain name to drive people to the site. You can do this with your direct marketing items, your business cards, bumper stickers, advertising, car door & trunk signs, billboards, etc.

The second way to make it work for you is to use *pay-per-click*. This is a service through Yahoo or Google where you bid for *pay-per-click* ads on a search page. When someone searches using your search key words, you pay for a link ad at the top or right side of the search page. These are the *sponsored links* that you see when you search for something. You decide what your budget is going to be, and if you bid the amount required to place your domain name on the search page, whenever someone clicks your link, you are charged for that click. You are charged for each click until your budget is reached and your ad then stops showing up on the page.

The third way to make a website work for you is to optimize your site to show up on the first or second page of the *organic* listings. This means that when someone uses the search engine to find sites with key words matching those of your site, they show up high in the organic listings, or the various search results that you see on the main body of the search page.

Website optimization is extremely technical and requires an expert in search engine optimization. A good search engine optimizer (SEO) can make certain that your website shows up on the first page when someone searches for your solution to their need. Search engines rank every site with a number score that is calculated from algorithms. As your site is optimized, the score is raised in competition with the scores of other sites. In addition to search engine optimization, creating a blog and updating it every one to three days can add to the likelihood that your site will show up in a search by greatly increasing the *organic* score. Creating links from your site to other resources that people will utilize when they are on your site will increase the your search engine score for an organic search. Using your blog and other people's blogs to link back to your site will also increase your site's organic score.

If you are serious about building a website, be careful if you are using your affiliated national real estate entity's free websites. Some of those sites are *framed* which makes it easy for you to design using their templates, but a search engine cannot read data in frames and your site may not be able to score high enough to show up on the first pages of a search window. There are rules for scoring high, and a good SEO can make that happen. You can also learn how to properly optimize your website, and more information about this can be found in the *Short Sale Business Manual*.

Whichever way you use your website, it is most effective if you can create a *viral marketing* activity. Viral marketing is finding a way to create a buzz, get others to pass on your advertising, spreading your site by word of mouth or page. Entering an abbreviated entry into a popular blog where you contain a link to your website blog for a more complete discussion, will utilize the popular blog to drive people to your site. For other ideas, enter the search terms *viral marketing* into a search engine to find really smart people with unique ideas for viral marketing.

In deciding which marketing type you should use for your primary marketing, it is very clear who your target populations are: real estate agents, and homeowners who are behind in their payments. Targeting real estate agents is relatively straight forward and they are obviously good targets for direct marketing by mail, email, or utilizing the services of a direct marketing company. The problem is that real estate agents receive a lot of direct marketing pieces, so your challenge is to make something that will stand out and be read by them. Some marketing companies maintain lists of agents, and they have technology that prevents your email from ending up in the junk mail box. Many agents work hard to find unique ways to get the word out to other real estate agents. Some use training sessions, training webinars, gifts, various offers, etc. Others find a way to personally meet as many agents as they can through events, attending open houses, providing food or snacks to real estate offices, etc.

When you target agents, it is important that they understand specifically what you want from them. If you want them to refer short sales to you, then you will need to pay them a

Marketing For Short Sales

referral fee upon closing. The referral fee should be whatever is customary for your area, and is generally in the 25%–33% range. Most agents see short sales as too much work for the amount they receive, so are only too happy to refer them out and will do so for a smaller fee, depending upon what your competition pays. Many large real estate offices will have one or two agents who specialize in short sales so they may get the majority of the referrals, but there are often agents who will avoid referring cases to their in-house competition, so they may be willing to refer short sales and loan modifications to someone else outside the office.

Finding homeowners in trouble is easy. Before a lender commences foreclosure action, they file a *Notice of Default* with the County Clerk or Recorder office. The NOD will contain at least the name and address of the homeowner and property. Utilizing direct marketing, your challenge is to be the one out of many direct mail pieces the homeowner receives all claiming to have the best solution to their problems that is selected by them to call. There are some excellent online resources from whom you can, for a fee, obtain the names and addresses of homeowners *before* the NOD is filed, so you can get to them earlier. These companies watch for payments being missed and will provide you with a regular report of homeowners in given zip codes.

My Personal Marketing Rules

I am the most difficult personality to whom to market anything. I am repulsed by telephone calls and have never and will never buy a product or service from a phone call. The same with sales people who show up at my door. Most of my junk mail goes into the trash without ever being read. When a marketing piece does catch my attention, I scan, not read the piece looking for key words that tell me to throw it away or it deserves more attention. If it is a letter, I will read the first few lines and then scan the rest. I do not watch TV commercials. I zone out during radio commercials in the car. I will never buy anything from spam email.

So, how would you market to someone like me? Here is a set of rules that can reach me by direct mail, email or advertising such as by radio.

1. I have to *feel* a need for your service. If I were a homeowner who has missed my payments, I may be either quietly searching for solutions, or I may be emotionally frozen and doing nothing. Actually the former is likely the way I would respond, but for most homeowners the latter is more likely than not to be true.

2. I have to believe that you may hold the solution for me. You must word the solution in such a way that you do not sound like everyone else who *claims* to have the solution for me. You see, from my view, bankruptcy lawyers only want me to file bankruptcy, mortgage lenders only want to sell me a loan, credit counseling centers only want me to use their service, investors only want to take advantage of me, and real estate agents only want to sell my home in a short sale, whatever that is. This is

Marketing For Short Sales

the way that many people have learned to respond to marketing. You must address that you have a number of solutions and you are out to help *me*, and convince me that you are not just helping yourself. So stating that you have a number of alternatives to foreclosure and that one of those alternatives may be right for them may be effective. Stating these alternatives using solution-oriented language may be helpful for them to see there are a number of ways. Be careful that you do not word the solutions in ways that they may misinterpret the solution and assume the so-called solutions are worthless. Use terms that leave questions.

3. Do not be pushy. Yes, I know that in sales, it pays to be aggressive, but when people are emotionally frozen in financial troubles, aggressiveness can be fatal to your marketing. Today, before writing this, I heard a commercial on the radio that caught my attention about marketing a business. I am always looking for great ideas and information. One statement about how difficult it is to move a small business from one level to another caught my attention, so when they stated that their email reports provide the solution to this common struggle, I became curious and made the call. Like I said, I am always looking for new methods and information. The pushy sales person who answered my call pulled the *bait-and-switch* tactic of attempting to sell, instead of the free reports, a $200 webinar series of training

with some so-called *expert* I never heard of. So, I played his little game and he stayed on the phone with me for 45 minutes arguing with me. To me, it was great entertainment, but finally, I had to literally hang up on him to get him off the phone.

Another example. I have, from time to time, been forced by need or to find the lowest price to go into a *Best Buy* store. I hate that place because every time I shop there, some young sales person who does not know as much about electronics as I do is too aggressive in selling to me. I usually buy at *Circuit City* or *Staples* if the price is close, because there the sales staff are less pushy and more courteous. But now Circuit City is closed. Some people like a good aggressive sales person and may need their help to make a decision. But that is not the case with homeowners in financial trouble. They seldom respond well to pressure. Rather, these emotionally frozen homeowners must sense from you a lack of pressure, a lot of understanding, and that you have a number of tools in your toolbox with which to help them.

4. Under my rules, your identifying my need, the possible solutions, and your words that capture my attention must be in the first few lines if you send a letter, or in your main topic headings if a flyer, brochure, or commercial piece of some kind.

Marketing For Short Sales

5. You should include a statement that you have found solutions for other people that I trust. If you don't have a name, then at least make a statement that you have provided solutions for people such as medical workers, factory shift workers, pastors, teachers, firemen, police officers, doctors, lawyers, etc., so that I can relate to you as someone who understands people like me. Referrals from trusted people is best though.

6. Give them the option for you to either bring an instructional report by or to meet with them to discuss their situation. If they are not emotionally ready to meet with you and feel more comfortable reading your material first, then do not pressure them for a sit down meeting. I provide some reports concerning the alternatives to foreclosure in the *Short Sale Business Manual*.

7. Make sure that you know what you are talking about, and do not guess at answers unless you make it clear that you are making an educated guess, but that you will find out the answer.

8. Really help them to make their own informed decision about what to do. Do not try to close the deal; rather, give them time to think.

These rules are the rules to which I have held for over 20 years of law and real estate, and they have not failed me. I am not a good sales person, but I am great at *solving problems*. Some people can sell an elephant to an apartment-dweller, but I can solve problems. When people become comfortable that I can solve *their* problem, I rarely lost them as a client.

Sample marketing letters to homeowners and real estate agents are provided in the *Short Sale Business Manual*.

Red Light, Green Light

As a child in the 1950's, our three most favorite recess activities were *kickball*, *dodgeball*, and *red light, green light*. For those of you who are unfortunate and deprived former children, here is how *red light, green light* is played, although there are many variations.

One person is assigned the *stop light* position on one end of the field, and the rest of us would line up at the other end of the field anywhere from 25 to 50 feet away. The *stoplight* would turn facing away from us and place hands over the eyes. The *stoplight* would say "green light" and at any point would then say, "red light". The *stoplight* would then immediately turn and if he or she saw anyone with a foot off the ground, that person would be sent back to the beginning. The game was over when the first person reached and touched the *stoplight* or recess was over.

Many years ago, I read a recommendation in a book written by a marketing expert to use the concept of *red light, green light* when testing marketing activities. I wish I could recall who it was that I got this from, but it makes sense. The idea is that you try a limited test marketing and see if there are results. If you obtain good results, then try a larger test. If the result does not expand with your larger test, then it is a *red light* and you proceed to a different marketing approach.

This makes sense with short sales, particularly with sending direct mail pieces to homeowners in trouble. Try a letter or a flyer. If you get poor results, try a different approach with the same people. *Red light* you stop doing ineffective activities, *green light* you expand the activities.

Writing Letters

Sending a marketing letter to homeowners and real estate agents seems like a logical approach to marketing to these target population groups. Agents have reported mixed results, with some having great success, while others have experienced very poor success. The appearance and content of the letters are likely determinative.

The agents and investors who meet with success do so because there is something in the letter that caught the attention of the homeowner over all the other marketing pieces. Some people have included a dollar bill with the letter, indicating that this is one of the dollars needed to solve the homeowner's problem and that the sender has available the rest of the solution. Others have addressed how the homeowners must feel in a way that connected with them. In the *Short Sale Business Manual*, we have sample marketing letters to homeowners in default as well as to other real estate agents from whom you are seeking referrals of loan modifications and short sales.

Summary

I have outlined two forms of marketing: Primary and Secondary. We also discussed the types of marketing: brand, direct, and media. Direct marketing to real estate agents may be effective, especially if you can create some form of viral marketing to obtain referrals. Marketing to homeowners is relatively easy because you can check the NOD listings at your county clerk's office. You can also subscribe to an online service that will provide you with the homeowners who have missed a payment, or two or three. Homeowners have a tendency to be emotionally frozen, so you need specialized methods for reaching them. Using common sales techniques to them often are not effective and may backfire on you. Some emotionally frozen people are often effectively reached by using methods proven effective for reaching strong difficult personalities. There are some rules for effectively working with emotionally frozen people, and it is often most effective to put away your salesman hat, and just be a problem-solver for them. Using a *red light, green light* approach, test different methods of marketing, including marketing letters, but they must stand out from those sent to them by the crowd of agents and investors marketing to defaulting homeowners.

In the next chapter, we will explore and discuss the alternatives to foreclosure that are available to defaulting homeowners.

CHAPTER 3

Alternatives To Foreclosure, Part A

When you meet with homeowners who are behind on their payments, keep in mind that they may be embarrassed, discouraged, desperate, fearful, defensive, angry, emotionally frozen, or a combination of these and other emotions. It is important for you to recognize these emotions and respond appropriately to them.

If you have made an appointment to meet the homeowners in their home, be friendly upon arrival, getting acquainted with them. Exchange names, ask about their work, their family, find something in the home to comment positively on that is interesting, and ask if you may gather at the kitchen or dining room table. When comfortable, ask them in a friendly and caring way to tell you their situation. *Do not interrupt*. When they stop talking ask questions of clarification, about what they have done to try to solve the problem, the results, and how they feel about their situation. When they share their feelings, connect with them by restating back to them their feelings and that if you were in their situation you would likely feel the same way they do and may not have handled things as well as they have.

This *reframing, restating,* and *affirming* approach is part of active listening, and will go a long way toward gaining their trust and respect for what you offer. This approach may help them move out of their immobilizing emotions and unfreeze them. It shows that you care, that you understand how we all

Short Sales & Loan Modifications

can have difficult times in our lives, and that you are there to help them.

In this chapter we will outline the alternatives that are available to homeowners in default. For every alternative we discuss, there is someone who fits that solution. You are there hoping for either a loan modification or short sale, and you will find many candidates who will be a good fit for those solutions. First, though, you must be there as a *neutral*, to help them, to inform them of all of the alternatives, and allow them to make an *informed* decision which alternative is best for them. If you try to *sell* them on one alternative, you are likely to have less positive results, because with time and thinking about it, along with talking to others now that you have unfrozen them emotionally, they may likely no longer trust you and select another alternative.

You must have the heart of a teacher, be sincere, be honest, be knowledgeable, be accepting of their ideas and opinions, gently correcting their misperceptions and misinformation, and you will win their hearts, trust, and respect.

Do Nothing

The first alternative is to do nothing. Sound crazy? In my law practice I have had many business owners and individuals come to me for a bankruptcy, and upon evaluation of their situation, knowing the laws that are available, doing nothing was the appropriate alternative in many situations. Of course, along with doing nothing, I would offer counsel in better managing their income and expenditures, and help them make some major decisions to get back on track.

Alternatives To Foreclosure, Part A

Doing nothing is allowing the foreclosure to happen. In a judicial state, the attorney for the lender files a court action with a Summons and Complaint (or Petition), giving the borrowers the statutory number of days to respond or a Default Judgment will ensue. The Summons is served on the borrowers. After the statutory number of days has passed, the attorney will file a Motion for Default Judgment, which merely is a statement to the court that the time to respond has lapsed and you are asking for a Judgment of Foreclosure. On the date of the hearing on that motion, the Judge will accept from the attorney the Default Judgment and will sign it. It is then entered into the court's record. Every Judgment becomes final after a certain number of days set by state statute, and after that time has lapsed, the attorney submits a request for the Sheriff to hold a Sheriff's sale to dispose of the property. If no one appears at that sale, the lender bids in the amount due that they obtained in the Judgment plus costs and takes possession of the property. After the sale, the lender may then obtain a Writ of Possession from the court that will allow the Sheriff to remove the occupants and their belongings from the property. Now, the length of time it takes and the titles of these documents may vary from state to state, but that is essentially the process.

In a non-judicial state, the owners signed a Deed of Trust when they purchased the home. The actual title ownership is vested in a trustee who may be an attorney, a title company, or perhaps the trust department of a bank. Upon default, the trustee sends notice as required by state statute, and then advertises the sale of the property for the statutory number of weeks (usually three) in the local legal notice publication. On the day of the sale, the trustee bids in the lender's account balance and takes possessory ownership of the property. The lender can then obtain the Writ of Possession and seize the property.

Remember, *everything I say is true, except when it is not*. I have experienced lenders who have asked the now former owners to stay in the property and take care of it rent free. Although unusual, lenders who have customers who were cooperative and took good care of the property recognize that having the property occupied will keep the collateral safe and make it easier to sell. The more that the lender can get for the property, the lower will be their losses and any deficiency balance to assess against the former owners. Sometimes the way to see if this can happen is to merely call the attorney for the lender and make that offer, agreeing to show the property and move out prior to closing. Sometimes they will be willing to do this for no payment; other times they can agree to an appropriate rental amount. I have seen lenders who have paid $1,000 or more move-out money when a resale of the property closes.

In a non-recourse state, like California, the lender can only collect on their debt by the proceeds they obtain from the resale of the property. These states may have very specific situations in which this applies; for example, applying only to the original purchase-money loan obtained to purchase that property and may not apply if the loan was refinanced, and only if this is the owner's primary residence. In recourse states, the lender may resell the property using usual and customary sales like assigning it as a *bank-owned* or *REO* (Real Estate Owned by the lender), or at a well-advertised auction. Upon the sale, the lender calculates the amount they received from the judgment along with accrued interest and expenses and subtract from the total

Alternatives To Foreclosure, Part A

the net amount they received from the sale, leaving a *deficiency balance* that is billed to the borrower.

What can they do now? They can sue for the additional amounts and obtain another judgment for the total amount owed. Then what? They can garnish wages, levy on bank accounts owned by the borrower, and attach property. Sounds ominous, doesn't it?

Actually, for many people, this is not so bad. In each state, there are laws stating the value of certain property of a debtor that may be *exempt* from creditor action. Exempt means that the stated property can not be taken from the debtor. This does not apply to the IRS but it does apply to all judgment creditors, including the lender. These exemptions vary from state to state, and links to these state exemptions are included in the *Short Sale Business Manual*. Exemptions may include the wages for a stated number of hours per week times the minimum wage, a dollar value of their furniture and furnishings, a specific dollar value of equity in an automobile, pension earnings, social security earnings, IRA accounts, 401(k) accounts, even the entire value of equity in the home in some states like Florida and Texas.

A debtor who is retired or disabled, with furniture they've had for many years, who may possess an old car or is financed without equity, living off pension or retirement income, and do not keep their money in a bank account in their name, may not have assets in excess of their exemptions, and may therefore be *judgment proof*.

When talking with a homeowner, it is important to inquire into their future plans, whether they are retiring or disabled, what assets they owned, whether they are moving in with

Short Sales & Loan Modifications

relatives, or if they are moving into a home they own in Florida or Texas. If they are judgment proof, and do not plan to ever purchase another home, they may elect to merely do nothing and allow the foreclosure to happen.

You may be asked what they should do about the creditors calling them all hours of the day, every day, and calling their friends and neighbors. There is a federal law called the *Fair Debt Collections Practices Act* that prohibits creditors from calling outside certain hours and from calling you, your friends, work, or neighbors if you send to the creditor by certified mail a notice demanding them to no longer telephone you, your family, coworkers, neighbors, or acquaintances. Usually merely making this statement over the phone is sufficient, but the letter by certified mail is the procedure. Over the last twenty years, I have only very rarely experienced this procedure to fail. For that creditor, it was worth paying a lawyer to send them a demand of no contact letter.

Even people who are judgment proof may profit from one of the other alternatives, including a short sale. So, make certain that you do not recommend that they do nothing even if they are judgment proof; just make the statement that that this alternative may be one of the alternatives to consider.

A note here. Be careful that you do not advise the homeowner which alternative they should take in their circumstances. That is the practice of law and it is vital that unless you are a lawyer licensed to practice law in that state, that you always, always, always caution them that you are not providing legal advice and that you are encouraging them to seek legal advice for any legal questions or advice they are seeking.

Alternatives To Foreclosure, Part A

Payoff/Refinance

For the homeowner who is about to default on a mortgage, paying off the mortgage or refinancing may be an alternative. Some homeowners have untapped resources in the family who are only too happy to help by paying off the mortgage and holding the note, thus allowing the homeowner to then make reasonable payments to that person or family business. Always ask the homeowners if there is someone they know who could and would help them. They may have merely not yet gotten up the nerve to ask. Many people have such available resources and may have just been waiting to find out if there is another alternative that fits better.

Refinancing may also be an option. Why would a lender loan money to debtors whose home may have dropped in value, who may no longer have great credit, or who are about to be in foreclosure? Because many lenders have been caught up in the relatively recent mortgage scandals and fraudulent ARM loans, and may be eager to provide refinancing into a reasonable fixed interest mortgage loan. Some lenders who are not of that variety may offer a loan that has a higher interest rate to cover the risk of a subprime customer, particularly if there is equity in the property securing the loan.

When meeting with the homeowner, be sure to discuss this option and find out if they have recently gone to see a mortgage broker about refinancing. Hopefully you have a list of mortgage brokers with whom you have networked and that you know will do anything they can to help the homeowner qualify. You should always encourage a homeowner to check out this option to see if this an alternative to consider.

Reinstatement

Reinstatement is paying off the entire default amount plus interest, attorneys' fees, late fees, taxes, HOA fees, missed payments and other fees. It may seem like a no-brainer, that if they could do this they would have already done it. However, experience shows that here again there may be a relative or family business that would loan or give them what is needed to bring them current.

It is all too common that people wait and make the problem worse through indecision and inaction. Never assume that people have done everything they can early on. My 20 years of experience in law shows me that very often people have easy solutions at hand, or was at hand had they only made a decision and acted early. I have filed many bankruptcies that might have been avoided except for this indecision and inaction.

Sometimes people have assets that could be used to secure loans or be sold to cover the costs. I know one family that I met with for a bankruptcy. The wife brought pictures of their home and I observed that they had so much *stuff*, that I encouraged them to have a yard sale before deciding on a bankruptcy. They lived on a busy highway and held a daily sale for three weeks. They sold furniture, cars, PWC, a boat, some old tractors and farm implements, and tons of clothing, tools, child toys, etc. They raised enough money in those three weeks to pay off the amount of default plus fees, bringing their payments current. The wife enjoyed the selling so much that she started a business of selling other people's *stuff* in weekly yard sales and flea markets, sharing 50% of the proceeds with each contributor of the *stuff*.

Alternatives To Foreclosure, Part A

Forbearance

A forbearance is a temporary reduction or suspension of payment of the principal, interest, or both until the borrower's circumstances pass. Many lenders will approve this, particularly if the financial condition is a specific and temporary period of time like a layoff for a specified number of weeks, during recovery from surgery where the recovery period is known, or the loss of employment and a limited period of retraining with a strong likelihood of returning to gainful employment.

A forbearance is obtained by the homeowner calling the customer service number listed on their mortgage statement. A customer service department of the lender is just another name for their collection department. That department exists solely to make sure that homeowners make their payments, and have the power to grant or take applications for most of the alternatives listed in this chapter. Approving of a forbearance has become much more commonplace since the housing and mortgage crisis has forced so many people into foreclosure situations.

The forbearance can include a temporary reduction in the payment. Sometimes the amount the borrower must pay monthly is an interest only payment, but it is quite common that the homeowner is granted an outright suspense of payments for a temporary period of time. To obtain the forbearance, the homeowner will need to submit a financial statement either on a form provided by the lender or one they draft themselves. A form for this purpose is included in the *Short Sale Business Manual*. We will come back to this budget or financial statement shortly.

The amount due during this forbearance period does not go away. Sometimes it will be amortized over the balance of the note causing an increase in the payments at the end of the forbearance period. Other times it may be approved to put the entire forbearance amount at the end of the note plus accrued interest.

Partial Claim

A partial claim is a second loan from the lender for the amount of the arrearage plus accrued interest and costs. It may constitute another mortgage on the property, or it could have language allowing the collateral securing the other mortgage to secure this property as well. It could also remain an unsecured loan with the lender. Sometimes the original security agreement will provide for the property to secure all notes with this lender. This may vary from lender to lender and depend in part on the state laws regulating secured instruments.

Again, the homeowner would apply for this through the customer service representative for their servicing lender. They may or may not qualify for a partial claim depending upon their credit worthiness, but sometimes it is the preferred alternative of the lender and would not require the borrowers to qualify.

Deed-In-Lieu

A Deed-In-Lieu of Foreclosure is a legal document in which the homeowners merely deed the property back to the lender instead of the lender going through the foreclosure. Typically,

Alternatives To Foreclosure, Part A

a deed-in-lieu results in no deficiency balance as it is accepted in full satisfaction of the debt.

A deed-in-lieu has become increasing less common, and is usually accept only in cases of a Chapter 7 bankruptcy or in the event there is substantial equity. As an alternative to foreclosure outside of bankruptcy it is often the least preferred alternative for the lender.

For the borrower, a deed-in-lieu may be far worse than a bankruptcy on their credit worthiness for a new mortgage loan in the future, and may have the same ultimate consequence as a foreclosure. Many, or even most, mortgage loan applications will ask if the applicant has ever had a foreclosure or given a home back through a deed, and if so, this could bar the applicant from mortgaging a home in the near future, or even ever.

Alternatively, bankruptcy may bar a mortgage loan for a while, but not for long term. Many bankruptcy attorneys routinely have their Chapter 7 debtors surrender the home through a deed-in-lieu, giving little thought or legal counsel to the debtor about the impact that process will have on the credit future of their client.

If your homeowner has considerable equity and the lender is willing to accept the home back by deed, the homeowner should consider the future impact of such a decision. If the homeowner is of advanced age and plans to never purchase a home in the future, then the impact may be of no consequence to them.

However, do not give legal advice. Legal advice is giving an opinion as to the law and applying the law to their fact situation. Rather, it is best to give general information about the law and allow them to apply it to their fact situation themselves, referring them to a competent attorney.

Bankruptcy Chapter 7

A Chapter 7 bankruptcy is also called a *straight bankruptcy* or *liquidation*. It is called *Chapter 7* because the federal bankruptcy code is divided into various chapters. There is a chapter for wage earners to reorganize their financial estate (Chapter 13), for farmers who receive revenue seasonally, for businesses to reorganized (Chapter 11), and for municipalities (yes, even cities, towns, counties, and states could go bankrupt).

In a Chapter 7, the debtors must list all of their assets on forms called *Schedules*, along with their debts, creditors, income, and expenses. The debtors must disclose any payments made to creditors within a certain number of days prior to the filing of the bankruptcy (called *preferred creditors*).

The filing of the case with the court instantly halts all creditor actions to collect the debt or to impair the collateral. Creditors who repossess vehicles or who hold a foreclosure sale after the filing but before they receive notice, have to give the collateral back and sales are void.

Upon filing, the debtors' financial estate (income, expenses, assets, & liabilities) are placed in the hands of a trustee appointed by the court. The trustee is usually but not always a local attorney who is appointed to oversee the administration of the bankruptcy case.

The first hearing on the case is usually an informal hearing called the *Section 341 Meeting of Creditors*. That hearing is usually held not in the bankruptcy courtroom but in a meeting

Alternatives To Foreclosure, Part A

room set aside for that purpose. The trustee is usually seated at a table along with a number of attorneys who represent various creditors. It is common for one creditor's attorney to represent many creditors simultaneously. The trustee will have numerous cases and call the cases one by one according to the Hearing Calendar for that day and hour.

When the debtors' case is called, the debtors and their attorney sit at the table. The trustee then looks through the Bankruptcy Petition and schedules, as well as the *claims* filed by the attorneys for the creditors. The trustee's function is to view the claims of secured creditors to make certain that they are properly *perfected*. When the buyer purchased their home at closing, there is a statutory number of days that is required of the lender for their security interest to be *perfected*. The same with automobile financing where the lien is perfected with the Department of Motor Vehicles. A mortgage lien must be perfected with the Register of Deeds or Recorder for the county in which the property is located.

The trustee will look to see when the liens were perfected. It is often the case that there is one that is not properly perfected, so in that case, the trustee will *void* or set aside the lien. If the trustee finds assets that are in excess of the debtors' statutory exemptions, or assets in which liens are voided, then the trustee seizes those assets and sells them at auction. The trustee is entitled to a percentage fee of the proceeds and the balance is distributed to unsecured creditors who file liens.

A bankruptcy Chapter 7 case in which the trustee finds assets that are available for distribution to unsecured creditors is called an *Asset Case*. Likewise a case in which there are no assets that can be seized to distribute to unsecured creditors is called a *No Asset Case*. What many attorneys do not realize is that unsecured creditors who were inadvertently not listed as a creditor and therefore received no notice of the bankruptcy will be discharged the same as if they had been listed, but only if the case is a *No Asset Case*. This is always true except when it is not. The United States federal court system is divided into nine Circuit Courts of Appeal. Bankruptcy law is rarely reviewed by the U.S. Supreme Court, so the decisions on bankruptcy law by each of those circuits is binding on all of the bankruptcy courts in the states that make up that circuit. This discharge of unlisted debtors may not be true of all of the circuits, especially since court-made law is fluid and continuously subject to change.

After the case has been administered, usually about three to four months after it was filed, the debtors will receive a *Discharge* of their debts sent by the court. That discharge means that the debtors have received a forgiveness of those listed debts and no longer owe them. It is an absolute defense to any collection action brought against them by a creditor whose debt was discharged by the court.

A discharge of the debt does not mean a discharge of the creditor's lien on secured assets, unless voided and seized by the trustee. Therefore, a homeowner can either *reaffirm* the debt if they so desire and if the creditor is willing, meaning that they can sign a *Reaffirmation Agreement* with the creditor and they will continue to be liable for the debt, or they can *surrender* the collateral and owe nothing.

Remember when I stated that the trustee will look to make certain that the lender's lien is properly perfected? If it is, then he will *abandon* his interest in the property, meaning he will release the property out of the bankruptcy to be disposed of according to law or as agreed between the debtor and creditor. This means that the debtor can either surrender the home back via deed, or the creditor may proceed with the foreclosure. In this case, there would be no deficiency balance because the debt has been discharged.

Bankruptcy Chapter 7 is a good solution for a homeowner who has a lot of other debt and is in great financial trouble that can be resolved no other appropriate way. Under recent law changes, the debtor must meet certain criteria of income, counseling, etc., but if they qualify, a Chapter 7 is appropriate for many debtors who need a general forgiveness of their debts and to start over.

Bankruptcy Chapter 13

Also called *debtor reorganization* and a *wage earner plan*, Chapter 13 starts out substantially similar to a petition under Chapter 7. One notable exception is that along with the schedules, the attorney writes a *Chapter 13 Plan*. This plan is a one or two page document that first lists the secured creditors, the value of the collateral, the amount the attorney proposes that the trustee pay under the plan monthly, and the interest rate to which the secured creditor is entitled.

The second section lists how priority claims are to be handled, like child support arrearages, student loans, taxes, etc. The plan will then state the percentage that will be paid to unsecured creditors, including the amounts owed to secured creditors over and above the dollar amount secured by the collateral.

The plan payment is calculated first by determining the debtors' income and allowed expenses. This part is critical, and debtors seldom properly calculate their expenses. A lot of objections to plans occur over the budget, and a lot of Chapter 13 plans fail because attorneys fail to properly guide their clients in the construction of the budget. The amount of income over the debtors' allowed expenses constitutes the amount that the debtors must pay into the plan. If that payment will pay off the unsecured creditors in full over the 5 year plan, then the plan is called a *100% Plan*. If it will pay 70% of the unsecured debt, then it is a *70% Plan*, etc.

At the Section 341 Meeting of Creditors, the Chapter 13 trustee will go over the plan. Creditors' attorneys can ask questions, and if anyone objects to the plan, and believes they have a legal basis for that objection, they can file an *Objection* and the debtors and their attorney will appear in the bankruptcy court and respond to any legal objections. It is usual that prior to their case coming before the judge that the attorneys work out an appropriate deal, but I have argued many objections in court. If the attorney has drafted the *Chapter 13 Plan* properly, he will usually prevail.

Before discussing how this type of bankruptcy is useful as an alternative to foreclosure, I should point out that there are 3 kinds of bankruptcy attorneys. The first are those attorneys who will only file Chapter 7 cases. These attorneys are less concerned with the needs of the client than they are with making money. They do not like to write Chapter 13 Plans or other aspects of the Chapter 13 system, and they have a *one size fits all* mentality that thinks that everyone should file a Chapter 7

Alternatives To Foreclosure, Part A

bankruptcy. In my bankruptcy practice, I usually had almost equal numbers of both Chapter 7 and Chapter 13 filings.

The second are those attorneys who will do both, but are not willing to think outside the box to use a bankruptcy to solve other problems for the debtors. They do not care about the credit impact, or are ignorant as to the impact of Deeds-in-Lieu or foreclosures as part of the bankruptcy on the debtors' future plans. They likely know very little about loan modifications and short sales. Anecdotally, I have found that very few attorneys even know what a short sale is, let alone how to use bankruptcy planning to solve various problems. They see the bankruptcy itself as the problem solver for all financial ills.

The third are those attorneys who care deeply about the debtors and their financial situation, the impact the bankruptcy on their lives, and the future plans of the those debtors. These are attorneys who understand all of the alternatives to foreclosure and will use the bankruptcy to meet those needs and plans.

A Chapter 13 plan can be used as a solution for certain specific problems and to accomplish objectives. Now the flexibility of these Chapter 13 plans may vary from district to district, but where the trustees, the attorneys, and the court judges are flexible, the Chapter 13 plan can be written very creatively.

There are some common situations that are well suited for a Chapter 13 Plan. Suppose the homeowners want to sell their home in a short sale so that the lender's losses are mitigated, but little time remains before the sale. The agent or investor attempting to work the short sale discovers that although the lender appears to be cooperative, the secondary market investor or MI carrier prohibits the rescheduling of a foreclosure sale. If the court permits, a Chapter 13 Plan could provide for the property to be sold in short sale, consent obtained to employ the agents to work the deal, and if the lender does not object, the Plan is then *confirmed* and the sale is allowed. Remember, the foreclosure sale is halted at the moment of filing of the bankruptcy petition.

Another situation that bears consideration is when a short sale is approved by the first mortgage lender but a second mortgage lender refuses to consent. I have seen several cases when a second mortgage holder blocked the sale solely because they wanted to hurt the borrower. In this event, a Chapter 13 Plan could be written as we discussed in the previous situation.

This situation provides an interesting opportunity. Remember how we stated that different circuits may have different laws concerning bankruptcies? The bankruptcy reform act of 2005 prohibited *cram-downs* of mortgages on primary residences, which in a Chapter 13 is paying only the amount of the value of the collateral in the secured section of the Plan. This means that the Plan must provide for the full monthly payment of both mortgages, even if the second *could* be paid off before the end of the Plan and there is little or no equity securing that second mortgage.

However, some circuits have construed the law to permit *lien stripping* where if there is not even one dollar of equity available to secure the loan, the court can strip that mortgage of its lien and this second mortgage then is paid without interest, without a preferred payment, and paid along with other unsecured creditors in the Plan. Not all circuits agree, so this solution to short sale second mortgage holder resistance is very state-specific.

Alternatives To Foreclosure, Part A

Be very careful about referring homeowners to bankruptcy attorneys. It is sometimes difficult to find a bankruptcy attorney who understands short sales and who is willing to utilize the system to truly help the debtors. You want them to see an attorney who understands that foreclosure may be more consequential to the homeowners than a bankruptcy, and that a Chapter 13 is a tool that may be creatively drafted for their clients' benefits.

The use of bankruptcy to work on behalf of homeowners in default has been the subject of a lot of debate in congress, and it is likely that the concepts of cram-downs and lien stripping will often be included in these debates and discussions in the future.

Selling the Home

If there is enough equity in the home to sell the property for what is owed, plus the costs of sale including real estate commissions, then one viable option is to sell the home. This will protect the credit of the homeowners. Often people are reluctant to sell the home out of fear of where will live or they just have a distaste for renting again. They may like their neighborhood and their children may be in great schools and they do not want to tear them away from their friends.

It is often the case that people allow emotions to cloud their judgments and to blind them from the obvious. It is important to gently and kindly ask them if they lose the home to foreclosure what will happen then. Give them time to process the answer. Sometimes they will make statements, little by little, that they are coming around to the proper conclusion.

However, if there are pauses during this, remain quiet and let them slowly arrive at the conclusion themselves.

If there is not enough equity in the home to pay the mortgage off plus all these costs of sale, including the real estate broker commissions, then a sale of the home is still possible, with the mortgage lender taking a reduction in the amount they will receive. This is called a *short sale*, *pre-foreclosure sale*, *short payoff sale*, or *discount payoff sale*. That is what this book is about.

If they do not want to sell the home, and none of the other alternatives seem to fit, then a *loan modification* may be the alternative best suited for them. We will discuss loan modifications in Chapter 13.

Summary

We discussed the alternatives to foreclosure and the importance of your being a knowledgeable resource for the homeowner. I intentionally omitted loan modifications from this discussion and we will revisit this alternative in chapter 13. We discussed how doing nothing, paying off or refinancing the mortgage, reinstatement, forbearance, partial claims, a deed-in-lieu, bankruptcy Chapter 7, bankruptcy Chapter 13, and selling the home are all viable alternatives for differing situations. By being knowledgeable of the alternatives, you can provide the homeowner with a number of options that best fit their situation, of course which alternative is best should be the informed decision of the sellers. It is important that you do not advise them which alternative you think is the best choice, but you may tell them, if you are an agent, that you may help them with either a loan modification or short sale. If you are an

Alternatives To Foreclosure, Part A

investor, you can tell them that you can help them by purchasing their home in a short sale.

In the next chapter, we will discuss the listing or buying presentation, and the documents and information that you need to collect.

CHAPTER 4

Listing Presentations and Collecting Documents

"Hello, this is Ken Lawson."

"Hi, I'm Ed Homeowner, and I'm calling because I received a letter from you."

"Yes, I appreciate your calling me, how may I help you?"

"Well, your letter says there are a number of options, and that one of them will be the perfect solution for our situation. I don't know what to do. Can you tell us what those options are?"

"Yes, I can. I am available tomorrow at 4:00 p.m. and Thursday evening at 6:00, which of those times will work for you?"

"Well, do you have a pamphlet or something that will explain those options?"

"I do have a list of options that I could email to you, but they will not explain how options can be adjusted to work in your situation. How about I email those to you tonight and tomorrow we meet to show how to make some of them work for you? There is no obligation and it will not cost you anything."

"Why would you do that if you are not going to try to sell me anything?"

"Because I have learned a long time ago that when you use your business to help people, your business will prosper. I am a real estate agent, and sometimes selling the home is the right choice and sometimes it is not when people want to keep their home. Regardless, if I can help you, you will likely tell other people about the helpful way I do business."

"Sounds good to me, but can you make it at 5:00 tomorrow instead of 4:00?"

"Sure, but may I ask you a few questions first?"

"Yes, you can."

"Will each person who owns the home be present at the meeting?"

"Yes, it's just my wife and me."

"Excellent. Have you talked to anyone else about finding a solution, like a financial counseling firm or attorney?"

"We talked to a bankruptcy lawyer, but we don't want to declare bankruptcy if we can find another way to handle this. We want to protect our credit, and this mortgage is the only thing we're having trouble with."

SCRIPTS

Listing Presentations and Collecting Documents

"Ok, that's good to know. I will see you tomorrow at 5:00 and we'll work together to find a solution."

"Thank you so much!"

 Agents love scripts! When I was selling real estate, I was impressed by how successful agents were able to use just the right words to calm their potential clients, answer questions, address concerns, handle objections, and to put people at ease. Other agents who seemed to me to also be very good with people would often ask other successful agents if they had a written script.

 Scripts are important and they represent that someone has taken the time to choose carefully the words they use to convey a word picture. Many people just talk without giving much thought to their words, consequently causing ill feelings or lack of trust or respect. Carefully chosen words are especially important in sales. I cannot tell you the number of times I have had a sales person end up unintentionally insulting me when responding to my resistance or even mere questions. One sales person stated to me, "I'm not trying to argue with you, Mr. Lawson, I just know that I know more about how this webinar will help you than you realize." What arrogance! Those words say that at twenty-something he knows more than I do about my skill level, my knowledge, and that I am coming up short and need the webinar in order to successfully run my business. The words he chose believing that he was conveying to me a helpful sales pitch were in fact insulting me.

 I went out to eat with some family members to a popular Italian restaurant chain. When I gave my order, I told the server that I wanted my spaghetti with sauce covering the entire pasta. I don't like primarily noodles with a dab of sauce in the middle. When my food was delivered, the plate was about ¾ covered with noodles with a few tablespoons of sauce in the very center. When I reminded the server that I asked for sauce to cover the noodles entirely, he argued with me and eventually said that the sauce is expense and they don't want to *waste* it. The words he chose conveyed the meaning that my eating the sauce is a waste! He was undoubtedly thinking that I would leave a lot of sauce on the plate. To this day, I bristle whenever someone suggests going to a restaurant with an olive in the name. Actually, that restaurant serves great food, and all of my experiences prior to that event and since have been positive, and no else has failed to deliver me great pasta with as much sauce as I desire. But the effect of a subtle but unintended insult has a strong emotional impact.

One of my greatest struggles in practicing law has been articulating well in court. Like many other attorneys, I would write out my opening statement, questions for witnesses, various cross examination strategy questions, and a closing statement summarizing the law and the facts. That process takes a considerable length of time, but it became easier and faster to do this over the years. I always admire attorneys who seem to so easily articulate in a very persuasive manner.

Scripts accomplish the same thing. They help you to articulate statements and responses that are persuasive and break down barriers. The right words paint a clear picture in their minds of the message you truly are attempting to convey to them.

Listing Presentations and Collecting Documents

Many of you are likely much better at writing scripts than I, however, there are a number of suggestions for you to consider when drafting your script for an in-home presentation.

You are meeting with people who are stressed, embarrassed, maybe even desperate. They may also be very skeptical and wary of you.

Be accepting. Accept their circumstances as being ok. It is ok to feel stressed, angry, depressed, fearful, and desperate. Your response: *"if I were in your situation, I don't think that I would have handled it as well as you have. The fear of losing your home to foreclosure can be very oppressive and I think you are doing great."*

Be affirming. If they indicate that they are angry, affirm to them that they have a right to be angry. If they seem really fearful and especially if they say they don't know where they will go if they lose their home, do not say they will find some place to go; rather, say *"yes, I can see how facing that possibility is difficult."* Affirming their feelings and perceptions helps them to see that you are giving empathy to their dilemma. It builds trust.

Show interest in their family, their lifestyle, and their home furnishings. Find something in their home to talk about. A guest that comes into my home that points out how much they like the dining room table that I built and uses words such as *awesome*, is a welcome guest any time.

I remember many years ago attending a training session in which the instructor presented the FORD approach to getting acquainted and breaking the ice when making sales calls. I have no idea where this originally came from but the idea was to first talk about their family (F), then their occupations (O), what they do for fun or recreation (R), and finally their hopes and dreams (D) for the future. They may say that their home was their dream and now their dreams are going down the toilet. If so, use that as the perfect segue to tell them that's why you are here. They may have to readjust a bit, but you can help them to find the solution that will help them recover their future and their dreams.

Ask to gather at their dining room or kitchen table. There are a couple of reasons for this. The table is not only the place where people are comfortable to eat their meals, but it is also a place for family business. You have papers to hand to them and to go over with them, and the table presents that environment. Secondly, you are at the same height as the others, and that makes a major difference in their comfort level. Physically not towering above them helps them to feel a sense of equality and sense of empowerment.

Keep all of these introductory conversations as close as possible to ten minutes. You are here for a purpose and you should be able to sense when the normal stranger to stranger barrier begins to drop and they are beginning to relax.

Now let's review a sample listing or purchasing script. *A* represents the agent (or investor) and *H* represents the homeowner.

> A. It is certainly great to get acquainted with you folks. As I told you over the phone, I am a real estate agent (or investor) and my normal business is selling homes (or purchasing homes). However, part of that process is to help folks like you to solve foreclosure problems and I have discovered that if I truly help people find a solution that is just

Listing Presentations and Collecting Documents

the right one for them, then enough business will come my way to make it all worthwhile, even if selling (or buying) *your home is not the right solution. I can assure you that in the list of alternatives, we will likely find the solution you will select as the best possible one for you and your family.*

H. *That's good to hear, but we want to stay in our home. We can't sell it.*

A. *Then you already have been considering different alternatives. Now, here is a list of alternatives. Let's go over them one by one and talk about them.*

This is the time to pull out the document *Alternatives to Foreclosure* that we provide in the *Short Sale Business Manual*, and go over the alternatives one by one. Make certain that you at no point tell them that they should or should not choose any given option. Remember, if you are not a licensed attorney, you cannot give legal advice. Rather, describe what each alternative means, list the pro's and con's of each option and then give them time to digest the alternative and to either ask questions or tell you that the alternative is or is not right for them. If they say that option is not the right one for them, say to them, *"tell me the reasons this alternative is not the right one for you."* Do not ask with the word *why* because that term often makes people defensive. Just suggest to them to *tell* you the reasons.

In Chapter 3 we discussed each of the alternatives available to them except for short sales and loan modifications, so I suggest that you not go on a listing or purchasing presentation until you have finished the book. Keep your discussions simple yet complete.

There are some common objections that we should address here. In the following scenarios, it is important to clarify and correct common misconceptions and misinformation. Let's take each alternative and address objections or misinformation. The importance here is to learn to articulate each one so you may correct their misperception or misinformation and to set aside stereotypical thinking.

Do Nothing.

> H. *I can't just do nothing, they will harass my family and take me to court.*
>
> A. *I understand how that would be stressful. However, we can show you how to stop them from doing that.*
>
> H. *But it will destroy my credit!*
>
> A. *If you are judgment proof, it will be much easier for you to live and do business without using credit. You will be in a better position to save up an emergency fund to take care of those unexpected emergencies.*
>
> H. *But to get an apartment, I need good credit.*
>
> A. *Actually most landlords will understand the loss of a job, catastrophic medical situations, or how many homeowners were pushed into adjustable rate mortgages and some fraudulently*

Listing Presentations and Collecting Documents

by greedy mortgage people. Besides, even if some landlords require good credit, there are always landlords who will not require it if they can get a sense that you are good people and will take care of their property.

H. *They will take me to court.*

A. *That's ok. They will get a judgment, but if you do not have more than a certain dollar value of assets like furniture, personal items, retirement funds, they cannot take that from you. I can show you how to protect your personal property.*

A. *Maybe this is not the right alternative for you. It is important though to think accurately about these alternatives and to consider whether this alternative is the best one for you or not. That is a decision you will make. My responsibility is to provide you with accurate information so that you can make an informed decision.*

Payoff/Refinance

H. *I'm behind in my payments, my credit is now shot. Nobody's going to loan me any money.*

A. *Maybe that is true. Maybe your credit union, bank, or second mortgage lender will see this situation is worthy enough for this kind of loan, since you have real property it shows stability. Or, perhaps you have a friend or family member who would cosign with you.*

H. No, I would not ask anyone to cosign for me.

A. That's ok, have you tried to get a loan to cover the arrearage on your home mortgage?

H. Yes, I talked to both the mortgage broker who helped us buy the home and my credit union. We can't get a loan.

A. Ok then, we know now that this alternative may not be the right one for you. Let's just put an X by this one on our sheet.

A. Maybe this is not the right alternative for you. It is important though to think accurately about these alternatives and to consider whether this alternative is the best one for you or not. That is a decision for you to make. My responsibility is to provide you with accurate information so that you can make an informed decision.

Reinstatement

H. Where am I going to get all that money to pay all the payments and fees?

A. Do you have a relative or friend from whom you can ask for the money? Can you raise funds through the selling of any assets? Do you have an IRA or investments that you can pull the money out of to bring your home current?

H. I have a 401(k), but I will have to take a penalty if I pull it out.

Listing Presentations and Collecting Documents

A. *If you lose your home to foreclosure, is that possibly a greater penalty than you will pay in taxes on your 401(k). If you are able then to make your payments timely, this option may be one you should put on list of possible alternatives to consider.*

A. *Maybe this is not the right alternative for you. It is important though to think accurately about these alternatives and to consider whether this alternative is the best one for you or not. That is a decision for you to make. My responsibility is to provide you with accurate information so that you can make an informed decision.*

Forbearance or Partial Claim

H. *When the bank called about my payments, they said that there was nothing they can do to help, that I had to get the money or they were taking my home.*

A. *That is merely a collection tactic, and that person may have lied to you. Rather than asking these questions when they call you, you call the customer service number, tell the person that you are having temporary financial difficulty and you would like to apply for a work-out. If they ask you what kind of work-out, say you are thinking about asking for a forbearance or partial claim. If the representative tells you that they do not accept work-outs or a forbearance or partial claim, then ask to talk to their supervisor. If the person argues, ask if they are refusing to allow you to talk to a supervisor. Often the supervisor will be willing to get you in touch with the right person to help you apply for a work-out. If they tell you they* will send you an application, then you should receive it in a few days. If they do not then call you, call them back.

H. What if they only allow me to leave a message with the supervisor and they don't call me back.

A. Then call again and do the same thing. However, maybe this is not the right alternative for you. It is important though to think accurately about these alternatives and to consider whether this alternative is the best one for you or not. That is a decision for you to make. My responsibility is to provide you with accurate information so that you can make an informed decision.

Deed-In-Lieu of Foreclosure

H. Will they be willing to take the home back?

A. They might. This is usually done if there is a lot of equity in the home so they will not be taking a big loss, or as part of a bankruptcy. I should caution though, that it could possibly keep you from buying another home in the future, just like a foreclosure.

H. We don't have much equity in our home.

A. Then Maybe this is not the right alternative for you. It is important though to think accurately about these alternatives and to consider whether this alternative is the best one for you or not. That is a decision for you to make. My responsibility

Listing Presentations and Collecting Documents

is to provide you with accurate information so that you can make an informed decision.

Bankruptcy

H. *Oh, we will lose everything we have.*

A. *Actually, the laws allow you to keep most of your personal belongings and home furnishings*

H. *But won't it destroy our credit?*

A. *Actually a bankruptcy does not normally harm your credit as much as a foreclosure. You can recover from bankruptcy and purchase a home perhaps even in the near future. A foreclosure can bar you from financing another home for a long time, if ever.*

H. *Oh, we are Christians and it is a sin to go bankrupt.*

A. *It is true that the Bible teaches us to pay our debts regularly when due, but the Bible also provides a plan for when we are unable to pay our debts, we can receive forgiveness of those debts. Even Jesus taught people to forgive debts. Actually modern day bankruptcy comes right out of the Bible and is similar to the system taught in the Old Testament.*

H. *The only financial trouble is this home. If we can find a way to solve this mortgage problem, then we don't need bankruptcy.*

A. *That's good thinking. Perhaps this is not the right alternative for you. It is important though to think accurately about these alternatives and to consider whether this alternative is the best one for you or not. That is a decision for you to make. My responsibility is to provide you with accurate information so that you can make an informed decision.*

Selling the Home.

H. *We can't sell our home. Our children are settled into their schools and we can't tear them away from their friends.*

A. *I understand. You are living in a great area. What will happen if the bank forecloses? Will you be able to find a place to live here in the same school district or will you have to move and take them on a great adventure? Children like to stay in the same place, but they are very resilient and adjust to new situations a lot better than we do as adults.*

H. *What will we tell our family and friends?*

A. *Real friends don't care. They only care about you.*

H. *But there is not enough equity.*

A. *Ah, there is a process called a short sale where you can obtain bank permission to sell the house for less than what is owed. These mortgage lenders have a standard procedure for reviewing and approving of short sales, so the house can be sold*

Listing Presentations and Collecting Documents

without a foreclosure and they lose less money. The benefit to you is that you get to start over again, reserving the likelihood of buying another home when your financial condition improves, and you don't have a foreclosure on your credit record.

H. What does it do to our credit

A. *There may be a small to moderate hit to your credit, but not nearly as severe as a foreclosure, or even a bankruptcy.*

H. *How does it work?*

A. *Well, we first agree for me to sell your home (or purchase if you are an investor). As an agent, I will list the home and find buyers for the property. Once we find a buyer, I will draft a short sale proposal and submit it to the lender for their approval. This process takes a long time, maybe even a few months, but once we have the approval, the property will close like any other sale. The lender provides an approval for less than what is owed, and at closing they accept the reduced payoff.*

H. Will I owe the rest of what is due that the short sale did not pay?

A. *Most first mortgage lenders will accept the short sale in full satisfaction of the debt. In those rather less common cases that they do not, then the deficiency balance will be much less than if they foreclose and sell the property for a much bigger loss. If that happens, they will accept very reasonable payments, and sometimes they ask the borrowers to sign a note for only a portion of the anticipated balance. A second mortgage lender though will likely receive very little in the short sale and it is common that you will still owe the balance to them. Whether they will forgive the balance or not, again, it is much better than a foreclosure.*

H. Will I have to pay taxes on the amount of debt that is forgiven?

A. *That depends upon your tax status, and you will need to talk to a good tax accountant about that. Actually, I can tell you that there was a law passed that made it so that many owners do not have to pay tax on the forgiven deficiency balance for a primary residence (be careful that that law is still in place), but again only a tax professional can tell you what will happen in your circumstances.*

H. Well, I talked to the bank when they called about my payments. I told them I was thinking about a short sale and he told me that they would 1099 me if I did that and that I would have to pay a lot of taxes on it.

A. *First, the collection department is only trying to get you to pay them. They have nothing to do with another department that works the short sales. These collectors will often lie to you in order to pressure you. Besides, even if you receive a 1099 after a short sale, that is only a report the bank is required to send; it does not mean that you owe any taxes on it. Only a tax professional can tell you whether you a short sale would be a taxable event for you.*

Listing Presentations and Collecting Documents

The most common conclusion that homeowners will arrive at will be the short sale alternative if they want to sell the home and a loan modification if they want to stay in the home. It is the law of numbers. By the time you are in the home, the other alternatives will likely have been tried and rejected as viable options. Well, that is true except when it is not.

There may be a number of homeowners who will qualify for a loan modification. We will discuss loan modification in Chapter 13. The thing about loan modifications is that if they attempt it, much of the time they are not approved and you get it back as a short sale. If you are willing to take on the processing of a loan modification, then you can charge a fee and make some money off that as well as the short sale.

Collecting Documents

What do you do next? The same as a normal sale, but with some extra documents. If they select the short sale alternative, it is important that you assess their willingness to be cooperative. Cooperating means more in short sales than it does even in normal sales. If the lender detects *any* lack of cooperation on the part of the borrower, they will often immediately deny approval.

Before completing the listing contract, it is important to go over a list of what will be needed. Here is that list:

> Recent mortgage statement from the lender
> Last 2 months of pay stubs from each borrower (when you have a buyer)
> Last 2 bank statements (again at the time you find a buyer)

Short Sales & Loan Modifications

Last 2 years of tax returns
Possibly will have to fill out a budget worksheet

You need to also ascertain their willingness to prepare the home for showing and sale the same as you would with a normal sale. This means deep cleaning, de-cluttering, yard clean-up, and even painting if needed and they are able. This may not be required if they are investors and the property is low income rental property. Any hint of resistance to cooperating is a cause to not work with them. This level of cooperation is very important. If they are living in the home, they need to stay in the home, or abandonment can cause the short sale to be short circuited and accelerate foreclosure.

In the *Short Sale Business Manual*, there will be additional documents to aid you in collecting all of the needed information including a *Short Sale Addendum* to the listing contract which has the language specifically related to this sale as a short sale. For investors, there is an *Investor Addendum to Purchase Contract*. There are also various disclosures and other agreements for your use.

A word about disclosures. I have regularly had agents question me about the need for the many disclosures that I provide. However, I know that as an agent, your risks may seem very low, but as an attorney I have seen everything go wrong that could go wrong. We are living in a very litigious society and a liability lawsuit is only one non-disclosure away. Even though you may have E&O insurance or an umbrella liability policy, you could be sued for far more than the policy limits. Even perhaps more importantly, a judgment for any amount of money will have an impact on your credit report and cause you a great

Listing Presentations and Collecting Documents

amount of stress and time. One cannot have enough disclosures! Well, that is true except when it is not. It is highly recommended that you prevent any foreseeable issues and complaints through the liberal use of disclosures.

In your listing presentation, whether it is the first meeting or second, you will likely have time only to go over the listing contract and the normal documents such as the *Seller Disclosure* and the like. You may need to return for another meeting to review and obtain signatures on the rest of the documents.

Summary

In this chapter we discussed the need for good scripts. Being able to properly articulate the answers to questions and objections is vital to being able to help them form a correct mind picture of how the alternatives apply or do not apply to their situation. Even though I provided some script material, there are many excellent agents who are far more gifted in articulating to homeowners than am I. For those of you who have these skills, feel free to work your magic on the basic framework that I provided.

Do not underestimate the importance of disclosures, and although I cannot guarantee that the disclosures that I provide to you in the *Short Sale Business Manual* will protect you from all possible liability, and although I am not providing to you any legal advice or representing that the documents will meet all of the requirements for your state, I have endeavored to provide you with as much educational material and support as possible. I strongly recommend that you check with your local attorney about the adequacy of those disclosures and documents as applicable under your state laws.

In Chapter 5, we will discuss more about liability, so that you have a better understanding of when and how you may become vulnerable to lawsuits and protect yourself from them.

CHAPTER 5

Understanding Liability

Now isn't this what you would expect an old lawyer to put in a book, a chapter on liability? Well, I don't want to disappoint you. However, I am not going to say much about it, but anyone going into business dealing with homeowners about to lose their home and who yet may indeed lose it to foreclosure, should understand the basic principles of liability.

But, you say, you have E&O insurance, right? Or perhaps a liability umbrella policy? So you don't need to know anything about it? Wrong. Even if you have insurance, most policies have a number of exclusions, and those liability lawsuits will cause you a lot of stress and sleepless nights. You will be put under a microscope and people will be saying that you are the bad guy. Those plaintiffs will be the ones you will least expect. They will be the ones that you went out of your way to help. Every nice thing you did for them, all those conversations will be twisted into more evidence against you.

In addition, you may be sued for a lot more than the insurance policy limits. You may need to hire your own attorney. What? You've been told that the insurance company will hire a lawyer to represent you? Oh, you mean that attorney who is paid by the insurance company to look out for their interests first and foremost? I have seen some insurance-paid attorneys properly represent the insured, but I have also seen the insured's interests not protected as well.

We are primarily discussing potential liability toward your clients, but there are others who may also hold you liable. What about the cooperating agent who brings a buyer and then the bank says they will only approve the short sale if the agents take a 1% reduction in total commissions. The other agent may agree because his buyer wants the property, but later, the agent comes back at you stating that you advertised a specific BAC commission and he wants you to pay it, the agreement notwithstanding. In my opinion Boards of Realtors are not reliable to follow the law with respect to complaints they receive. I have seen very poor quality leadership in some of those organizations and it is important to protect yourself, for I don't think that organization always will.

In the next chapter, we will discuss how to best protect yourself from liability for reduced commissions and what disclosure steps to take in the listing of properties and BAC.

Wouldn't it be a better idea to not have those lawsuits in the first place? Great concept, isn't it? This chapter is all about avoiding liability. There's not much that needs to be said about it, but what is important is that you understand its basic principles, the need to disclose properly, and the need to have great evidence in the event of a dispute.

A person is liable when a judge or jury makes a finding that they are liable. It is also when an insurance company decides to settle a case. You are left with that smear on your character and credit report, not them.

The laws of every state have a body of law called *Common Law*. Common law is the law that is established by the courts. In common law, liability is actually the finding when a defendant is found to have committed a *tort* against another person.

Understanding Liability

Tort liability makes up the majority of court cases outside of family law cases. There are different kinds of torts. Some are intentional torts as when you assault somebody. You have committed a criminal assault against someone for which you may be criminally charged in criminal court. You could also thereafter be sued in civil court for the tort of assault. The criminal courts can put you in jail, assess a fine, or place you on probation. The civil courts however cannot put you in jail but you are sued for civil damages which is reduced to a judgment stating a dollar amount you must pay to the plaintiff.

Intentional torts are generally those lawsuits for assault, trespass upon chattels, injuries sustained as a result of drunk driving, in which there has been established either the *intent* by the defendant to cause the loss, or *gross negligence* resulting in that loss. Intentional torts allow not only for the actual damages that the plaintiff suffered such as medical bills, rehabilitation, medical expenses, psychiatric expenses, therapy, or in real estate intentional tort cases, moving expenses, loss of equity in the home, and any other expenses directly related to the loss, but they also allow for punitive damages and attorneys' fees. Punitive damages could rise into the millions and could be assessed by the judge or the jury.

Unintentional torts are usually call *negligence* cases. Negligence is the tort basis for most traffic accidents, slip and fall cases, and real estate cases involving a loss claimed to be caused by someone who either mistakenly *misrepresents* a fact, or was in possession of knowledge that could have helped the plaintiff and that plaintiff claims they were induced to rely on those misrepresentations or undisclosed information to their detriment and loss.

A good example in a short sale situation would the homeowner who was facing foreclosure. The agent told them that he could sell the home and the lender would likely approve the sale. The agent found a potential buyer and started negotiating with the lender. The lender approved the short sale, but did not reschedule the foreclosure sale and that sale took place prior to closing. The homeowners never disclosed to the agent that there was a sale date set and the agent did not ask the lender. The agent was found to have not exercised *due diligence* to find out whether there was a sale date scheduled and request the sale date to be rescheduled or the closing earlier. The court found that the failure to exercise due diligence was sufficient to find negligence to render a judgment of liability.

Liability cases are usually due to alleged failure of the agent to disclose information to the plaintiffs in order for the plaintiffs to make informed decisions or neglect of their duties to their client. Short sales are never a sure thing and homeowners should always explore various options. There are a number of disclosures that a wise agent will disclose to the homeowners, and those disclosures that are obvious to an attorney or that I've seen in some case reports are included in the disclosure forms in the *Short Sale Business Manual*.

Please Note

This is a good place to tell you that this book is intended for educational purposes only, and nothing herein is intended to represent that any of the laws, information, suggestions, recommendations, steps to take, or other material is consistent with the laws in any given state or the correct decision to make

Understanding Liability

in every situation or in your specific fact situation. I am providing general educational and practical information. It is your responsibility to determine the laws of your state and let those laws guide your decisions. You should always seek the advice of an attorney licensed in your state for any legal question and a tax professional for tax questions.

Potential Risks

There are four primary liability situations that you should keep in mind even with all of the disclosures. The reason for this discussion is that even though you properly disclose, you are still assuming certain *duties* of care toward the parties. First, you have a duty to find out when a foreclosure date is scheduled, if any. To do this, you ask the homeowners for any and all documents they received concerning foreclosure or court action. You also should ask the lender to inform you if there is a sale date scheduled. Finally, if the foreclosures are posted on a website, that website should be checked. This would likely meet the duty of care toward the homeowners.

Secondly, if there is a sale date scheduled and getting close, it is wise to inform the sellers that while you are attempting to obtain short sale approved, they should at least talk to a good bankruptcy attorney for a possible alternative solution if the closing cannot occur prior to closing and the lender is refusing to reschedule that sale date. If they then refuse to see an attorney, you have met your duty of care toward them. Also, they should see an attorney especially if they purchased the home between 2001 and 2006 because the majority of home loans contained RESPA or TILA violations. If the attorney finds such a violation, it would most certainly have a positive impact on a short sale or loan modification proposal.

Third, it could happen that you receive notice that the short sale was denied by the lender just a day or so before closing, leaving little time to consider other alternatives, like bankruptcy. Some of the cases have alleged that even though the agent cautioned them that it might not be approved, the agent was so encouraging and positive that the plaintiffs claimed they were led to believe the approval was imminent, notwithstanding the disclosures to the contrary. Here is where the power of positive thinking can bite you in the proverbial butt.

Finally, your agency relationship itself may create a liability. In normal home sales, the agent makes certain that there is a binding contract for the seller to accept. If the buyer backs out, they lose the earnest money. It has become common to accept the amount of earnest money to be *liquidated damages*, that is, that amount will suffice as the damages suffered by the seller for a buyer's breach of contract. All the seller needs to do is place the property back on the market. In short sales however, if the buyer backs out of the deal, there may be a much greater and more devastating consequence for the sellers. If the bank approves the sale and the buyer backs out, there may not be enough time to find another buyer before the foreclosure sale. The earnest money hardly suffices to cover the losses to the sellers.

It has become commonplace, because buyers' agents know that it may take a long time to obtain approval and that approval may not even be granted, for those agents to make the purchase contract, or offer, nonbinding so that they can easily get out of the deal. I always recommend that only

Understanding Liability

binding contracts be accepted by the sellers. The best contracts are "as-is", but if not, then buyers should be encouraged to hire an inspector early to perform only an inspection of major systems affecting habitability for a fraction of the usual inspection fees. Then, if the buyer still wants to buy the home, they should amend the contract to accept it "as-is" with no additional inspection. If the offer is a good return on investment dollars for the buyers and it is worth the time, then it should be worth committing to a binding contract subject to third party approval within 120 days of the contract.

Then, if they back out, and the buyers want a mutual release, you should advise your sellers to talk to an attorney first, because of the devastating result if they back out and you are not able to find another buyer prior to the foreclosure sale. I made this recommendation to an agent friend of mine, and that very thing happened. The buyers wanted out just before the bank approval, the agent referred the sellers to an attorney, the attorney threatened the buyers with a lawsuit if they did not perform as agreed in the contract, and the buyers went ahead and purchased the home. They were actually happy that they did buy it. They had only been anxious because of the length of time the process was taking.

This lesson brings out two rules for the agent here. First is the strong recommendation that the agent makes certain that the purchase contract is binding. If it is not and the sellers agree to accept it, then you should make sure that you send a letter to your seller confirming that you have advised them about the possibility of the buyer backing out too late to find another buyer and that the sellers could lose their home, and confirming that they have elected to accept the contract against your advice and counsel.

The second lesson is that if the buyers do attempt to back out, that you do what my agent friend did and refer your sellers to an attorney. If you do this, you will have met your duty of reasonable care toward your clients. Having a conversation about these risks with your sellers in advance goes a long way toward the sellers understanding all of the ramifications of their decisions and preventing later feelings that you should have done more.

Liability is an important concept to always keep in mind. Preventing liability should always be a consideration in every aspect of your business. Using the appropriate disclosures along with exercising due diligence is critically important and should always in the back of your mind to guide your decisions and communications.

This chapter is so very important, that you should read it a second time. I will help you with that. Here it is again:

Understanding Liability

Now isn't this what you would expect an old lawyer to put in a book, a chapter on liability? Well, I don't want to disappoint you. However, I am not going to say much about it, but anyone going into business dealing with homeowners about to lose their home and who yet may indeed lose it to foreclosure, should understand the basic principles of liability.

But, you say, you have E&O insurance, right? Or perhaps a liability umbrella policy? So you don't need to know anything

Understanding Liability

about it? Wrong. Even if you have insurance, most policies have a number of exclusions, and those liability lawsuits will cause you a lot of stress and sleepless nights. You will be put under a microscope and people will be saying that you are the bad guy. Those plaintiffs will be the ones you will least expect. They will be the ones that you went out of your way to help. Every nice thing you did for them, all those conversations will be twisted into more evidence against you.

In addition, you may be sued for a lot more than the insurance policy limits. You may need to hire your own attorney. What? You've been told that the insurance company will hire a lawyer to represent you? Oh, you mean that attorney who is paid by the insurance company to look out for their interests first and foremost? I have seen some insurance-paid attorneys properly represent the insured, but I have also seen the insured's interests not protected as well.

We are primarily discussing potential liability toward your clients, but there are others who may also hold you liable. What about the cooperating agent who brings a buyer and then the bank says they will only approve the short sale if the agents take a 1% reduction in total commissions. The other agent may agree because his buyer wants the property, but later, the agent comes back at you stating that you advertised a specific BAC commission and he wants you to pay it, the agreement notwithstanding. In my opinion Boards of Realtors are not reliable to follow the law with respect to complaints they receive. I have seen very poor quality leadership in some of those organizations and it is important to protect yourself, for I don't think that organization always will.

In the next chapter, we will discuss how to best protect yourself from liability for reduced commissions and what disclosure steps to take in the listing of properties and BAC.

Wouldn't it be a better idea to not have those lawsuits in the first place? Great concept, isn't it? This chapter is all about avoiding liability. There's not much that needs to be said about it, but what is important is that you understand its basic principles, the need to disclose properly, and the need to have great evidence in the event of a dispute.

A person is liable when a judge or jury makes a finding that they are liable. It is also when an insurance company decides to settle a case. You are left with that smear on your character and credit report, not them.

The laws of every state have a body of law called *Common Law*. Common law is the law that is established by the courts. In common law, liability is actually the finding when a defendant is found to have committed a *tort* against another person. Tort liability makes up the majority of court cases outside of family law cases. There are different kinds of torts. Some are intentional torts as when you assault somebody. You have committed a criminal assault against someone for which you may be criminally charged in criminal court. You could also thereafter be sued in civil court for the tort of assault. The criminal courts can put you in jail, assess a fine, or place you on probation. The civil courts however cannot put you in jail but you are sued for civil damages which is reduced to a judgment stating a dollar amount you must pay to the plaintiff.

Intentional torts are generally those lawsuits for assault, trespass upon chattels, injuries sustained as a result of drunk driving, in which there has been established either the *intent*

Understanding Liability

by the defendant to cause the loss, or *gross negligence* resulting in that loss. Intentional torts allow not only for the actual damages that the plaintiff suffered such as medical bills, rehabilitation, medical expenses, psychiatric expenses, therapy, or in real estate intentional tort cases, moving expenses, loss of equity in the home, and any other expenses directly related to the loss, but they also allow for punitive damages and attorneys' fees. Punitive damages could rise into the millions and could be assessed by the judge or the jury.

Unintentional torts are usually call *negligence* cases. Negligence is the tort basis for most traffic accidents, slip and fall cases, and real estate cases involving a loss claimed to be caused by someone who either mistakenly *misrepresents* a fact, or was in possession of knowledge that could have helped the plaintiff and that plaintiff claims they were induced to rely on those misrepresentations or undisclosed information to their detriment and loss.

A good example in a short sale situation would the homeowner who was facing foreclosure. The agent told them that he could sell the home and the lender would likely approve the sale. The agent found a potential buyer and started negotiating with the lender. The lender approved the short sale, but did not reschedule the foreclosure sale and that sale took place prior to closing. The homeowners never disclosed to the agent that there was a sale date set and the agent did not ask the lender. The agent was found to have not exercised *due diligence* to find out whether there was a sale date scheduled and request the sale date to be rescheduled or the closing earlier. The court found that the failure to exercise due diligence was sufficient to find negligence to render a judgment of liability.

Liability cases are usually due to alleged failure of the agent to disclose information to the plaintiffs in order for the plaintiffs to make informed decisions or neglect of their duties to their client. Short sales are never a sure thing and homeowners should always explore various options. There are a number of disclosures that a wise agent will disclose to the homeowners, and those disclosures that are obvious to an attorney or that I've seen in some case reports are included in the disclosure forms in the *Short Sale Business Manual*.

Potential Risks

There are four primary liability situations that you should keep in mind even with all of the disclosures. The reason for this discussion is that even though you properly disclose, you are still assuming certain *duties* of care toward the parties. First, you have a duty to find out when a foreclosure date is scheduled, if any. To do this, you ask the homeowners for any and all documents they received concerning foreclosure or court action. You also should ask the lender to inform you if there is a sale date scheduled. Finally, if the foreclosures are posted on a website, that website should be checked. This would likely meet the duty of care toward the homeowners.

Secondly, if there is a sale date scheduled and getting close, it is wise to inform the sellers that while you are attempting to obtain short sale approved, they should at least talk to a good bankruptcy attorney for a possible alternative solution if the closing cannot occur prior to closing and the lender is refusing to reschedule that sale date. If they then refuse to see an attorney, you have met your duty of care toward them. Also, they

Understanding Liability

should see an attorney especially if they purchased the home between 2001 and 2006 because the majority of home loans contained RESPA or TILA violations. If the attorney finds such a violation, it would most certainly have a positive impact on a short sale or loan modification proposal.

Third, it could happen that you receive notice that the short sale was denied by the lender just a day or so before closing, leaving little time to consider other alternatives, like bankruptcy. Some of the cases have alleged that even though the agent cautioned them that it might not be approved, the agent was so encouraging and positive that the plaintiffs claimed they were led to believe the approval was imminent, notwithstanding the disclosures to the contrary. Here is where the power of positive thinking can bite you in the proverbial butt.

Finally, your agency relationship itself may create a liability. In normal home sales, the agent makes certain that there is a binding contract for the seller to accept. If the buyer backs out, they lose the earnest money. It has become common to accept the amount of earnest money to be *liquidated damages*, that is, that amount will suffice as the damages suffered by the seller for a buyer's breach of contract. All the seller needs to do is place the property back on the market. In short sales however, if the buyer backs out of the deal, there may be a much greater and more devastating consequence for the sellers. If the bank approves the sale and the buyer backs out, there may not be enough time to find another buyer before the foreclosure sale. The earnest money hardly suffices to cover the losses to the sellers.

It has become commonplace, because buyers' agents know that it may take a long time to obtain approval and that approval may not even be granted, for those agents to make the purchase contract, or offer, nonbinding so that they can easily get out of the deal. I always recommend that only binding contracts be accepted by the sellers. The best contracts are "as-is", but if not, then buyers should be encouraged to hire an inspector early to perform only an inspection of major systems affecting habitability for a fraction of the usual inspection fees. Then, if the buyer still wants to buy the home, they should amend the contract to accept it "as-is" with no additional inspection. If the offer is a good return on investment dollars for the buyers and it is worth the time, then it should be worth committing to a binding contract subject to third party approval within 120 days of the contract.

Then, if they back out, and the buyers want a mutual release, you should advise your sellers to talk to an attorney first, because of the devastating result if they back out and you are not able to find another buyer prior to the foreclosure sale. I made this recommendation to an agent friend of mine, and that very thing happened. The buyers wanted out just before the bank approval, the agent referred the sellers to an attorney, the attorney threatened the buyers with a lawsuit if they did not perform as agreed in the contract, and the buyers went ahead and purchased the home. They were actually happy that they did buy it. They had only been anxious because of the length of time the process was taking.

This lesson brings out two rules for the agent here. First is the strong recommendation that the agent makes certain that the purchase contract is binding. If it is not and the sellers agree to accept it, then you should make sure that you send a letter to your seller confirming that you have advised them

Understanding Liability

about the possibility of the buyer backing out too late to find another buyer and that the sellers could lose their home, and confirming that they have elected to accept the contract against your advice and counsel.

The second lesson is that if the buyers do attempt to back out, that you do what my agent friend did and refer your sellers to an attorney. If you do this, you will have met your duty of reasonable care toward your clients. Having a conversation about these risks with your sellers in advance goes a long way toward the sellers understanding all of the ramifications of their decisions and preventing later feelings that you should have done more.

Liability is an important concept to always keep in mind. Preventing liability should always be a consideration in every aspect of your business. Using the appropriate disclosures along with exercising due diligence is critically important and should always in the back of your mind to guide your decisions and communications.

Summary

Every agent should have errors and omissions (E&O) insurance, and you should read your policy carefully. You should discuss the policy with your insurance agent to make certain that it will cover the particular risks involved in short sales. Then it is important to understand that you may be liable not only for intentional torts involving gross negligence, but negligence torts as well.

It is important that you provide disclosures to your client, and that you go over each disclosure with them. Even with the disclosures and insurance, you still could face potential liability by not exercising due diligence to determine if a foreclosure sale date is imminent. Also, you should advise your clients to consider other alternatives if the sale date is approaching and you do not yet have approval from the lender. Additionally, if the sale date is very close and the lender will not reschedule the date, then you should advise your clients to seek legal counsel to discuss using a bankruptcy Chapter 13 Plan to stop the foreclosure sale and permit the short sale as part of a plan to mitigate damages for the lender and at the same time the losses to the client.

Finally, it is highly recommended that the agent ensure that all buyer contracts are written so as to be binding before they are accepted, or that you obtain a signed waiver from the client prior to their accepting a nonbinding contract. Then, with a binding contract, the clients should be referred to an attorney if the buyers want out.

In the next chapter, we will discuss some of the issues with listing and marketing the home.

CHAPTER 6

Agency Responsibilities, Establishing Hardship, and Pricing

Now that you have a signed listing agreement and other documents that you normally collect when you list a property, there are additional documents and disclosures related directly to handling it as a short sale that must be reviewed with the sellers. These documents are available to you in the *Short Sale Business Manual*. It is important to not merely place these documents in front of the sellers to sign after you give a short summary. To provide full protection from liability, you should go over each document with them point by point, making certain that they fully understand the disclosures and terms of agreement.

Seller Forms and Information

Since a short sale differs somewhat, a *Short Sale Addendum* providing language specific to short sales should be added. In some states there is a form specifically designed with language required by state statute. The *Short Sale Business Manual* contains a *Short Sale Addendum* containing important additional language. If you have a state form, you can add the language from the provided *Addendum* to the state form. You may be required to use the state-required document, but you should be able to add the additional language into the state form, or request the sellers to sign both. Of course, any language in the form provided in the *Short Sale Business Manual* which contradicts what is required by law in your state must be deleted or amended to conform to state law.

Discuss and obtain approval from the seller for a strategy to reduce the price at periodic intervals. We will discuss this shortly, but you would complete and have them sign the *Price Reduction Strategy Addendum*. This is an addendum to the listing contract authorizing you to make periodic and automatic price reductions of the list price or to hold the price if activity looks like an offer is imminent.

Short sales are handled quite differently from normal sales, and short sale homeowners can often be very challenging. Some may start the relationship being very cooperative and then suddenly stop cooperating. It is advisable to have them sign the *Short Sale Termination Agreement*, also an addendum to the original listing contract. This agreement places them on notice that if they cease cooperating, you will terminate your agency relationship. This agreement has proven quite effective and has greatly helped homeowners to stay motivated. Some agents are reluctant to take such an authoritative stance for fear of offending the clients. However, there is a time for touchy-feely encouraging and understanding, but there is also a time for exercising wise business practices. Business is business, and this is the time for business. You need to be clear that if they choose to stop cooperating, that slowing down or stopping their cooperation will likely cause the short sale to fail and you need to be able to go on to other cases that have a chance of success.

The *Foreclosure Disclaimer* form discloses to the seller certain ramifications for attempting a short sale, such as their not

Agency Responsibilities, Establishing Hardship, and Pricing

being able to receive any of the proceeds of the sale. Again, this is true except when it is not. There are some loan products for which HUD may be offering some cash for helping to mitigate losses and to reward the borrowers for moving out and leaving the property in good condition. Other disclosures involve possible tax ramifications, that their agent is not providing tax or legal advice and the recommendation to seek professional counsel in these areas, and that there is no guarantee of avoiding a judgment of foreclosure or losing the property. The disclosure also permits the agent to purchase the property either in a short sale or at a foreclosure sale, and to necessarily disclose the sellers' negative financial condition for necessary purposes such as listing the property as a pre-foreclosure or short sale.

There is a *Mediation Request* in the event the services of a mediation firm are sought to process and mediate the short sale. My firm regularly provides these services, however there may be other mediators who provide similar services. Be careful about mediation firms and especially other third party short sale companies. Make certain that the mediator is also an attorney, as these professionals are much better suited to handle the peculiar problems that can arise in short sales. It is recommended that you avoid non-attorney third party short sale companies, as they are usually agents or investors who consider themselves experts, but really *do not know what they don't know*.

Mediators are particularly concerned with ethical standards. Serving as *neutrals*, the mediator is not representing any party, but is protecting the *interests* of each party. They are obsessive about confidentiality, and they have very effective methods and techniques for working through issues and problems that may arise.

We have already discussed the *Seller Alternatives to Foreclosure* which the sellers need to sign after a full review. This form lists and provides a brief explanation for each of the alternatives they have for their financial condition as it relates to their mortgage.

An *Authorization and Release* is required for each lienholder and use a separate form for each entity. Make certain that the account number is accurate. Also be sure you are provided with a mortgage statement for each entity so you may verify the account numbers and the correct legal name. It is common that I receive releases only to discover that the handwritten account number is missing some digits or numbers are transposed. Before you leave the home, compare the account number on the statement with the number handwritten on the release.

The *Authorization and Release* must be signed by *each* borrower. Sometimes other related and unrelated parties are also on the note as a borrower or co-borrower, so the release must be signed by each of them. The same with the listing contract and other documents. Make certain also that the sellers enter their social security numbers and dates of birth as this information may be required by the lender as confirmation that the voice on the phone is the same as on the release.

Let's be very clear here. Every *owner* must sign the listing and sale documents. Every *borrower* (even if a person who signed the note is not on the ownership deed) must sign the *Authorization & Release* and provide a hardship letter and supporting financial documentation.

There are many illegal aliens present in the U.S. and some of them have been permitted to finance mortgages. Not having a valid social security number, they may have used a

Agency Responsibilities, Establishing Hardship, and Pricing

fraudulently obtained number, or a number provided by the Social Security Administration or IRS for this purpose. It is not your purpose here to judge, but it is important that if you sense this may be the case, assure them that everything they provide to you is confidential and you need the number they provided on the mortgage loan application, whatever it is.

Also, make certain that on the release where handwriting is printed, that it is very clear and readable, and is written in *dark, black ink*. The process of faxing and imaging can cause a great amount of degradation, so it is important that the signatures and hand written data on all documents are clear and readable.

Hardship Letter

Two common mistakes made by realtors and investors processing short sales that results in rejection involve the hardship letter and production of financial statements. These agents merely request the borrowers to write a hardship letter and fill out their budget and they then forward what is submitted to the lender without reviewing them for accuracy. Wrong!

Most people have watched *Law & Order* or some other police or court shows enough to know that if someone is arrested for a crime and then appears for trial, that the prosecution must prove the case beyond a reasonable doubt. To do this, they must take the state statute that was alleged to have been violated and prove each and every *element* of that crime. The case turns on the technicalities of each *element* having been proven.

In short sales, the lienholders are able according to law, regulation, and contractual restrictions to approve short sales, but one of the elements that must usually be "proven" is that the sellers are in hardship circumstances, and hardship is carefully defined. That hardship is shown by a properly written *hardship letter* and *financial statement* completed by the borrowers. In the *Short Sale Business Manual*, I provide you with a sample letter for this purpose, along with a list of elements that should be addressed in the hardship letter.

Although there may be some differences between lenders as to what is required in the letter, there are some common elements that should be addressed. The letter should state what the borrowers' financial condition was when the home was purchased and how they could afford the mortgage at that time. It should state their care of the property to maintain its condition and value within the level of their ability.

The letter should state the events that created the hardship, that is, the *involuntary* circumstances that caused the hardship. Going to prison is *voluntary* (the voluntary criminal act being the precipitating cause). Divorce is considered to be involuntary. So is being laid off from work. Getting sick, having a baby, or undergoing surgery and rehabilitation is accepted as involuntary. Going back to school is voluntary and does not constitute a hardship, unless that return to school is part of a layoff or job retraining program. Being fired is considered to be voluntary, even if there is a personality conflict and the employer is difficult to work for.

The letter should state how the borrowers attempted to overcome the hardship and what prevented their financial rehabilitation. The efforts they made to make the payments in spite of their circumstances and what prevented those efforts from being successful should be described.

Agency Responsibilities, Establishing Hardship, and Pricing

The letter should address how the borrowers attempted unsuccessfully to work with the servicing lender's collection department, without complaining about the lender's employees. Those complaints are not believed and not accepted as a valid excuse to not attempt some kind of workout. HUD requires that borrowers attend credit counseling with a HUD approved counselor as part of the attempted workout activities. The letter should address those efforts.

The letter should address the borrowers' understanding that the lender will be losing money, their regret for this happening, and their willingness to cooperate with the lender to get the house sold for the highest price possible. The borrowers should describe in the letter what they will do to make this happen, such as getting the home in show condition, cleaning, painting, yard work, and anything else they can do to show a high level of *partnering* with the lender to sell the house for the highest price.

The letter should then make a plea for the lender to approve the short sale, and their gratitude toward the lender for doing so. This request to have the lender approve the sale may seem to be obvious because it is part of the short sale proposal, but this is an element that must be in the letter with some lenders, to literally ask them to approve the sale.

They should end the letter by thanking the lender for entrusting them with the loan and the desire to refer friends, family, coworkers, and neighbors to the lender in the future for their mortgage needs. This is merely a point of courtesy the value of which should not be overestimated. Borrowers often do not consider that real human beings review the short sale proposals and little courtesies can help motivate these reviewing decision-makers to make that extra effort to get the short sale approved.

The letter should be handwritten clearly, printed clearly, or typed. It should be on a standard 8½ x 11 sheet of paper. If the letter is multiple pages, each page should be numbered. The letter should follow standard formatting with indented paragraphs. It should be dated, include the borrowers' name and address, along with the account number. The letter should not have crossed out words, but should rather show that the writer took their time to provide a good letter.

It does not matter if the writer has spelling errors or grammar problems. What is more important is that even an unsophisticated borrower helps the reader to understand that the hardship was not their fault, that they did everything reasonable to solve the problems, and were unable to resolve them.

The letter must bear the signatures of all borrowers. However, if the borrowers are not living together, then they should each write separate letters because their circumstances are different. Separated husbands and wives, parent and child, former cohabitating partners, should have separate letters, each of which needs to conform to these elements.

Budget/Financial Statement

The financial statement is the other item that often tanks the proposal. Both the letter and the financial statements demonstrate or do not demonstrate the hardship that legally or contractually permits a short sale. A personal financial statement is required to meet technical requirements in bankruptcy cases as well, and I have seen many bankruptcy lawyers experience

Agency Responsibilities, Establishing Hardship, and Pricing

problems with their cases due to this technical nature. When I have received financial statements or budgets, very rarely are they drafted properly and accurately.

A financial statement for most married couples is merely a budget, listing income and expenses. It also includes a list of assets with their current market value and a list of liabilities. If either of them own a business, then separate financial statements must be provided for their share of that business.

I have included in the *Short Sale Business Manual* an asset and liability worksheet, and an income and expense worksheet. These worksheets will suffice as financial statements if the lender does not require them to be on their branded forms. The financial statements are actually required by the SMI, so their requirements rule. Some do not require the financial statements at all; others want them on their specific forms; and still others just want the information and the supplied forms are acceptable.

One point of issue with financial statements completed by homeowners is mere calculation errors. These calculation errors are not just errors in arithmetic; they include errors in how many weeks are in a month or a year. If a worker gets paid weekly, then his income is not multiplied by 4 to obtain the monthly amount. The weekly amount is multiplied by 4.33, because there are an average of 4.33 weeks in a month. There is also a difference between bi-weekly and semi-monthly. Getting paid twice per month is 24 paydays per year and bi-weekly is 26 paydays annually. Bi-weekly is getting paid every other week on the same day of the week. Semi-monthly is on set dates twice per month, such as on the 15th and 30th of each month. To calculate monthly income from bi-weekly pay amounts, multiply the bi-weekly amount by 26 and then divide by 12 to arrive at the monthly amount. For semi-monthly pay periods, merely multiple the semi-monthly by 2 for the monthly amount.

If the financial statement has space for deductions, then you enter the gross pay so long as the deductions are calculated into a net income amount on the form. If not, then enter the net pay as the income. Do not include deductions for credit union or voluntary retirement accounts as those are voluntary and not counted to show hardship.

Most people when they buy groceries, also buy cleaning products, personal care supplies, paper products, and other necessary miscellaneous items at the same time. Thus, the amount for food should include these budget items unless the form provides a specific category. I have seen several forms have separate lines for food and cleaning supplies. So, they would separate out the regular budget amount monthly for cleaning supplies and the rest on the food expense line.

Mathematics again here. If they buy groceries and other items weekly, then multiply the weekly budget amount by 4.33 to obtain the monthly amount since there are 4.33 weeks in a month.

Another budget mistake involves automobile expenses. If the vehicle uses oil regularly, then include that with the gas expense. There are two areas of automobile expenses: gas & oil that most people buy weekly, and automotive maintenance. Gas & oil expense weekly is multiplied by 4.33 to arrive at the monthly amount.

Automotive maintenance and repairs is a bit more complicated and most people fail to insert a realistic amount for

Agency Responsibilities, Establishing Hardship, and Pricing

this category. Let's say that you have two vehicles and you use synthetic oil in the vehicles and change the oil and filter every 6,000 miles. One of the vehicles achieves this about every 4 months. The other vehicle may reach this mileage in 6 months. Suppose you change your own oil and filter and this costs about $50 for the oil and Napa filter (only use quality filters). Suppose also that you need to change your air filter each time as well, and again only use Napa filters. So, about another $10 is added for this cost. The oil and filter changes costs about $60 each times 3 oil and filter changes per year, or $180 per year for the first vehicle, and 60 x 2 = $120 per year for the second vehicle. The total is $300 per year. So this expense is 300 divided by 12 = $25 per month.

In addition, suppose your truck requires tires about every 3 years, an expense of approximately $700, or $234 per year. The car tires costs about $1100 each two years, or $550 per year living in a mountainous area. Other maintenance or repair items include brake pads & rotors, wheel alignment, tire rotation and wheel balancing, bi-annual changes of thermostat, hoses, vacuum lines, cooling system flush, transmission servicing, car washes, annual waxing, interior detailing, air conditioner servicing, etc. Cap, rotor, and plugs require changing periodically as well. These are all maintenance items needed to keep the vehicles properly maintained for many years.

Then we must add the anticipated cost of repairs. If the car is fairly new, then this expense will be quite low. Over time, there are things that wear out and need replacing. Your truck is 14 years old and you decide to keep it for another couple of years.

Keeping a vehicle well maintained will make it so that you will seldom brake down. You try to make certain that you replace parts *before* they wear out. When a vehicle's mileage turns over about 110,000 miles, it is time to replace the alternator, the starter, and other items that tend to wear out at that time. Some cars have timing gears or chain, so that should be replaced at an appropriate intervals so the vehicle will not break down.

The Universal or CV joints should be checked and replaced if wearing. Keep track of differential fluids, wheel bearing grease, and tire wear patterns, replacing seals, repacking bearings, or having tires rotated and balanced, and wheels aligned as necessary.

It is important for borrowers to anticipate and calculate projected expenses over the course of a year and divide that amount by 12 to obtain the monthly amount and enter that amount as automobile maintenance.

Many people pay tithe and offerings at church. This will be acceptable as budget items as long as they are kept to 10%. In the bankruptcy court district I was in, when debtors argued to the judge that their budget needed 15% for tithe because they were absolutely required by God to give 10% tithe plus 5% offerings. The judge would listen and on one occasion I overheard him tell a couple that the Bible teaches that we are absolutely required to live a perfect sinless life, but when we fail, He is the first to forgive us. Likewise, he told them, the Bible absolutely requires that we pay our debts regularly when due, but when we fail, the Bible teaches a bankruptcy forgiveness of debt, and God is the first one to forgive, meaning that in this situation, during financial recovery, God does not hold

Agency Responsibilities, Establishing Hardship, and Pricing

us to that obligation. Some people may argue with that logic, but the laws, the courts, and yes, a person's mortgage lienholders have a right to limit giving to a church for purposes of a permissible budget item for short sale approval. A 10% giving is usually seen as reasonable.

The point to this section is that you should review the sellers' paystubs to ensure that their budget compared to their net pay does in fact evidence a hardship and that the budget items are reasonable under their particular circumstances.

The financial statement does not need to be completed immediately upon listing. It is needed when you find a buyer and prepare the proposal. It may not be needed at all, but you should have it completed early so that with re-writes, it will be ready when you submit the proposal.

Note – if the borrower is a small business owner, owning the majority of stock in a corporation or LLC, they will need to financial statements completed for those entities, and a separate personal financial statement for themselves personally.

Listing the Property

For real estate agents, you will want to list the property with the local Board of Realtors MLS or BLC. When you have collected all of the documents necessary to list the property, then enter it into your multiple listing service (MLS) or BLC, the name that some boards are now using. The hardship letter, financial statements, paystubs, and the bank statements are not required up front, but will be submitted after you receive your first accepted offer. In fact, you should direct the borrowers to keep and be prepared to provide you with the *most recent* two months of paystubs *at the time proposal is submitted to the lender*.

It is important that you follow your local Board of Realtors' rules for entry. Different boards have different rules. Some agents have had a great deal of trouble with the way their local boards have interpreted the rules. In law there are attorney jokes based upon the great amount of greed and dishonesty by a minority of attorneys who give the rest of us a bad name. Likewise, in real estate there are some brokers and agents, some of whom may be connected with some local boards, who give realtors a bad name.

We will address those problems in a moment. But first, when you are completing the MLS entry form, you should check the disclosure boxes that would indicate that this listing is *"pre-foreclosure"*, *"possible short sale"*, or other similar wording to that effect. If both of those are available, check them both.

Most entry forms allow you to insert language in *Agent to Agent Remarks*. If so, I suggest the following wording: *"Possible short sale. By showing this property, you agree to the attached media. Obtain short sale instructions from listing agent before submitting offers"*. The idea here is that it is important to disclose to them clearly that there are required terms and language that must be included in an offer. Also, there is a possibility, and it happens about half the time that the lienholders may require real estate agents to accept a reduction in commission as a condition of approval. More about this in a moment.

Attach the document *Before Showing This Property* as a media attachment. This document is included in the *Short Sale Business Manual* and is merely a one page sheet that tells potential buyers' agents about the possible commission reduction,

Agency Responsibilities, Establishing Hardship, and Pricing

and that they should discuss this possibility with the listing agent and reach an agreement as to how they will divide any such reduction in the event it is required. In the *Short Sale Business Manual*, there is a *Commission Modification Agreement* for this purpose.

In a normal sale, you would offer a BAC (Buyer Agent Commission) to the cooperating agent who finds you a buyer for the property. This BAC is entered either as a specific percentage of the sale price or as a specific dollar amount. Most commonly it is the percentage. Some agents have a listing agreement for a total commission of 6%, or 7%, or more or less. They sometimes will offer to split that percentage equally (e.g. 3.5%) for the BAC. Other times, them may offer something less (or more) than half of the total commission percentage.

Let's take a closer look now at the possibility of reduced commissions. After following the above procedure, you now have stated in the listing the amount of BAC that you are paying the cooperating agent at closing if the short sale is fully approved. However, sometimes but not always, the lienholder may require that the agents voluntarily accept a reduced commission as a condition to approval by that lienholder. If that condition is accepted by the parties, then the cooperating agent would not receive the full commission published in the MLS listing. They will have voluntarily agreed to modify their commission. This is permitted under the National Association of Realtors Standards of Practice.

Follow this reasoning now: the above procedure provides for a specific percentage published in the MLS as the BAC. The agent to agent remarks have directed the agent clearly to a media attachment before they show the property. The media attachment clearly states that the short sale requires third party lienholder approval, and that the third party lienholder *may* require the agents to accept a commission reduction as a condition to approval. The cooperating agent is directed to discuss this possibility in advance and reach an agreement as to how they will divide any such reduction, if it happens. With this procedure, no agent could reasonably come back later and claim that he or she did not know that there might be a reduction, and they were directed to reach agreement in advance before they became obligated as an agent to a buyer under a purchase contract.

However, there arose a problem in one local board. Even though it appears that in a possible lawsuit, an agent would be estopped from claiming that he was fraudulently induced to receive a reduced commission and not the published commission, this local board leadership stated that notwithstanding the disclosures and agreements, that the agent should pay the published BAC. In addition, I received anecdotal evidence that an agent serving as an arbitrator for the local board made public statements that he would rule that the agent was entitled to the published BAC regardless of any disclosures and agreements.

If this is true, then this would fly negatively in the face of logic! First, the arbitrator, if this happened in fact, is violating ethical standards by "ruling" on facts not before him, showing extreme bias. Second, the above procedure was established to meet legal and ethical standards. There is no way to know if a lienholder is going to condition approval on a reduced commission, and *you cannot get a full commission if you do not ask for it.* I have often seen approvals for 6%, 7%, and even 8% commission.

Agency Responsibilities, Establishing Hardship, and Pricing

As far as I know, this issue has only arisen in one local board of a large metropolitan area. I can only outline a procedure designed to meet the legal issues of disclosure and contract. If there is any doubt that your local board or grievance arbitrators are going understand and support this procedure, you may want to consider either conforming to their idiocy or be prepared to have your managing broker or a good attorney ready to represent you.

There are stupid people everywhere, and in every profession. I once was in a judge's chamber in Tennessee and I overheard the judge talking to an attorney in a divorce case involving the alleged sexual abuse of his baby daughter by the father. The judge stated that he did not think that molesting a child hurt the child any, and as *proof*, he told the story about how he, the judge, was molested as a child and it did not hurt him any. Yes, stupid people everywhere and in every profession.

Most of you have really good quality and professional leadership in your local boards, but you should remain alert for problems and circumstances with which you must deal. It is best to not be caught off guard by stupidity and unfair bias.

Determining a Price Strategy To Generate Offers

You will already have calculated the fair market value of the property and determined that it is less than what will pay off the mortgage note plus the costs of sale. Now let's talk about a price reduction strategy.

First, you need to understand how short sales are assessed and approved by the lenders. When borrowers obtained their mortgage loan, they obtained the loan from a lending institution such as a bank, credit union, mortgage company, or investment company. At that point the lender no longer had in its possession that $100,000, $200,000, or $300,000 that had been loaned. Obviously you cannot make too many loans before there is no more money to lend. So the federal government and private investment entities established *secondary market investors* (SMI) to channel capital funds back into the market for more loans. The lender that made the loan then sold the mortgage loan *note* to the SMI, and as part of the sales contract, retained certain *servicing rights*. Those servicing rights permit the lender to accept the payments, retaining part of the payment as its fees, forwarding the balance of the money received to the SMI.

The borrower is notified when the note is sold, but borrowers often do not understand the notices when they are received, so may not be aware that the bank or mortgage company they are sending their money to is not the entity that actually owns their loan. Secondary market investors include Fannie Mae, Freddie Mac, Ginnie Mae, and a host of private investment entities and publicly traded securities entities.

Additionally, when the loan was made, the borrower may have been required to pay for *private mortgage insurance* (PMI) on the loan. That insurance pays the face value of the policy to the lender in the event of a default by the borrowers. Sometimes the lender or even the investor may purchase that insurance, so the borrower might not even be aware of its existence.

All three of these entities, the servicing lender, the SMI, and the private mortgage insurance carrier (MI carrier), if any, also have the right to approve or not approve the short sale. Although you are submitting the short sale proposal to the

Agency Responsibilities, Establishing Hardship, and Pricing

lender, you are really seeking SMI and MI carrier approval. So the proposal should be drafted to meet the needs of those entities. In this book, I use the term *lender* rather loosely, sometimes referring to the servicing lender and sometimes using it to refer to all of them, the servicing lender, MI carrier, and SMI.

How do you know who that investor is? Often you will not. Servicing lenders are not required to tell you, especially if the investor is a private company. So how do you know how to tailor your proposal? You draft it to the highest standards possible.

So now, when you submit a proposal, it will be analyzed by the servicing lender. The person may have the title of *negotiator* or *analyst*, but those are really misnomers. That so-called negotiator may have little or no discretion in the approval of the short sale. The negotiator or analyst merely reviews the proposal for the necessary elements, information, and documents, orders an appraisal, and submits the proposal to the MI carrier and SMI. The SMI will analyze the proposal for legal elements present (found in the hardship letter, financial statements, tax returns, pay stubs, and bank statements) to determine if they can permit the short sale, and an analysis to determine if the short sale price is sufficient.

Besides making certain that the borrowers have proven a hardship, there are two methods of determining if the short sale can otherwise be approved. In one approach, the investor compares what they will likely lose if they foreclose and seize the property, selling it as a bank-owned or REO property. This *comparison analysis* means that if your short sale purchase contract nets to the bank more than would reasonably be obtained from selling it as an REO with the associated costs of management and other expenses, then the short sale will be approved.

Another approach that is becoming increasingly more prevalent, is a *minimum threshold percentage*. The SMI sets the minimum percentage of the fair market value (fmv) that the net amount received by them in the sale must yield. If the offer price is equal to or greater than that threshold percentage, then the sale will be approved. If not, then the proposal will be rejected, often outright with no opportunity to negotiate, and you might be required to start all over again in order to resubmit a new offer for consideration. Occasionally, the SMI will respond with a report back via the servicing lender informing you of the minimum net receipt amount they will require, but often the proposal is merely rejected.

So how do you know what that percentage is? You likely will not know in advance. Most commonly it must be above 80%, but 82%, 85%, 88%, and 92% of the fair market value of the property is also common. Some are lower and some are even higher. HUD keeps changing their rules, so you should consult their website to find out what they are currently requiring as the minimum threshold percentage on FHA or VA loans.

This makes working short sales quite difficult. You likely will not know which approach is being utilized to evaluate the short sale by the SMI, because you are unlikely to know who the investor is unless it is a HUD backed loan. So you likely will not know if it will be approved at 70% of the fmv or if 92% is required. You do not want to *not* submit a proposal just because you do not have a high percentage fmv, so in many cases you must simply use your best judgment. In this respect a short sales is somewhat of a gamble. I can guide you to not

Agency Responsibilities, Establishing Hardship, and Pricing

make common errors, but even so there is a bit of gambling in this. It's like going to Las Vegas and playing blackjack by counting cards. You are reducing the risks through carefully developed principles, but there is still a certain amount of gambling to it.

This discussion is important in developing a pricing strategy for the home. You need to obtain offers for the property and pre-foreclosure or short sale properties are going to attract lower offers. So I recommend that you very carefully calculate as accurately as possible the fair market value of this property. Not a range, but the actual price you will stake your reputation on as the one-number value of this property at this time. Then I recommend that you set the first list price at 95% fmv. That may net to the lender less than what the investor may approve, but you have to start somewhere that will get offers quickly.

Then I suggest that you begin reducing the price each week or every two weeks. Ideally, you would determine a weekly or bi-weekly price reduction strategy over an 8 week period. If you choose to drop the price every two weeks, then you would drop the price by a larger margin than if you use the weekly reduction strategy.

The amount to reduce the weekly price should be determined by the end price point after 8 weeks. That amount should net to the lender at least 82-88% fmv. This is true except when it is not. There are other factors to consider, including how well pre-foreclosures and shorts sales are selling in your area. A glut of short sales may not be bringing in any offers above 65% fmv and you need offers. One location that serves primarily as a bedroom community for a mountain resort area never had pre-foreclosure sales until recently and they have no buyers desiring at this point in time to move into this community due to the economy. The only buyers are local wealthy people who are only willing to buy them for pennies on the dollar.

There are many times when the amount the sellers owe is much greater than the fair market value of the property, and the lenders can be quite sensitive about setting the initial list price too low. If you have sellers who owe tens of thousands of dollars greater than the fair market value, you should consider adding some weeks to the front of your 8 week plan to start the pricing closer to, or even half way between the fair market value and the amount of the debt. This will provide evidence to the lienholder that you attempted to mitigate their losses but that no one is going to submit an offer for more than the value of the property, especially in a pre-foreclosure situation.

Summary

If the sellers have decided to list the property with you as a possible short sale, there are a number of documents to review with them. Some are legal disclosures, terms and conditions in the form of addendums, and various information and documents the borrowers are required to produce for submission to the lender.

Of special importance is the hardship letter and financial statements which most people do not accurately provide and this accounts for many rejections of short sale proposals; however, agents often do not discover the real reasons their proposal failed. Budget items must be calculated carefully, and weekly, bi-weekly, semi-monthly, and annual expenses properly converted to a monthly amount.

Agency Responsibilities, Establishing Hardship, and Pricing

The information entered into the MLS listing should include special disclosures to prevent misunderstanding and complaints from cooperating agents who may not otherwise realize that their commission could be reduced as a condition for approval by the lenders. The agents should discuss and reach an agreement as to how they will divide any such reduction in commission if so required.

You should calculate the list price strategy carefully, starting out with a percentage of the fair market value and leveling off about 8 weeks later with a net to lender amount that may still receive approval by the majority of investors, somewhere around 80–82% of the fair market value. When the amount of the debt far exceeds the value of the property, adding some weeks where you list the property at a price point between the fair market value and the amount of the debt will help the lenders see that you are attempting to mitigate their losses.

In the next chapter, we will discuss marketing the property and managing offers.

CHAPTER 7

Marketing the Property and Managing Offers

The great thing about short sales is that aside from listing the property in the MLS or BLC, you do not really need to market the property. It is a good idea to list the property with online sites and there are a few sites where you can submit the information and they will forward the data to around a hundred or so different sites. Marketing short sales is essentially free.

There is also no need for an open house. No paying for advertising. Just list the property and adjust the list price according to your schedule. Of course, make absolutely certain that your sellers are going to be cooperative with showings at all reasonable hours and days. They may need you to help them remain motivated throughout the process.

If you reach a point in your price reductions strategy when you receive a good offer and there is still a fair amount of showing activity, you may wish to hold the line on that price point and not reduce it further for a while, unless you do not receive any more offers. The idea is to have more offers and it is a good idea to keep the published listing in whatever category that will allow you to accept multiple offers. You do not want too many offers though. Two or three is perfect.

Your goal is to obtain offers that will net to the lender the highest percentage possible of the fair market value. The nice thing about real estate investors is that they will often value the property by the return on investment analysis which may be higher than the fair market value of the property. This is particularly true in low income housing or in blighted neighborhoods.

If you are a real estate investor, it is a good idea to calculate the value of the property using both approaches. If you do not have access to the MLS to accomplish a CMA (comparative market analysis, similar to an appraisal), then you could pay a real estate agent to work one up for you at a reasonable cost, or even pro bono if they see the value in knowing and networking with an investor.

If there is no one living in the property, and the property is in an urban area with a high crime rate, you may wish to consider *not* having a *For Sale* sign visible. Purchase some cheap window coverings so the house will look occupied. A few outside decorative items could also help here. There is a major problem in many areas with drug users who break in and use the property as a drug den, or unsupervised youths may break in to vandalize.

Buyer Packet & Commission Modification Agreement

After you list the property, your published listing has disclosed the possibility of a reduced commission, so the cooperating agent (BA or buyer's agent) should call you to discuss this before showing the property. Let the BA know that there is language that is required for any offer to be accepted and that you will send them a *Buyer Packet*. This buyer packet is provided in the *Short Sale Business Manual*. The packet will provide them with specific language that should be included with an offer or you should have your sellers not accept the offer.

Marketing the Property and Managing Offers

At this time, you should also talk about the possibility of a reduced commission and that there may be about a 50-50 chance it could happen. If the agent objects, then tell them had you not done it this way, you would have been required to arbitrarily set the BAC much lower and they would never have the opportunity for a full commission. This way, you are looking out for the BA's interest as well as you attempt to obtain approval for the highest commission possible.

I do not recommend including the *Commission Modification Agreement* in the *Buyer Packet*. I provide it as a separate document in the *Short Sale Business Manual* because it is important for you to discuss this with them and send it to them already completed with the proper paragraph selected.

This agreement has two options. First, the option is to share in a reduction equally. If you are evenly dividing the commission between the two agents, then if the lienholder requires a reduction, dividing it equally between you is the fairest approach.

However, if you are not sharing the commission equally, then dividing the reduction equally is unfair to the BA. For example, suppose the total commission is 7%, and you are keeping 4% and the BAC is 3%. That is approximately a 57/43% split. You get around 57% of the total commission and the BA gets about 43% of the total commission. Let's use for our example a $200,000 sale with a 7% commission, or $14,000. Here you would receive about $8,000 and the BAC is $6,000. If the lienholder is a secondary market investor for whom there are regulations or contractual restrictions that permit only a 5% total commission, this would result in a *reduction* in total commissions of 2% for a resulting total commission of $10,000. That is a $4,000 reduction.

In this example, if you divide the reduction equally, then you would each reduce your commission by 1% of the sale price, or $2,000, with a resulting commission of $6,000 for you and $4,000 for the BAC. Whereas originally you have an approximate 57%/43% split, you now have a 60%/40% split. This is not fair to the BA.

The best approach in this case would be to divide the reduction *pro rata*. A 4%/3% split is calculated by the formula 4/7 = .571429, or 57.1429% of the total for you. The BA share is 3/7 = .428571, or 42.8571%. Let's check our numbers with the above example. The total commission is $14,000 and your share is 14000 x .571429 = 8,000.006 rounded to the nearest dollar, or $8,000. The BAC is 14,000 x .428571 = 5,999.994 rounded to the nearest dollar, or $6,000. A 2% reduction then would result in a $4,000 reduction. Your reduced share *of the reduction* is 4,000 x .571429 = $2,285.72. $8,000 − 2,285.72 = $5,714.28 resulting commission for you. The BA's reduced share is 4,000 x .428571 = $1,714.28. $6,000 − 1,714.28 = $ 4,285.72 resulting commission for the BA. Checking our work, the reduction is $2,285.72 + $1,714.28 = $4,000. Total resulting commissions are $5,714.28 + $4,285.72 = $10,000.

This example merely demonstrated that if the commission is divided equally, then the fair method of dividing a potential commission reduction is to divide the reduction equally as well. You would check that box on the *Commission Modification Agreement*. However, if you are not splitting the commission equally, then the fair method of dividing the reduction is *pro rata* and you would check that box on the agreement.

Marketing the Property and Managing Offers

Understand that the agreement is not how you are splitting the *commission*, but how you are splitting *the reduction* in that commission. This was purposely drafted this way for flexibility in dividing the original commission in one manner and the reduction in another manner, which some agents may choose. The agreement is provided to you as it is. Feel free to re-write it and modify it in any manner you wish.

The buyer packet provides specific language that should be inserted into the purchase contract. If this language is left out of the offer, then you should instruct your seller to either counter with the language included or to reject the offer. The packet also contains a document entitled *Disclosures and Memorandum of Understanding*. Likewise, if that is not returned with the offer, then the offer should be rejected. Actually, this happens often and the easiest way to deal with is to simply make a call and ask the agent if they forgot the language or if they forgot to return the signed *Disclosures and Memorandum of Understanding*.

If you attempt to persuade an agent to properly follow the instructions, and that agent argues with you or is otherwise difficult, you should consider requesting your seller to reject the offer. The reason is that difficult people usually remain difficult people, and some controlling agents cause so much trouble as time progresses that you will likely be very sorry you worked the case. Do not feel that you have to tolerate troublemakers merely because you think you owe it to your seller. Most experienced agents refuse to tolerate verbal abuse or being telephoned repeatedly with constant demands, and in short sale cases those same difficult agents only become worse with time.

Purchase Contract Language

When you receive your first offer, review it to ensure that the required language has been included and that they understand that the contract is subject to third party lienholder approval within 120 days. What is very important is to ensure that your seller is going to have a binding contract. If not, then you should request your seller to sign the *Binding Contract Waiver* available in the *Short Sale Business Manual*. If the contract is accepted within the appropriate number of days, then it should be binding subject to any contingencies contained in the contract.

The 120 day period is important for two reasons. First, it can take anywhere from about 2 weeks to 120 days to obtain approval for a short sale from the servicing lender, the MI carrier, and the SMI. This places your buyer on notice to expect up to that length of time to obtain approval, and helps them to remain more patient.

The second reason the 120 day period is significant is that an outside boundary is necessary to make the contract enforceable. Merely making the contract subject to third party lienholder approval may be unenforceable because no court would enforce it if the contract required the buyer to wait an *unreasonable* amount of time, and without the language, that *unreasonable time period* is subject to interpretation by the judge. However, stating the 120 day approval period enables the court to determine the reasonableness of the clause.

All time periods such as obtaining financing (except for pre-qualifying which should be done in advance), setting a date for closing, etc., should commence with the receipt of lienholder approval for all lienholders. If arbitrary dates or time periods are inserted, then the contract is not binding unless all parties agree to amend to extend. Of course, the acceptance of the contract itself should be required prior to submitting the proposal to the lender. You should always insist on binding contracts.

There is another reason for requiring binding contracts, other than the potential liability to your sellers. Some lenders, MI carriers, and SMIs may not approve a short sale that is not likely to close. They will almost always require a copy of the contract and the contract will be reviewed to determine if it is enforceable and their approval means that the sale will close, They want to be assured that their efforts to process the short sale and seek approval from the various decision-makers who must sign off on the deal will not result in a loss of the buyers leaving them with no alternative but to foreclose anyway.

Cooperating agents will very often object to having a binding contract, and will most assuredly want to keep the option open for their buyers to walk away if the process seems to be taking too long. They make a strong argument and that argument is reasonable. In some states, the law provides for their right to cancel the contract and walk away. Remember, though, you have both a potential liability here and a responsibility to your sellers to get the home sold and obtain approval before the foreclosure sale. These are difficult and polar positions, and you should give great thought to your stance. One way to decide your approach to it may be that if your sellers are real estate investors and there is no foreclosure action commenced, then leaving contracts nonbinding may be reasonable. If this is the sellers' primary residence and the foreclosure sale is only a month or two away, then locking that contract up and making it binding may be the reasonable thing to do.

Whether or not to have a binding contract is a complex issues and there exist strong arguments for each position. The most important lesson from this discussion is for you to review it on a case-by-case basis, use good judgment, discuss it thoroughly with your clients and your managing broker, and make sure your clients sign a *Binding Contract Waiver* if they decide to accept a nonbinding contract.

Another topic that is related to the above discussion is the inspection contingency. If the inspection is to be made *prior* to bank approval, and the buyers will then purchase the property *as-is*, the proposal is much stronger and there is a greater likelihood of approval by the SMI. However, inspections cost a substantial amount of money and if the proposal is denied, the money will have been wasted. If there are multiple offers, the SMI may select a lower offer simply because that offer is made *as-is* and therefore more likely to close. Since we just discussed the need for binding contracts, an offer that is *as-is* or which specifically accepts the property subject only to inspection *for major systems affecting habitability*, is stronger and more binding.

This is an area where buyers' agents often place opting out language. They will use language like *"subject to inspection and approval by the buyers,* or *in the event the inspection reveals defects not acceptable to the buyers, they may cancel the contract and their full earnest money shall be returned"*. Contract with this opting-out language commonly will not close, because the buyers have not committed themselves to the purchase and often get tired of waiting. When they go so far out of their way to make the contract unenforceable, you can count on the likelihood that the deal will not close.

Marketing the Property and Managing Offers

One solution that is often found acceptable by both sides, is for the buyer to go ahead and pay for an inspection for *systems affecting habitability only*, which can be done for a fraction of the cost, and then if the home is found habitable, they are able to amend their purchase contract and make it *as-is* and waiving inspection long before the proposal is reviewed by the SMI. This will satisfy the fears of the buyers and make the proposal more enticing to the lienholders.

A common problem in short sales is the common practice of many agents who fax a nice, clean contract not degraded by multiple faxing, along with only the signature page signed by the parties, obviously with multiple faxing. When you submit the short sale proposal, it is imperative that you submit a complete signed legal document with the signature page for that document. Some legal cases have involved later allegations that the document they signed was not the exact same document that was submitted with the signature page. You can help protect yourself from potential liability by always requiring that when someone scans and emails or faxes a document to you, that the full document with signature page is scanned or faxed altogether. Always do business with as few liability doors open as possible.

The media attachment that we provide also places agents on notice that multiple offers will be accepted. That language is included in the packet sent to the buyers as well. The reason is that your proposal may have a substantially greater chance of approval if the lienholders know that you are forwarding to them any offers that may be better, and that you are inviting more offers. They will realize that with the door open for more offers, time shows it obvious that they likely have the best offer obtainable. For this reason, accepting multiple offers is a benefit to both the buyers and the sellers.

Be very careful to observe the rules of your local Board of Realtors in the listing. Some local boards have rules that make it difficult to keep the listing active. However, your *Agent to Agent Remarks* section directs other agents to the media attachment that prominently discloses that fact to them before they show the property.

After you have inspected the purchase contract and made certain that it is either binding or you have a signed *Binding Contract Waiver*, and that all of the necessary language is inserted, then request the sellers to accept the contract. Every contract that you are going to submit to the lienholders should likewise be accepted. There is no problem accepting multiple offers because they are all subject to third party lienholder approval and the lienholders are only going to accept one of them. So have your sellers accept them all, so long as they meet the standards for short sale.

When accepting multiple offers, it is best to not disclose or even hint at whose offer is better when talking to the agents. If you do, then a lower offer is most assuredly going to walk. I have mediated a number of cases with multiple purchase contracts, and while some have gotten tired of waiting, most of them have stayed in there not know whether they will be the one that is approved or not. I do make a practice though of sending at least weekly updates. Several have commented that those Friday updates have been really helpful and made the difference in keeping all of the buyers hanging in there waiting for approval.

Marketing the Property and Managing Offers

Investor Purchase Contracts

As an investor, you want to obtain the best return on your investment as possible. If you are planning to rent the property out, you will likely use a return on investment analysis to determine the price you should pay for the property. It is worth the effort, however, to establish a relationship with a real estate agent. You may be able to help that agent network with you and you steer business his or her way. In return, the agent may be able to provide you with a CMA (basically, an appraisal) for the property.

What should you propose as the purchase price? You should calculate the rate of return if the property is going to be rental property to ensure that you do not pay too much. However, since short sale approval will likely be based upon a threshold net to lender percentage of the fair market value, that fmv needs to be first calculated. Then, contact a title company and tell them that you are going to need an estimated HUD-1 because you are going to purchase a short sale property. Make certain you tell them that you are going to use them for the closing.

Now, here's the deal. If you are planning on just putting offers in on multiple properties and then just taking the first one that comes through with an approval, you are taking unfair advantage of these agents, title companies, and homeowners, leaving them to suffer the losses. That is unethical and, depending upon all of the facts, could be fraudulent. That is the fastest way to build a bad reputation and could feasibly land you in court.

Short Sales & Loan Modifications

When I was selling real estate, there were a lot of investor names being passed around among the agents and title companies who were just taking advantage of these professionals. Many of them have taken courses offered by TV gurus marketing get-rich real estate schemes. I highly recommend that you do not become one of them. A real estate investment business can be highly profitable if you stick to proper ethics. It is ethical to make a great profit, but not if it results from someone else's loss. By that I do not mean the homeowner, because in a short sale, you purchasing the property at a great deal does not negatively affect the homeowner but in fact is helping them to get out from under the mortgage. I also do not mean the lender because they have savvy employees and fully staffed legal departments so they are at least on an equal bargaining position with you.

However, it would be unethical and may perhaps make you vulnerable to liability if you submit a low percentage net to lender for a home, your proposal is rejected, and the homeowners are left with no time to find another buyer. If you are going to make the proposal, you will owe a duty of care toward the sellers to submit a good faith proposal and that you do not turn down a reasonable minimum threshold percentage the SMI will accept.

I am primarily referring to the way you treat real estate agents and title companies. They are typically very giving people who will often provide free CMAs (agents) and HUD-1s (title companies). Generally, the title companies provide free HUD-1s to agents because they refer closings to them. If the title company charges you up to $75 for a HUD-1, that is still a good deal and worth it. They will likely amend them as needed

Marketing the Property and Managing Offers

without charge. If you take unfair advantage of them and they find that they are doing work for you and you give them nothing in return, many doors of opportunity will close on you in the future.

You will need to assess whether you wish to take a conservative approach to working short sales or an aggressive approach. A conservative approach is to make an offer on the property that after deducting the closing costs is about 92% of the fair market value. This approach maximizes the likelihood that your offer will be approved by the lender, and is recommended if you are close to the foreclosure sale date. An aggressive approach is to offer net to the lender 80% of the fair market value. That is fairly low, but still captures a good share of the minimum threshold for a number of SMIs. Below 80% minimizes your chances, but in some situations is actually the right thing to do. Why? Because there are some areas in which short sales cannot bring in more than 60%, 65%, or 70% of the fmv. It is important to find out what short sales are going for in your area. How do you do that? By contacting some real estate agents from different companies in your area who work short sales, tell them you are an investor, and ask them. Some may be open and honest with you.

Generally, though, a middle of the road approach provides you with the best approach if there is no pending foreclosure sale and time is on your side. I recommend a minimum net to lender percentage of 82% of the fair market value. My reasoning is that it still is acceptable to a large percentage of SMIs and MI carriers. Then, if that is inadequate, they will either reject and you merely re-submit, or they will come back and tell you what the minimum amount is they will accept.

If you are purchasing the home through an agent, the net to lender will be much lower, by the amount of the commissions. The advantage here is that the agent will assist you with completing the purchase contract. If you are comfortable with doing that on your own, or if you make an arrangement to pay an agent to help you with one, and you are making an offer on property you found through your direct marketing, then you will not have to pay commissions and your offer will be much more attractive to the SMI.

Prior to completing your offer, there is an important step that you must not overlook. You need to obtain a seller disclosure form for your state and have the sellers complete it. Also, if the home was built prior to 1978, you will need them to complete a lead-based paint certification. In many states, if not all, they are required of every seller. You can usually obtain these forms from any agent, your local Board of Realtors, or from a title company.

You will need to obtain from the homeowners many of the same documents, information, and disclosures that we have recommended for agents to complete. In the *Short Sale Business Manual,* I indicate the forms that you would or would not need to utilize.

Summary

As lengthy a process as short sales tend to be, they still close faster than many normal sales. One advantage is that you merely list the property in the MLS or on property websites. You usually do not need to spend money marketing them such as flyers, advertisements, or open houses.

Marketing the Property and Managing Offers

You should always make certain that you and the buyer agent (BA) will agree on how you are going to handle any reduction in the commission if required by the SMI or MI carrier. An equal split of the reduction is fair if the published BAC is one-half of the total commission. However, if there is originally an unequal split, then the reduction should be divided pro rata and so indicated on the *Commission Modification Agreement*.

Real estate investors will not need to allow for commissions, so your purchase contracts will have an advantage and be more attractive to the lienholders. Be sure that you do not take advantage of real estate agents or title companies, making certain that you always reward them in some acceptable way for the valuable information and/or documents that they provide to you. They will in the future open many doors of opportunity to you if you do not damage your reputation with them.

The *Short Sale Business Manual* provides and identifies documents and forms needed by agents as well as those required by real estate investors.

In Part 2, Chapter 8, we turn now to working with lienholders. You will be provided with the knowledge needed to minimize the common mistakes made by agents working short sales, to draft professional proposals, and to negotiate effectively with the lenders.

PART TWO – BE A GREAT NEGOTIATOR

CHAPTER 8

Systems For Effective Organization

Before you receive your first acceptable offer, it is advisable to arrange your office for easy processing and review, and set up case files. This chapter is about getting organized and staying that way. Many of you are experienced in running a business, getting organized, and staying that way. However, some of you are agents or investors who are brand new to real estate. Many people drop in and out of the real estate business looking to make a great living. Almost all of the new agents I met when I sold real estate have since left the business in order to make a living.

Many of you who will read this book may be looking for a way to survive in real estate when more traditional methods have not worked for you. I also know that some of you are making some money in real estate but your lives are so busy that you have no time for yourself or for your family. This chapter may be of help to you.

Effectiveness and efficiency in business is about *systems* consisting of equipment, supplies, checklists, or procedures with simplified steps for breaking down complex tasks. Organizational *system*s begin with the layout of your work space and setting up your case files. Its purpose is the efficient processing of all your tasks and avoiding the *bottle-necking* that wastes so much of our time. There are some things that will naturally slow you down, and those items or tasks need *systems* to prevent that from happening, or at least prevent it from happening again in the future.

A *system* is merely anything that reduces complicated or time-consuming tasks into smaller components for easier and faster action. A *system* could be simply a checklist of steps to take so that you don't have to think your way through it. A *system* could be a computer program designed to cut your time or to increase accuracy. *System*s could be certain office supplies to make tasks faster and simpler.

Shortly after opening my own law firm, I contracted with a computer programmer to develop a database so I could easily access client information; insert notes into a log; track time and charges; invoice clients; track payments; organize trial evidence, witnesses, and exhibits; maintain a prioritized task list; and to track deadlines and statutes of limitations. In that environment, the database was a major timesaver and it helped to efficiently maintain accurate control over those activities. In addition, *system*s of checklists were developed for staff members to simply enter in data according a specific set of rules so all of the information in the *system* would be consistent and accurate. So, *system*s (instructions and checklists) were developed to work other *system*s (the database).

Closed files were filed by file number. People change their names over the process of time and it was important for us to determine if we had ever represented a new client in the past, a former spouse, or a relative in order to avoid potential conflicts of interest. The database could be searched by name or by case number.

We leased a large and very fast network copier that also served as printer and scanner for the entire staff. The copier

Systems For Effective Organization

was placed in a workroom that had cabinets and a counter top specifically designed as a *system* to efficiently assemble documents and copies, which were then placed in bins for filing with the court, hand delivering to attorneys, or processed for outgoing mail. However, we each had local printers within reach of our desks for printing initial drafts for quick review.

When clients came to the office for the first time, they completed an information sheet specifically designed for easy data transfer into the database, legal document-drafting (e.g. divorce petitions, etc.), or into the bankruptcy software.

Interview rooms were designed for efficient management of time with clients. When clients completed the information sheet, an assistant escorted them into an interview room and informed the attorney that the clients were ready. The attorney retrieved the information sheet on the way into the room, met with the clients long enough to determine their needs and provide them with needed legal advice, and then moved to the next interview room. The assistant collected any additional information that might be needed from the client, explained the process involved in their case, answered additional questions, and made arrangement for the fees. Meanwhile, the attorney was interviewing the next client. Using this *system*, the attorney could to meet with and provide services to almost double the number of clients other attorneys typically handled. *Systems* are the key to saving time, and maintaining control and accuracy.

A *system* then is any task made easier by simplifying that task with procedures, steps, equipment, office supplies, and/or checklists. A *system* is created by analyzing any complicated task or tasks that slow you down or waste time, and developing easier, faster, and more efficient ways to perform those tasks, with a checklist or written procedure for yourself or others to duplicate.

A short sale and loan modification business is not complicated like a law firm. I have a database available to me that is actually quite good, but I do not use it in my mediation practice. The reason? Some activities take longer by computer than manually. I still use *systems* for virtually everything I do, and some of these *systems* are provided in the *Short Sale Business Manual* for use in your processing and negotiating of short sale and loan modification cases. They are provided for both real estate agents and real estate investors.

Many real estate agents use a popular online contact management program to utilize for everything from an appointment calendar to managing emails and performing marketing functions. For those of you who do, great! However, when I sold real estate, I chose not to incur the cost because I did not really need everything the expensive service provided. I know many agents who utilize Microsoft Outlook as a contact management program, as do I, and are happy with it. Outlook can be utilized to efficiently manage emails for each case and it is a great *system* for a short sale and loan modification business. More specific tips and instructions for using Outlook are provided in the *Short Sale Business Manual*.

You must manage your emails efficiently if you are working a number of cases because you will receive a lot of emails. Email is a primary communication method with agents, homeowners, buyers, title companies, and some of the lienholder negotiators. Outlook enables you to organize all of those incoming and outgoing emails very effectively and if you need to look quickly

Systems For Effective Organization

to find certain emails while on the phone with a negotiator or agent, you should be able to locate them in short order.

Many people including myself, no longer use the computer for a task list, appointments, deadlines, or notes. Many utilize a cell phone calendar program for appointments and deadlines. Most people keep their cell phone with them at all times, and it may allow you to set reminders as needed in advance for important deadlines and appointments.

Tasks and notes for each case can be logged on the case Activity Log. For a task list, I use a three-ring binder with special forms for that purpose. I will explain that shortly. Although you could utilize a database *system* for notes, I find that just handwriting notes into the case Activity Logs is actually faster when on the phone with negotiators.

Many agents use a white board on the wall to maintain a list of properties for quick review. This *system* works great for short sales and loan modifications too. I suggest that you write the property address next to the number of that property corresponding to its number in the casebook. I will describe that shortly. To the right of each property write the status of that case in color coded abbreviations for *pre-submission*, *post-submission* (but prior to being assigned to a negotiator), and *in negotiations*. A different color could be used to indicate the pending foreclosure sale date. A complete list of sample abbreviations for various *systems* is provided in the *Short Sale Business Manual* for your use if you find them helpful.

Anyone can develop their own abbreviations though, and I do not claim to have the best. I merely utilize abbreviations like "wtg4hud" for *waiting for HUD-*; "wtg4as't" for *waiting*

Short Sales & Loan Modifications

for assignment of a negotiator; "N2propo" for *need to draft proposal*; "wtg4docs" for *waiting for documents from the agent*; etc.

For a law practice, malpractice insurers require a three-tiered *system* for keeping track of statutory deadlines, to avoid the possibility of missing a deadline through simple clerical errors or forgetting. I still follow that requirement by entering all of my foreclosure sale dates into my cell phone calendar, on a cheat sheet in my casebook, and listing it on the white board on my office wall. I recommend you also maintain such a three-tiered *system*.

Aside from using Outlook for emails, The *Windows Explorer* software is excellent for managing electronic documents and for drafting and assembly of the proposals. *Explorer* is the software that pops up a window when you click on *My Documents* or some other icon when you want to find files. Another method is to hold down the *Windows* key on your keyboard plus touch the *E* key. You can also easily put an icon for this on your task bar. Oh, be aware that *Windows Explorer* is not the same as the Microsoft Explorer you may be using as your web browser.

Now, the casebook. You need a *system* for organizing your case notes and activity log entries. One effective *system* is to obtain a moderately-sized three-ring binder to use as a casebook. In it place 12 section dividers corresponding to each of 12 cases. Use a separate casebook for each 12 cases. If you have more than one casebook, you could organize them geographically or by price point, whichever you may prefer. I suggest limiting each casebook to 12 cases because more than that makes the casebook more cumbersome and difficult to use, as well as making it more difficult to find information.

Systems For Effective Organization

In each section, insert a *main cheat sheet* containing all of the information you may need for that property, including information about the sellers, buyers, agents, lienholders, and status. Include addresses, telephone numbers (both preferred and alternate), email addresses, loan numbers, and the dates of birth and social security numbers of the sellers. A sample is provided in the *Short Sale Business Manual*. You will likely use this cheat sheet every time you work on the case and it is much faster to use than a computerized database, in my opinion. If your information was more complicated or detailed, then a database would be faster.

Place another one-half sheet size cheat sheet in the binder for offers, the fair market value of the property, the net receipt to the lienholder, the terms of the offer, and notes of counter-offers from the lienholders. This cheat sheet is also provided in the *Short Sale Business Manual*. The sample also includes the name and type of SMI as well as counter-offers or minimum threshold amounts from the lienholders.

Inside the binder insert an *Activity Log* in which all activity on this file is entered by hand. Notes of every email to and from anyone; all telephone calls; periodic updates to the parties; status reviews, and faxes. The *Activity Log* is provided to you in the *Short Sale Business Manual*. The *Activity Log* is the central focus of all the work on the file and should include everything that happens on this case. To make entries fast and easy, use abbreviations as shorthand for commonly entered data. A list of these shorthand abbreviations is provided in the *Short Sale Business Manual*.

Organize the casebook by turning it so that it is in the landscape orientation, with the cover opening away from you.

Short Sales & Loan Modifications

The cheat sheets and Activity Logs are all printed in landscape orientation, and are three-hole punched along the bottom so when you open a section, the main cheat sheet containing all of the property and parties' information is facing you but on the far side of the rings. The cheat containing the offer amount, net to lender, etc., is on a half sheet with two properly spaced holes in the bottom and placed so that it is on the right side but on the far side of the rings and covering the right side of the main cheat sheet. The Activity Logs are top-hole punched so they are on the near side of the rings directly in front of you for easily reading the notes and making entries.

Next is the *file system*. Some excellent databases provide an electronic method of organizing notes and documents for paperless processing, and there is software for modifying documents, even PDF documents. I have such a database, and while it is excellent, the casebook *system* in my opinion is much faster and easier to use and easily portable. For me, reading documents is also easier in printed form than on the computer monitor. If it is faster to manage and process paper, then paperless has not yet become profitable. You may find reading the monitor easier, but my almost-senior-citizen eyes make it much more difficult for me.

Every document that I receive is printed and placed in file folders, the old fashion way. When I talk about this with other attorneys, most of them still utilize paper *system*s for speed and efficiency. If you can easily read on-screen documents, and find that more efficient, then you could have a paperless *system*. We will discuss this in more detail in the *Short Sale Business Manual*.

Systems For Effective Organization

Create four file folders for each property file. Label them on the tabs with the property address, but close to the edge affix labels for the following four folders: *Case Notes*; *CMA*; *Seller*; *Buyer*. I recommend that you organize the documents as those coming from the seller, the buyer, all documents relating to the value of the property going into the CMA folder, and general case notes. If you request agents to fill out and send you contact information sheets for the buyers and their agent, that will go into the case notes file. Place any title information and estimated HUD-1 forms there as well.

The four folders for each file can be inserted into large pocket expansion folders to keep them together. The open top expansion folders with no flaps are great because they make finding the right files easier, and easier to retrieve a folder and insert documents. The files should be stored within easy reach of you at your desk or work table.

You should have room on your desk to easily use your computer, the casebook, and the file on which you are working.

I recommend having an all-in-one printer, copier, and scanner within reach of your seated position, because when drafting the proposal and sending in post-submission documents to the lender, you will need to be able to quickly go back and forth between the computer and scanner. If you have a paperless system, this may not be necessary, but you will need to have the ability to modify PDF files and insert individual PDF pages into a Word document.

Everything in your office should be organized for quick, easy task work with nothing slowing you down. You should have within reach binders containing the proposals that were submitted for easy grab and reference when a lender calls. If you have a paperless system, then you will need to set up quick access codes for fast retrieval of the proposal.

The idea here is to create simple *system*s to make your work activities fast and efficient with the fewest number of steps to perform, and the less you must get out of your chair while you are working on the case files, the more work that will be accomplished in the least amount of time.

I mentioned a binder for my daily task lists. I use a form with only ten numbered lines. Why ten? Well, it used to be six. Many years ago, I attended seminars in *Time Management* to increase my productivity. I also read a number of books in time management. I internalized many of those concepts and utilized them to build a successful law firm. The experts encouraged everyone to list the most important six tasks that needed to be done that day. The task sheets had more lines, but they only numbered six tasks. After obtaining a similar type of task list form from a friend that numbered the tasks to ten, I have discovered that by using *system*s as I do, I am easily able to perform ten tasks per day. I use the extra lines for notes, or additional tasks as I am able to perform them. Those tasks are not just related to the business. They include all tasks for both business and your personal life. It is important to accomplish at least six tasks every work day. Now I make it ten.

Other Business Systems

Many people have a telephone dedicated landline for a fax machine. The cost includes the monthly business line as well as the cost of paper and either toner or film. I have discovered that using the online fax service that I use costs me much

Systems For Effective Organization

less, is much easier to fax documents, never runs out of paper or toner, and is more easily managed than having my own fax machine with a dedicated phone line. The incoming faxes are sent to my email address and are sorted by Outlook according to the rules that are set up in Outlook. Outgoing faxes can be sent right from Word documents, but I prefer sending from the online site. This is described in more detail in the *Short Sale Business Manual*.

There is another business *system* that may be easier and faster to use than using computer software. For a successful law firm, a central database was utilized for all of our client invoicing and billing. However, like many other small businesses, we used Quickbooks Pro for our accounting needs. That software is great, and I have nothing negative to say about it. I would be an awesome spokesperson for them about the effectiveness of their software managing the finances of the firm.

However, a small business such as processing short sales and loan modifications, or even a small real estate or investment business, does not really need that powerful software. In fact, many people find that an old yet simple financial *system* may be much easier and faster. If you do not have employees, require sophisticated accounting needs including depreciation of equipment over time, tracking of sick leave, personal leave, and vacation time; and a host of various financial data to track, there is an easier way. You do not need to spend a lot of time working a sophisticated computerized financial program.

This easy to use *system* is great for lazy people, busy people, or people who just do not want to spend much time taking care of the business of running a business. A lot of people allow business receipts to pile up until a lot of time is spent playing catch-up.

Here is the system. Simply obtain a large three-ring binder. The largest they make. Purchase a package of 12 section dividers, one for each month. Also purchase a box of 5 x 9 envelopes (you could use larger envelopes). Using a glue stick, glue one envelope to the backside of the #1, or *January*, divider, and another envelope to the front side of the #2, or *February,* divider. Glue the envelopes so the flaps are visible. Repeat that with each month, and for the last month you can use a piece of cardstock behind the last envelope.

Next print your usual and customary expense categories on a page about the size of your envelope. Space the categories apart so the dollar amount of the receipt can be handwritten under the category. After printing 12 of these forms, glue them to the face of the business envelope for each month.

This is how it is used. When you are out of the office and incur business expenses, place the receipt either in the bag or in your pocket. When you arrive home or in the office, merely place the receipt in the envelope and write on the form the dollar amount under the appropriate expense category. At the end of the year, merely take about an hour or so totaling up each category for each monthly envelope and enter the totals for each month onto an Excel spreadsheet. You may then merely send that spreadsheet file to your accountant. The other envelope in the monthly section divider is for personal receipts.

Any depreciation amounts that you have may be entered monthly on the envelope as appropriate or recorded separately and added to the spreadsheet annually. With this easy to use

Systems For Effective Organization

system, you will not have the problem of receipts piling up and you will spend very little time with finances. To make it easier, keep a small table top on which to place the receipt binder, open to the monthly page you are using. It is simple to merely enter the amounts on the envelope and stick those receipts in the envelope. Simple, cheap, fast, easy, and effective.

When you pay bills online, print off the receipt and do the same with them. Merely fold your printed full size receipt in half and place it in the envelope.

For rent and utilities that are business oriented, or if you have a dedicated home office, keep your recurring monthly statements in a monthly-divided expansion folder, and enter the amount on your primary envelope *system*, or otherwise as you fine-tune your *system*.

Some people could never use a simple system like this. I know some personalities are very detailed and this would drive them nuts. Yes, I understand. For you, there is great software that you can use to spend all the time you wish to keep track in the most detailed fashion. This discussion was not for you.

Another *system* that saves time is the processing of faxes and emails. A short sale and loan modification business will receive many hundreds and even thousands of pages of documents from agents, sellers, buyers, and lienholders. As they arrive in Outlook, they can be routed by the software to their proper location through the use of *rules*. I will describe this in more detail later, but a printed checklist can be used to process those documents so that you never lose track as you print the documents, place them in the file, save the electronic document to an Explorer folder, enter the activity in the Activity Log, show the email as having been processed and move it to its storage location. This *system* is provided in the *Short Sale Business Manual* for you to utilize if you wish.

There is also a *system* checklist for completing a legal and market analysis, as well as another *system* checklist for drafting the proposal and scanning the required documents into a Word-generated proposal. More about this later also. These systems are all in the *Short Sale Business Manual*.

Many years ago, I purchased a mechanical stamp machine for my firm. I would take it to the post office periodically and have them enter the amount of postage I wanted to pre-pay for postage. Later, when an assistant would prepare the outgoing mail, the envelopes were stacked into the bin, the machine turned on, and the envelopes would feed rapidly, printing the postage on each envelope. The process took mere seconds, even for a large stack of outgoing mail. Then came the age of more modern technology and internet-purchased stamps. My postage then cost more, the machines were more expensive, and they processed the mail much more slowly. The post office halted the servicing of the older machines, so we went back to purchasing and using rolls of stamps because it was far more efficient than the new machines. I still use stamps, because I do not want to pay extra for purchasing stamps online. The stamps no longer need to be moistened, so it is faster. Besides, I am still kind of rebelling!

I suggest that any time you see that you are getting bogged down with time-consuming activity, develop a simple *system* for making tasks quicker and easier, create checklist forms for less thinking things through and simpler processing. In my law firm, we handled a lot of divorces and another attorney was brought to focus solely on those cases. By using the attributes

Systems For Effective Organization

of Microsoft Word – oops, we were using WordPerfect then, we were able to reduce the time that most firms would spend drafting initial divorce documents, from about one and a half hours, down to approximately twenty minutes. That included drafting a Summons, Court Cover Sheet, Complaint, Marital Dissolution Agreement, Parenting Plan, and Final Decree. Both of the document software mentioned have features that allow the merging of data into forms after the data is entered quickly by assistants into a data source. We utilized *quickwords* and *macros* for the many different paragraphs that needed to be written so many different ways.

Actually, everyone to some extent creates *systems* to cut time and costs. I know many buyers' agents who will show properties organized by location and will use mapping software for the least amount of time and expense driving clients around. Even memorizing scripts is a *system* because not only are you using the scripts to articulate correctly, they also cut the amount of time you need to discuss concepts and ideas.

As you set up your office to run a short sale business, whether you are an agent or real estate investor, I encourage you to arrange your business and set up your files for the highest level of efficiency and speed, creating a *system* for anything that could slow you down.

Summary

This chapter was about establishing *systems* to cut your time and allow you to accomplish more work in less time. Some *systems* work best utilizing high tech software, while other *system*s are more efficient and effective using old fashioned methods by hand.

Microsoft Outlook and Microsoft Office, including Word and Excel, are software *system*s that allow for efficient management of your information, emails, and documents. However, the proper use of binders and file folders still have their place even in this world of high technology. Sometimes modern technology is better and more efficient; sometimes it is not. Sometimes the old ways are the tried, true and best ways. Sometimes they are not. You decide.

Now let's turn to Chapter 9 and learn how to prepare a proposal for submission to the lender.

CHAPTER 9

Preparing the Short Sale Proposal

Throughout this book, I have been referring to two different types of investors, the real estate investor (REI) like many of you, and the secondary market investors (SMI) who purchase mortgage loans and put capital back into the system for new loans. There are many SMI entities, actually numbering into the many hundreds, who purchase mortgage notes. Some even bundle mortgage notes together and sell them as securities.

The SMI who actually holds the note is the lienholder. The bank or mortgage company who holds the first mortgage is likely only a servicing lender, that is they collect the payments, send the homeowners statements, and then forward the payments to the SMI after paying themselves for these servicing responsibilities. When the mortgage company or bank sells the note to an SMI, they form a contract between them outlining the various rights and responsibilities of each of the signatories to the contract.

The actual owner of the note then is the SMI. It could be Fannie Mae (actually abbreviated FHMA), Freddie Mac, Ginnie Mae, other publically traded SMIs, or private SMIs. The servicing lender operates under a contractual arrangement with these SMI entities. Those contractual responsibilities may vary from entity to entity and may even vary according to different loan products. You see, every loan has its own contractual responsibilities, rights and obligations between the borrowers

Short Sales & Loan Modifications

and the holder of the note, and these loan product terms will affect the terms of the contract between the servicing lenders and the SMI.

When you submit a proposal for a short sale, you are submitting it to the servicing lender. The servicing lender processes the proposal, orders the appraisal, and then submits it to the SMI. You will almost never talk to the SMI, only the servicing lender, however, it is the SMI that approves or rejects the short sale. They just do it through the servicing lender.

This is true except when it is not. There are times when the servicing lender will also be what is called the *holder in due course* of the loan instrument. That means that it either was not sold on the secondary market, or it was and upon default, they received it back according to the terms of the contract. In that event, the servicing lender would also be the investor.

Another exception may exist when a predominantly small regional bank or mortgage company makes home loans with money provided by venture capitalists or small to medium investment companies. In these cases, the servicing lender could by contract with the investment company have complete authority to approve or reject the short sale.

Unless you live in more rural areas, most of your short sales and loan modifications will be with SMIs via the servicing lender. You will almost never communicate directly with the SMI and you may never know who the SMI actually is. Recently, though, I did have an occasion to call someone I knew at Freddie Mac when the servicing lender negotiator lied to me, misrepresenting the amount a second mortgage holder could receive in the short sale. Freddie Mac was the SMI and my contact took care of the problem.

Preparing the Short Sale Proposal

The SMI is not the only entity with whom the servicing lender may have a contractual relationship. When the homeowners made the loan, they may have been required to purchase private mortgage insurance. This insurance may instead be purchased by the servicing lender or the SMI. In that case, the homeowners may not even know that there is mortgage insurance on the loan. If a claim is made by the lender to the mortgage insurance (MI) Carrier, that carrier likely has terms under their policy contract that may affect the short sale. They usually will have the right to dictate some of the terms of the short sale approval. Additionally, a loan might actually be paid off by the MI Carrier under a claim filed when the homeowners defaulted on the loan, and they may now hold the second mortgage. In that case, you would be submitting the proposal directly to the MI Carrier.

The result is that you must draft a proposal that will meet the needs of the servicing lender, the SMI, and the MI Carrier. Most commonly, you will fax the proposal to the servicing lender who will image it, or scan it, into the computer system server. Once imaged, it is then available to the analyst or negotiator who can also then forward it electronically to the MI carrier and SMI.

Early in my legal career, I occasionally had to work on personal injury cases that came into the firm. The senior partner of the firm told me that most attorneys would merely send a demand letter to the insurance company along with all of the documents that proved the damages to the client. However, they asserted, they discovered that if you draft a professional looking proposal, complete with proof of injury and medical expenses, a complete legal analysis, and a table of contents making it easy to locate all of the tables and supporting documents, they obtained much better results. The proposal would have to impress the decisions-makers with whom they could never communicate.

The same is true with both short sales and loan modifications. If you draft short sale proposals and loan modification proposals under the same principle, you will discover that the people who make the decisions and with whom you can never communicate will approve the proposals more readily.

The reality is, though, that some of the servicing lenders upon receipt of the proposal, merely image in only the documents in their list, discarding the rest of the proposal including the legal and marketing analysis designed to be of help to their analysis. However, a number of my SMI contacts inform me that the proposals often do make it through to them and I have received a lot of positive comments about the professionalism the proposal brings to them, and how the well-structured proposal helps them to analyze the value of the case. I recommend then, that every proposal be professionally drafted, provides a one or two page summary along with a compel legal and market analysis, contains a CMA or BPO (Broker Price Opinion, basically an appraisal) and contains each and every document required. If they choose to discard some of it, so be it. The proposals that do get through intact to the SMI will greatly increase the likelihood of approval.

The majority of real estate agents handling short sales themselves merely submit documents. They may never know if the rejection was due to the actual value of the case or that it lacked information and analysis to help them truly understand

Preparing the Short Sale Proposal

the value of the case. They will often not get honest answers from the analyst, negotiator, or other employee because there is a widespread dislike among them for real estate agents. So many agents have attempted to play hardball with or were rude to the reps, that there is a general dislike for agents.

They may not disclose this attitude because they are required to always remain professional and courteous. Although they often do not like agents, they do seem to really like attorneys. Go figure! However, throughout this book and in Chapter 10, you will discover how to change those opinions and find effective methods to accomplish your objectives.

Drafting The Proposal

Let's turn our attention the practical aspects of drafting the proposal. I use a specially drafted Microsoft Word cover page with my firm logo and graphics. This cover page doubles as a fax cover page. The second page is my letterhead and a letter to the lender describing my role in the short sale process. Third is the *table of contents* with each document listed also stating a page number.

Following the *table of contents* is the *summary* of the case. The *summary* describes the borrowers and their circumstances, plus statements that alternatives to foreclosure have been explored and found not suitable for these borrowers, and that the borrowers cannot be reasonably rehabilitated. Do not underestimate the value of this statement. There are sometimes legal (or contractual) definitions and terms that may make this statement critically important.

The *summary* also contains the age of the home and the date that the property was placed on the market. This is followed by an important statement that reasonable attempts to sell the home have not been successful.

Next the *summary* states the *reasonable fair market value* of the property, and you should state who it is that provided that opinion. If you are the agent who completed the CMA, then merely state "The property has a reasonable fair market value of $xxx,xxx".

If I am quite certain that a *comparison analysis* will be made between the value to the lender as a short sale and the value as a bank-owned property, then I would provide another CMA, but with the value of the property as a bank-owned property using comps that are all bank-owned and most similar to the subject property. Simply state, "The property has a reasonable bank-owned value of $xxx,xxx".

Next is a listing of the offers with the purchase price and terms. Following that, a paragraph statement of lender needs. A paragraph stating the real estate commission includes a recommendation that paying a full commission is in the lienholder's best interests.

Agents often say that their commissions are reduced, and they just accept that as a fact that it will happen. What they may not realize is that a reduction may be prevented. However, if a limited commission is required by regulation or contractual restriction, then it is absolute. So, it is almost always either the SMI or MI carrier who would have a reduced commission as nonnegotiable. So how do we know if it is negotiable or not? We will discuss that in Chapter 11.

Preparing the Short Sale Proposal

The summary ends with a specific request to the lender to do the following:

> Approve the short sale of the property to the buyers
> Cancel the Sheriff's sale if scheduled
> Set aside the Default Judgment of Foreclosure, if obtained
> Dismiss the foreclosure suit, if filed
> Forgive the deficiency balance
> Issue the bank release document
> Report the account satisfied to credit bureaus

All of the documents required to be attached to the proposal are scanned into this word document. I do this in two or three separate Word documents, depending upon how many attachment documents are needed to scan in. Some of the lenders' incoming fax software limit the number of pages they can receive with each fax. Additionally, if you use an online fax service, you need to keep the file size down.

There are a couple of ways to keep the file size down for faxing. First, you could just use a separate fax machine over a phone line. Normally, whenever you send a completed document by email, you should convert it to a PDF file so readers are unable to alter the document or view the Microsoft Word document private information hidden within the document file. However, PDF files can be almost as large as the word document with other documents scanned in as images. You do not need to use PDF files to send a document by online fax. There is an alternative method. When you have completed the proposal, use the *Print* command (ctrl-P) to bring up the print window. In the small window that displays your default printer, click on the drop down arrow and your print options will be displayed. Select *Microsoft Office Document Image Writer* as your print selection. This software is part of the Microsoft Office software. Then print. You will be prompted for a *save* location. Save it to the proper folder. To open and view this file, go to the Windows Explorer program (found in *My Documents* selected from the *Start* menu or windows key-E) and right click with your mouse on the file name. Wait for the window to appear and select *open with*. You should have the option for *Microsoft Office Document Imaging* as the program to use to open this file.

The result of using the *Microsoft Document Image Writer* is that your file size will be cut about in half. As previously stated, I normally break the fax submissions into two or three faxes and indicate the number of the fax this is on the cover sheet (e.g. *This is the 2nd of 3 faxes for this short sale proposal*). For Countrywide, I limit each fax group to 10 or 11 pages, so there might be as many as six separate faxes.

Before scanning, I organize the documents by their fax grouping. I print temporary cover sheets numbered from 1 to 3, then take the document pages and assemble them with paper clips to each temporary cover sheet, so the total number of pages in each section is no more than 20 or 21. Then I scan each assembled group of documents into my Word document for this group using a multiple page scanner. In Word 2003, this is done by clicking on the *Insert* menu and selecting *picture from scanner*. The first fax group contains the pages as I described above and then about another 16 pages are scanned in. The second fax group contains the fax cover sheet as the first page and then the next 20 pages are scanned in, and so forth.

Preparing the Short Sale Proposal

My first call to the lender is to find out if they have a short sale packet and request their list of documents needed. Some do, some do not. Some require specific documents to be completed by the borrowers. Obtain them and forward them to the borrowers to complete. When they are returned and you've checked them to ensure that they were completed properly and signed by all of the borrowers, you can then scan them into the proposal, making certain that the *table of contents* includes these required documents clearly and they are paginated correctly. Other lenders have merely a list of documents and they usually correspond to a standard list. This is the standard list of documents customarily submitted and in appropriate order:

    Authorization & Release
    Hardship Letter
    Lienholder financial statement (if required)
    Pay stubs (most recent 2 months)
    Bank Statements (most recent 2 months)
    Tax Returns (last 2 years)
    List Contract
    Purchase Contract (with addendums)
    Pre-approval letter
    Estimated HUD-1
    Listing Agent's Price Opinion
    (with all supporting documentation)

Of these documents, the Listing Agent's Price Opinion is usually not required but I recommend submitting it for usage by the SMI to compare with any appraisal purchased by the lender. Most agents provide me with a CMA and use a *Property Value*

Report that I provide them for assessing a precise one-number fair market value. Other agents utilize a CMA report that is finely tuned and detailed which then does not need the report that I provide. The *Property Value Report* is provided in the *Short Sale Business Manual*.

In my opinion, the CMA report is important and it is also important that you draft it correctly and you arrive at the correct valuation. If the appraisal ordered by the lender comes back substantially different, yours will form the basis for appealing that valuation. We will discuss this in more detail later. Is the CMA required? No, but I include it because my proposal is often forwarded intact to the SMI intact, the entity who will actually decide whether to approve or reject the proposal The CMA provides credibility and adds to the professionalism of the overall proposal.

A sample of the proposal is provided in the *Short Sale Business Manual*. More detailed instruction is also provided.

Legal Analysis

Prior to actually assembling the proposal, I complete a legal and marketing analysis. This is an important part of working the short sale and you can perform this same exercise. Those of you who are real estate investors, if you develop a relationship with an agent, that agent could provide you with some assistance in this.

The legal analysis is a review of the documents to ensure the proposal meets the legal requirements for a short sale. When I use the term *legal*, I am not using this term in some specialized manner that requires an attorney to review and interpret. I am

Preparing the Short Sale Proposal

using the term in purely a technical sense, like saying *"the legal speed limit is 65 mph"*. In our case, we use the term to indicate certain technical issues that must be reviewed and addressed by you.

First, it is important that you have a good relationship with a title company. You should request them to provide you with a *preliminary title report*. This can either be in the form of a *Commitment*, which is a formal document committing their company to the issuance of a *Title Insurance policy*, or it can be merely an email or printout showing the liens on the property. It is your objective to discover what liens exist that impair the sale of the property, along with their ranking superiority. Normally, the borrowers will be able to tell you who has the first mortgage and other liens. However, borrowers often forget about second mortgages, that one of their credit cards may actually be an equity line of credit, or other liens. The preliminary title report provides you with a list of all lienholders. The report may not indicate the current servicing lender or even the investor. It will give you the name of the original entity who filed the lien. You can make certain assumptions and match up the current servicing lender with the mortgage. For example, if ABC Mortgage is on the preliminary report and there are no other liens other than for taxes and HOA fees, then it is a safe bet that the original lienholder was ABC Mortgage, that the mortgage was later sold, and is now being serviced by the current servicing lender.

What is important here is for you to look for any anomalies, like a second mortgage or mechanics liens (building trades companies), former spouses, and others. In order for the proposal to meet with success, you must identify all liens on the property and obtain their release.

For the second part of the legal analysis, at the same time that you request the title company for a preliminary title report, request an estimated HUD-1. They will need you to provide them with the purchase contract, and an estimated closing date. Provide them with a possible closing date about 90 days out, but on a weekday. That will likely be the middle of a range of possible closing dates. An updated HUD-1 can be later provided. The title company will calculate property taxes and other amounts that must be allocated between buyers and sellers at closing.

Remember, title companies normally provide agents with these documents for free because agents have the ability to refer their clients to them. Be really, really nice to them with no pressure. They are doing it for free! If you are an investor, you may not be perceived in the same way as an agent, so they may charge you. If you are in a position to refer people to them, you should tell them up front, and then make certain they receive a benefit in return in the form of document purchases or closings. At least assure them that if the short sale is approved, you will utilize them for the closing.

When you ask for the HUD-1, you should indicate that the sellers are to receive nothing from closing. All proceeds are to go to the mortgage holder, and you should provide them with the servicing lender's name *exactly* as it is on the sellers' mortgage statement. Naming this entity correctly is important because there are many similar entities. For example you could have ABC Bank; ABC Mortgage Co., Inc.; and ABC Home Loans, Inc., all being separate entities even if they are related.

If there is a second mortgage, most SMIs will limit the amount that can be paid to junior liens. For example, Freddie

Preparing the Short Sale Proposal

Mac has loan products in which they by regulation only permit a short sale payout of 10% of the principal balance of a junior lienholder's account up to a maximum of $3,000. Most investors will permit from $1,000 to $5,000 to be paid to junior lienholders. If the 2nd mortgage holder is the same company as the 1st mortgage, then set that amount at $1,000.

If there is a junior lienholder, you should insert a paragraph in the *summary* stating the amount that will go to them. For now, state that amount to be $3,000. We will discuss this more fully in Chapter 11.

Review the HUD-1 to ensure that the sellers will receive nothing. Check to make sure that a large amount goes to the first mortgage and the correct amount to the second mortgage. If the second mortgage is the same mortgage company as the first, then the amount to go to the second should be $1,000. Check the property taxes and HOA fees to be sure that there is an amount there. If there is no amount or just x's or ?'s, that will mean that they do not have a report for what amounts are due or overdue for those items. Make a note that this will need to be taken care of immediately before final approval and to ensure the lender will sign off on those added amounts. It is also a good idea to check with the sellers to see if they are behind, obtain the amount they are behind, and then calculate the best you can what taxes and HOA fees will be due at your estimated closing date, both arrearages and pro-rations. The title person can help you with that. It is a good idea, though, to estimate the best you can and provide the information to the title company so that the HUD-1 will be complete and as close as possible to reality. Some investors will approve your proposal but not approve any later changes for such things as taxes and HOA fees. (*HOA means "homeowners association"*).

Another part of the legal analysis is to be certain that you have *all borrowers* included in the proposal. The purchase contract and listing contract may list multiple sellers, but sometimes all of those sellers are on the note and sometimes not. Sometimes there are other parties who may be obligors under the note but not owners of the property. The listing and purchase contract *only* list the owners of the property, not all borrowers if they are not owners. Likewise, the rest of the documents to be submitted need to include the documents from all borrowers on the note, even if they are not owners of the property. That will include an *Authorization & Release* from each *borrower* and all of the financial documents required *from each borrower*. If they are living together, then it is easy and the same forms will likely be joint. Otherwise, obtain separate documents from each one.

Check the *Authorization & Release* to ensure that it includes the dates of birth and social security numbers of each borrower. Check the account number and lienholder name. Make certain they are accurate. I often have to request new ones signed because the borrowers left numbers off or transposed numbers in the account number.

The legal analysis includes a review of all documents to ensure they are the correct ones that must be attached. I always request the most current two months of paystubs and bank statements, but it is common that I receive them for months previous to what is required, or a paystub is missing. Sometimes I receive bank statements that include the summary pages but not the detail. Your legal analysis should ensure that all of the

Preparing the Short Sale Proposal

detail is there, that they are the most recent documents, with nothing missing. I utilize a *Case Checklist* to review each document for everything that I need. It is provided with the *Short Sale Business Manual*.

Check the pre-approval letter from the buyers' lender. Make certain that the approved amount covers the amount of the offer less the earnest money. If it is to be a cash offer, then the buyers need to provide a *Proof of Funds* letter from the bank indicating that they hold funds on account for the buyers in at least the amount of the purchase price. This letter can be a simple one sentence letter on bank stationary and faxed or emailed to you. Be sure that the letter is signed. Sometimes banks will send the letter by email and not sign it because they cannot print it, sign it and scan it back in to email it. If they ask which method of transmission by which you want it to be sent, choose fax. If the buyers have the total purchase price in separate banks, then have them provide a letter from each bank with the amounts available (not the amounts in the accounts but the amount that the buyers are going to use for this purchase), making certain that the amounts in both letters total the purchase price.

Check to be certain that you have the paystubs from each working borrower. The same with the bank statements and tax returns. If they, or one of them, also own a business and it is a corporation or LLC, make certain that the bank statements and account statements for that entity are provided as well. Also for each entity, a profit and loss statement is required if the borrowers are the sole owners of those corporations, LLCs or Limited Partnership.

A legal analysis includes comparing the paystubs to the bank statements to make sure that a hardship is evident.

The borrowers must meet the definition of hardship which is demonstrated by the *Hardship Letter* and the financial information. Compare these documents with the tax returns, as well as the financial statement, if required to be part of the initial proposal submission.

If you are certain that everything is complete, all of the information is up to date and accurate, and the proposal indeed shows a hardship, then you are ready to perform the market analysis.

Market Analysis

Growing up in the 1950's and 1960's, my math teachers all required us to check our work when calculating math problems. After calculating the answer, it was a simple matter to check to make sure that we did not make any errors. Throughout my legal career, I was keenly aware of how appraisers vary widely from each other when valuing property. Indeed, in contested cases, we were often required to obtain three separate appraisals and average them together.

When I sold real estate, I took a particular interest in learning everything that I could about valuing property. I found several agents who were particularly adept at it and learned their methods. I discovered that they all had differing approaches to valuing property, but there was one agent who stood above the rest in his ability to value properties.

Now I find it easy to drawn on those skills to check the work of agents who submit CMAs to me. There is a lot riding on the accuracy of the appraisals. I require my own analysis, so if a lender hires someone else to do it, I want to make certain

Preparing the Short Sale Proposal

I can tell if their appraisal is accurate, especially if the lender's net receipt is a minimum threshold percentage of the fair market value. So far, it has proven effective. I have on often appealed a lender's appraisal and succeeded in changing the fmv calculation.

The most common approach by successful agents is to prepare a detailed CMA and then adjust their subject property to match the comps by adding and subtracting the values of certain features. They then calculate a resultant fair market value of the subject property. For example, they may add a value of $5,000 for a fireplace, or $15,000 for an extra garage bay. Perhaps they may add $5,000 if the entry is a two-story entrance (open to second floor ceiling). That's the way many successful agents and appraisers do it.

The problem with that method is that they are attempting to use arbitrary values to explain the differences in the *sold* prices of the comps. Who provides those values of each feature? Good question. I have been provided with cheat sheets listing a number of different features and their approximate value ranges. Ring a negative buzzer here!

There is no set price for features. Just as any house is valued by what a person will pay for it, so are the features. To find the value of a given home, the appraisers must look to *historical data* to find the *values* of properties that recently sold or are pending in that subdivision or general area. They may look back as much as a whole year to obtain that data. Home values can fluctuate greatly over the course of a year.

The features also fluctuate over the course of a year and from one subdivision to another. For example, who says that a fireplace adds value? In many places there are many, if not more, people who do not want a fireplace. Fireplaces often lose energy, may be dangerous to small children, and may occupy a room which limits furniture placement and decorating. So. in a given subdivision it is often the case that a fireplace will actually *reduce* the value of the home.

Likewise with two-story entryways. The feature value lists suggest that a two-story entryway will add value to the home and suggest a value range. However, in many places, the predominant buyers do not like two-story entries. A two-story entry removes that entire area of square footage from the second floor, making the house smaller. In fact, two-story entryways often lower the value of the home.

Similar arguments exist for pools, landscaping, outbuildings, workrooms, and basements. It is very common to find appraisers and many agents who use this approach to appraising properties but it also results in a great amount of variance from one appraisal to the next.

A more accurate approach, and the approach that I utilize to complete a market analysis is this. When agents use my mediation services to mediate a short sale or loan modification, I request the agents to send me *Quick CMAs*. This is a CMA that is a printout in grid format for all of the properties in a given area that are most similar to my subject property, and are listed by the status of the property (Active, Pending, Released, Withdrawn, Sold). Search parameters are used to eliminate properties not similar to the subject property. The search parameters are such things as the level (one story or two story), basement (Y/N), a range of square footage, lot size, garage bays and whether attached, and year built range. Other features may be added to or subtracted from the search depending upon the number of properties culled. The search can cull for properties by date range, going back 3-, 6-, 9-, or 12-months, depending upon the number of properties culled. Of course, the closer in time of these *Solds* and *Pendings*, the more reliable. *Pendings* are properties that are under contract but have not yet closed, and should substantiate your final result.

The CMA grid will list the sale price of the homes as well as the price per square foot. By analyzing this full grid, a pattern will emerge showing that homes larger than the average size home for that area will have a lower price per square foot (the principle of regression), and homes smaller than the average size home for that area will have a higher price per square foot (the principle of progression). The properties most dissimilar to the subject property are eliminated from the grid, leaving the most common three *sold* and/or *pending* comparables. You will now know what regression and progression factors exist, so a comparison of the price per square foot of the three comps can be made, obtaining the average if you assume these three are very similar. Taking that average price per square foot, you multiply it by the square footage of the subject property to obtain its raw value. You then look at the pictures and determine to the best of your ability whether there exists any condition differences to explain variances, making discretionary modifications to your raw value.

It is not done yet, however. It seems that many if not most agents over-value properties. They do this for what I consider to be a dishonest reason. Sellers have the notion that you should set the price higher than it is worth to allow for *negotiation* downward. However, it is not a used car that you are selling or an item at a flea market. I have read reports of studies that have demonstrated that properly valuing the property at or just below market value brings the highest dividends from a sale. The only real reason these properties are over valued is because sellers like it that you are seeking a higher amount. In reality, homes overpriced in the beginning yield a lower sale price. When buyers search for homes, they enter what they can afford in the search criteria. Homes priced higher than they are worth are found in searches that will compare this home with more expensive, nicer homes or homes with better features. Agents know that if the home is overpriced, there will be many buyers who will not find this property and their *For Sale* sign will be in the front yard for a longer period of time, generating more business for the agent.

I once helped a buyer from my church to find a condominium to purchase. She wanted this condominium within a one mile radius of her place of employment so she could walk to and from work. I searched the area and found no condos in her price range in the area. I did, however, find a number of nearly-new condos all of which were priced $20,000 higher than she could afford. I completed some CMAs and found they were all—yes, all overpriced by $20,000. I helped her submit an offer on one of them for lower than market value, and it was immediately accepted. She bought the home.

We're still not done with our analysis. Looking at the *Actives*, you look for trends. Understanding the tendency to over price, you can see if the properties are going up in value or down. If the *Active* listings are showing lower prices per square foot, then you can see that the trend is down and that your historical data may need to be adjusted downward. The properties

Preparing the Short Sale Proposal

that are *Released* or *Withdrawn* indicate properties that have been rejected by the market.

This approach to valuing properties is used by many agents, so if this is the approach that you already utilize, you should *check your answers* by also working your valuation through the common method used by the appraisers.

Summary

It is important to always draft a professional looking proposal, not just submitting the required documents to the lender. The reason is that although you may be submitting this proposal to the servicing lender, it is really for the benefit of the SMI and MI carrier, who are the entities who will approve or reject the proposal. You will not be able to speak with these decision-makers, so your only opportunity to impress and persuade them is through a professionally drafted proposal.

I utilize a form proposal drafted in Microsoft Word. The form contains certain features, a sample of which is included in the *Short Sale Business Manual*, obtained separately. The proposal contains a *table of contents*, a *summary*, the *Authorization & Release*, and all of the documents required by the lenders (which have been dictated by the MI carrier and SMI). The proposal also includes a CMA (comparable market analysis) or BPO (broker price opinion), which is virtually the same as an appraisal except performed by agents.

It is highly recommended that you perform a complete legal and market analysis. The legal analysis is a thorough check of each document, ensuring that everything is complete and accurate with nothing missing. It also includes obtaining a preliminary title report and checking for other liens and borrowers. It is vital that you include all borrowers, whether or not they have an ownership interest in the property, and that you include all the required information and documentation from each borrower.

A marketing analysis is critical to determine whether the appraisal obtained by the lender is accurate or not. If it is not accurate, the amount required by the SMI as the minimum net receipt percentage of the fair market value required by the lienholder will be affected. There are multiple ways that agents perform these valuations, and it is important to check their work, or even your own valuation, utilizing an alternate method for calculating value.

CHAPTER 10

The Seven Golden Keys To Negotiation

There is currently a popular TV show called *Heroes*, with a number of characters who have special powers. Some can fly, see the future, move at blurring speeds, read minds, control minds, make inanimate objects come to life, fix mechanical things with the mind, and other superpowers. Of all of these superpowers, I think mind control is the most useful. Just think, having the ability to control other people. For good, that power could stop bad people from hurting others. You could persuade wealthy people to buy your products or hire you for high wages. For you real estate agents, consider how you could convince anyone you wanted to list their mega-million dollar homes with you, and you could then persuade wealthy buyers to buy only your homes. Yes, that power has great potential.

See the connection with this chapter? If you can develop your ability to persuade people to your point of view in life and business, you would essentially have this super hero power. The power to persuade is the power to negotiate. It is the power to move a person from one level of thinking to another. The power to help people understand the reasons behind their positions or demands, and the power to persuade them to choose another plan that will still protect their underlying concerns.

I realized that I needed to work on my power to negotiate and persuade in 1981. I had been a state trooper in Wisconsin for about a year, and I saw how experienced fellow troopers, county deputies, and local police officers on numerous occasions would talk criminals and drunks into handcuffs without having to fight them. Conversely, I saw other officers and troopers who antagonized criminals and drunks into fighting. I compared my abilities with theirs and carefully watched their behaviors and words that either caused their arrestees to submit willingly or to fight. Years later, a fellow trooper and I started a little friendly contest to see who could talk the most drunks and criminals into submission rather than fighting. We had both become fairly adept and made a lot of arrests. I do not recall who won, but the desire in me to become better at persuasion only intensified over time.

I attended law school while continuing to work full time as a trooper, and resigned from the State Patrol just before completing my law degree. After I received my doctorate in law, I moved to Tennessee and went to work practicing law with my first firm. I started out predominantly representing creditors' rights and creditors' rights in bankruptcy. This firm provided me with some very good mentors who were quite skilled in talking defendants into settling their cases rather than taking the case to trial. As I did in law enforcement, I observed them carefully to see what worked for them, and what did not. I also observed other attorneys who struggled with this ability, making myself aware of those words and body language that either provoked negative reactions or positive responses.

I attended various legal seminars every year like all attorneys who must meet the requirements for continuing legal education, and I was drawn to those seminars that taught the various skills in articulating and working with people. Later, I received training in both family law mediation and general

The Seven Golden Keys To Negotiation

civil mediation. I continued that training with advanced mediation techniques in domestic violence cases.

As my skills developed, I discovered that I was settling increasingly more cases and having less actual trials in court. My negotiating skills were becoming more refined and I was enjoying it more. I added a professional mediation practice to my law firm in 1999 and discovered that with even greater frequency cases with very difficult and egocentric people were being settled with fair results.

Because of my experience and love for law enforcement, I developed a police training program in the management of hostile contacts and trained police officers from different departments. Watching other police officers improve their skills in managing angry people was great fun and brought a sense of satisfaction.

I have always been active in church, and seeing a need, I developed a church training program in conflict resolution and church conciliation. There was another popular training program in existence but I saw a number of serious flaws in that system that could actually create conflict.

With my mediation firm focusing on real estate workouts between lienholders, sellers facing foreclosure, and buyers wanting the best return on their investment, I see daily the need for agents and investors to develop their negotiation skills, and I believe that you, as an agent or investor, could greatly benefit from this training.

To train you to a high level of skill in a short time would require many hours of structured training in a classroom. However, I developed my own skills over the process of time, by observing the skills of others, learning to understand the concepts I was observing, and then practicing the skills until I became proficient at them. Likewise, you can also learn the concepts. If you study them until you understand these concepts intimately, and practice them to refine them into skills, you too can become proficient at negotiating.

Many of you may already possess natural skills in working with people and have highly developed powers of persuasion. However, even you may benefit from the structured system for developing negotiating skills in this chapter, and if you practice and refine each of the skill sets, your natural abilities will be greatly enhanced. Whether you have natural abilities or think you have none, this training chapter will be a benefit to you. The only difference will be how long you need to practice before your skills are refined.

This chapter is not a list of *tips* and *suggestions*, but a structured process of learning to negotiate. I will present each skill set as one of the *seven keys to negotiation*. Seven concepts. Seven sets of skills. Each *key* is a concept that must be practiced and turned into a skill. If you find that you already possess some of them, then great! You can focus on refining it. If not, then now is the time to dwell on each *key* concept, internalize it, and understand how and why it is important. Practice incorporating it into your conversations, at home, at work, at church, with friends and acquaintances. Practice them with your loved ones, including your children. Practice them until they are refined skills. The keys are universal, unlocking doors of possibilities and opportunities in all areas of life and business. They unlock many of the doors of barriers to agreement, allowing both of you in conversation to engage in higher levels of discussions toward agreement.

The Seven Golden Keys To Negotiation

The skill sets are golden because gold has precious value. The seven golden keys to negotiation are seven valuable skills that when understood, internalized, practiced, and refined, bring great results.

They will not help you if you merely read this chapter a time or two. These keys are effective only if you read them, understand them, *internalize the keys*, practice them, and use them. Although I have reduced my entire training program to just these *Seven Golden Keys to Negotiation*, with no opportunity to practice and develop them under tutelage, each one of you can, through the process of time and practice, develop these skills if you so choose.

In the context of this book, I am not limiting the discussion to negotiating with the lenders, as this would prove to be a disservice to you. Rather, I present them using a variety of life contexts, primarily drawing from experiences in law enforcement and law and they will apply to all of life's contexts from business to family, from sellers to lenders, from neighbors to fellow church members. The need to negotiate is everywhere. The concepts learned in the workplace will be applicable at home. The concepts practiced at church will assist you with negotiating with lenders. Skills learned elsewhere are applicable everywhere.

We all meet people from time to time who are resistant to the services we offer, a proposal we may submit to the lender, the ideas we present to solve problems, the beliefs we want to share about God or religious ideas, the requirements we assert from our position of authority, the enforcing of rules, or the persuasion we offer for mercy. They are everywhere around us.

This resistance may result from a variety of factors. It may result from a lack of true understanding of what we offer, and the difficulty in articulating in a clear way that will change an incorrect *picture* in the hearer's mind's eye of what we are trying to convey. It may result from fear, because of an incorrect picture formed out of prior negative experiences, interpreting what they hear and perceiving it to be no different than what they have experienced in the past. This resistance may come from bias, which is a preference for pre-conceived ways of thinking and behaving. It may also result from differences in personality, which we all experience from time to time.

Resistance resulting from a lack of true understanding of what we have to offer is most common. I was once asked to assist another police officer who was assigned to arrest someone as a material witness to organized crime. The reason for taking him into custody was not out of concern he might skip the area and not be available for trial, but for his own protection. The easiest approach would have been for the officer to merely explain to the witness that we needed him to come with us to the station to find a way to protect him, but there was an arrest warrant, and to make certain that the witness was legally bound in case he suddenly took off, the officer had to actually tell him he was under arrest and place a hand on the witness. The witness immediately envisioned being handcuffed in back, thrown in the back of the police cruiser and hauled off to jail where he would be thrown into the drunk tank with criminals and drunks, to be assaulted and molested. That witness did not envision a reality where he would ride in the front seat of a police car, getting to play a bit with the lights and siren. He also did not envision merely going to the station where

The Seven Golden Keys To Negotiation

we would meet in an office, fill out some paperwork, and then go to a hotel where he would be protected from death threats. His interpretation of the words were based upon conditioned thinking and pre-conceived visioning based on what he saw in television shows.

When we offer a different idea, a different alternative, a different plan than what the hearer currently believes, holds, or desires, the words we use can instill fear because of prior experience, or merely because we have not articulated enough of the idea for the hearer to form an accurate picture of that idea, alternative, or plan in his mind. It is vital that we think about the words we use to articulate these word pictures in advance. That is why scripts are helpful to real estate agents, because the right words form word pictures in the mind of the hearer to a overcome this natural resistance.

Anytime we describe an idea, the words we transmit to the hearer are received and interpreted by the hearer. The hearer then forms a picture in his mind about this idea. If that picture is the same as the picture in the speaker's mind, then communication has occurred effectively and there is a clear understanding. However, when the right words are not selected to properly articulate that idea, then an altered picture results. It is as though the hearer were looking through foggy windows with a distorted view of what you are attempting to present.

Sometimes you can articulate properly but the hearer, because of past negative experience, forms an incorrect picture. Their negative experience, completely unrelated to anything you said, raises fear within that the same negative result will again be experienced. It is your responsibility to watch and be aware when negative experiences may be affecting communication.

Short Sales & Loan Modifications

I once stopped a person for speeding many years ago. At the same time that I was stopping this vehicle, there were sirens from fire vehicles and an ambulance enroute to a call. My police cruiser was equipped with a European type siren that alternated high and low notes, so I activated this siren type so that the driver could distinguish between my siren and those of the other emergency vehicles and notice that I was stopping him. What I did not know at the time was that this driver had survived the death camps of Germany and associated that siren with his experience with the Gestapo so many years before. When I approached his vehicle, I could see that the driver was visibly shaken, could hardly speak out of fear, and he had even urinated. An extreme example to be certain, but it illustrates how fear can cause involuntary reactions to seemingly normal activity. Obviously no ticket.

The same is true in simple conflict. A child wants to do one thing, and when we as parents even attempt to discuss the child's demand, he may immediately fear he will not get what he wants, before there is even any evidence of it. When a salesman calls me on the phone, I immediately react negatively because I do not like telemarketing with me as a target.

I mentioned previously that a lot of lienholders do not like real estate agents. The reason? Because they may have experienced agents who were pushy, belligerent, belittling, or just downright rude to them, or they have heard the stories about these agents in the break rooms. It is often the case that when I call a negotiator, the person immediately raises strong defenses or will start lying to me. Once they discover that I am one of those strange lawyer types working on this case as a mediator, the discussion immediately changes. The reason? They seem to like lawyers, and immediately the defenses come down and they are more open and honest with me. Even if they did not like lawyers, by telling them that I am one of those *strange* or *weird attorney types*, using a bit of self-deprecating humor often offsets that fear as well as breaking the ice and placing us both on a friendly basis. Using self-deprecating humor can also be used effectively with children, spouses, and anyone *who thinks that you think* that you know more than they do. It removes you from the stereotype.

Resistance from bias immediately brings to mind racial or cultural differences. Cultural bias can most certainly create barriers to open ideas and discussion. Many people allow this bias to intervene and prevent the sharing of ideas, but most people are able to keep their biases subdued especially when it is in their best interests and commerce is dependent upon friendly discourse.

There are other kinds of bias that may interfere with reaching agreements. When people ask what my profession is and I tell them that I am a lawyer, some people immediately react with telltale signs of a negative bias. People form opinions of races, cultures, professions, and various groups based upon what they hear from parents, friends, even TV and movies. People can often recognize an obvious bias, but the majority of people are affected in varying degrees by even subtle bias, and it becomes evident especially in conflict and bargaining.

Bias can arise from differences in personality as well. In both my law enforcement experience and law practice, I encountered a lot of smooth talking personalities who were dishonest, abusive, or controlling, and I learned to mistrust anyone with that personality. The majority of people really respond favorably to these smooth personalities, and many people with this personality take advantage of the unsuspecting, and they often get away with their misdeeds. Many judges and lawyers fall for their gifted tongue. I've seen a lot of controlling, abusive husbands win in court against the wives that they have beaten or controlled. In one case the evidence proved that the husband controlled every move of his wife, permitting her to leave home only one day each week and even then he kept track of her mileage. He controlled what food she could eat, what she could read, what she could watch on TV. He was insanely jealous, continually accusing her of making eye contact with other men. He controlled her every move, and she was completely dominated by him. The result? The judge after listening to his smooth talking answers said in his ruling that what the world needs is more men like John Wayne and this man who take control of their families.

This is an extreme example and most people with a *sales personality* have learned that people respond favorably to them. Even though many sales people are honest and decent, my initial reaction is negative, and I continually have to set aside my stereotyping, listen for the substance of the conversation and watch for evidence of their character. I am often surprised when smooth, articulate personalities turn out to be great people, honest and trustworthy. However, this is a good example of how we are all vulnerable to bias. I have a strong, dominant personality and this personality fits well with my military, law enforcement, and law background. However, a lot of people react negatively immediately when they encounter my personality. I have often joked about how for some of you agents, when at an open house, people will gravitate toward you and you can get a lot of business from the open house. I joke that my experience is the opposite, and at an open house, the moment I walk toward visitors, they immediately turn and head for the door!

This is an exaggeration of course, but I did have a more difficult time selling than most agents who possess this sales personality. I did learn and improve, however, by instead of thinking of it as sales, I reverted back to my attorney mode of thinking of problem-solving. That is how I viewed my profession of law – helping people to solve problems they could not solve for themselves. I became fairly accomplished at that. By focusing on helping people by solving problems, I became functional in sales.

As a real estate investor (REI), merely the term *investor* may bring a negative first impression to the minds of homeowners in financial trouble. Negative stereotyping can cause them to assume you are only there to take advantage of them to their detriment. All it make take to overcome this negative first impression is a little self-deprecating humor and having them experience that you are open and honest, different from their stereotype.

Even subtle mannerisms or words can cause others to form barriers to negotiation. It is important to recognize these influences in our own lives. We cannot totally eliminate the characteristics about us, but we can reduce their influence on our communication. Each of us have our own *frogs and lizards*; we each have something about us that is a little different, a little strange, a little weird. The idea is for us to be honest with ourselves about them, accepting our weaknesses and imperfections, but to reduce their influence or impact.

You may be called upon to negotiate in a variety of contexts. One context is a listing presentation to persuade homeowners to use you as their agent. Articulating well is critical, and learning to convey accurately word pictures from your mind to theirs is essential for them to understand that you have the solution for their needs and to build their trust. At the same time, you must be alert to offset any negative bias they may have from past experience to your race, gender, personality, profession, or other factors.

When I sold real estate, I attended some classes at my brokerage in using scripts. The class was taught by a very gifted, articulate agent. He had memorized scripts that were absolutely some of the most clear and articulate expressions and responses. I was greatly impressed. However, if learning scripts was all that was needed, and you had the ability to develop and memorize scripts for every possible objection in life whether responding to your spouse, your children or anyone else with whom you might come into contact, then no one would need a course such as this one in negotiation. All you would need is a gifted negotiator who can write scripts for every situation in life and for you to memorize them all. I guess that would be absurd, wouldn't it? In fact, this agent did have some difficulty when someone raised a situation that was new and he had to figure out a response. It will be much more effective if you learn the actual concepts behind those great scripts and the reasons for them, so you may always respond appropriately to a variety of situations requiring negotiation.

You may need to negotiate to persuade a potential buyer to hire you. You may need these skills when speaking to opposing agents who do not want to pay your client's price for the

The Seven Golden Keys To Negotiation

home. These skills may be helpful with a spouse who is upset at your behavior, your plans, or your words. They are definitely worth learning for attempting to communicate with a teenager whose hormones are raging and who may be exhibiting a bit of obstinancy syndrome. In short sales you will have opportunities to utilize negotiating skills not only with servicing lenders but with other lienholders as well, including lawyers, former spouses, second mortgage holders, and tradesmen who have not been paid.

Will these skills always work? No! Some people have barriers to conciliation.

You will, however, be maximizing the likelihood of success. When mediating court cases, it was reported that of those cases that were set for trial, and where the attorneys were unable to negotiate a settlement, mediation was effective in settling and avoiding trials in approximately 51% of these cases. That is a great success! These are cases where they tried hard to resolve. Cases with experienced attorneys. Mediation is different from negotiation in many respects but there is a lot of overlap in the methods and techniques. If more attorneys would obtain negotiation training and refine the skills, they would resolve and settle even more cases. The attorneys who obtain mediation or negotiation training and then refine their skills resolve more cases and have fewer court trials. Likewise, the agents and investors who internalize, practice, and refine the skills taught in this chapter will resolve and settle more short sale or loan modification cases.

When negotiating with lenders, there will be some things you cannot control. Regulations or contractual restrictions limiting agent commissions or establishing minimum threshold percentages are not negotiable and must be merely accepted. However, learning good negotiating skills will help you to control where negotiating *is* possible.

As agents, you negotiate with inspectors, appraisers, mortgage brokers, title companies, other agents, contractors, and anyone else that you need to persuade to your view. The process of negotiating even minor conflicts is the same as negotiating with billion dollar corporate contracts. They require the same skills, the same mindsets, and the same control over your own emotions and biases.

As you approach the possibility of a conflict or communication in which you need to persuade your opponent to your view, especially with someone who thinks they may be your better, the Seven Keys to Negotiation are skills that can make the difference for you. They can be the skills that results in a *win-win* for both of you.

Key 1: Negotiate From Strength

Negotiating from a position of strength means that you must always seek the upper hand in your negotiations. It creates in your opponent's perception that what you have to offer is at least of equal or greater value than what he/she possesses.

To negotiate from a position of strength requires that you think through and plan your responses. You must prepare for negotiation, like a lawyer prepares for a trial. Only the foolish lawyer would go into a trial not having prepared *in advance* the evidence to be presented, the witnesses' testimonies, the

The Seven Golden Keys To Negotiation

questions that are asked of the witnesses, the questions to ask of the opposing witnesses, the arguments to the court, and both the opening statements and closing statements.

To negotiate from strength means to prepare *in advance* first your own attitude and mindset. You need to be confident that you have the solutions for their needs. What you have is valuable and it should be your purpose to plan the words needed to accurately convey that value in word pictures.

Preparing in advance allows you to gain strength not only by preparing your own mind, but it is the time to investigate, to determine the strengths of your positions and weaknesses, and your opponent's strengths and weaknesses, as well.

Right after obtaining my license to practice law, I did not know hardly anything about being a lawyer. I had been a pretty good police investigator, but was not yet much of a lawyer. Someone that I knew referred a young man to me who had just received a summons for a lawsuit. He had caused an accident and he was being sued for millions. The lawsuit was filed by an attorney who was nationally known, was one of the best trial lawyers in the country, never loses any of his cases, and he was seeking a judgment that the young man would spend his lifetime trying to pay.

I knew that I was in over my head, but before I referred him to another lawyer, I decided to investigate further. I had been an experienced accident investigator as a state trooper, so I studied the accident reports, went to the scene, made a number of mathematical calculations, and determined that the accident would not likely have caused major permanent injuries to the other driver, as was claimed.

As far as the attorney knew, our young man did not have an attorney yet. I knew an off-duty police officer who would do a little investigating for me, so at my request he conducted surveillance of the other driver. He was able to obtain a video of that driver removing, repairing, and replacing the engine of a car. The same man who was supposedly permanently injured and could not lift more than ten pounds.

I printed some stills from the video and had them hand delivered to the attorney's office. I attached a note with my business card which stated *"Call me when you decide to dismiss your suit."* The next day he called me and said he had done some checking and that it was very humbling being beaten by an attorney who had only been licensed a month.

How you prepare for negotiating determines the strength you have in bargaining. Most of the time your investigation is limited and you cannot gain enough *intelligence* about your adversary to really know their strength and weaknesses. What do you do then?

The U.S. Government has the CIA to gain this kind of information on their adversaries. Likewise, each branch of the government has intelligence-gathering agencies. Most of you will not have the ability to send spies into all of the companies who are your adversaries in negotiation.

Doing your homework with buyers of real estate is about knowing the answers to the questions they ask about the property. It does not matter if the MLS sheet is in your hands and you refer from it, but that MLS sheet will not tell you when the last time was that the septic tank was emptied. Doing your homework adds strength. But if you do not know what their arguments will be, how can you gain strength?

The Seven Golden Keys To Negotiation

In the same way as attorneys when preparing for a trial. You will need to make certain assumptions. Learn to think like your opponent and predict their arguments. Sit down with pen and paper and list of all of their arguments, carefully putting yourself in their shoes and thinking through the ways that you could argue their cause. In this way, you determine their strengths, as well as their weaknesses.

I once was preparing for a trial in which a fairly wealthy defendant owed a hospital a large amount of money. The problem was that hospital employees had treated him very poorly as his wife was dying in the hospital bed. They did take very good care of her, but they were rude and mean to her husband because of critical statements he made to them. Somehow they came to believe that he was the cause of his wife's condition. His wife passed away and now there was the hospital bill that needed to be paid.

I knew because of the man's emotional state that the entire trial would be more about how he was treated than what he owed, and I also knew that the judge would not limit his testimony to solely whether he owed the debt. The strength of the defendant's emotional argument with this judge might threaten to outweigh the debt this wealthy defendant could easily afford.

As I prepared for this case, I realized that I owed my client, the hospital, a duty to collect the debt. After all, collecting these medical costs from him and others like him meant keeping the hospital open to continue providing services to people in need. I made lists of all of the arguments for each side and the evidence that would be used to support those arguments.

From my list, I was able to see arguments that my opponent might make could have a stronger impact than mine, so I decided to nullify the impact of those arguments by conceding them myself. At the very beginning of the trial, I was the one who proved the bad treatment and disclosed the weaknesses of my client's position, and then went on to prove the debt. When it came time for the defendant to put on their case, most of their proof had been used up cross-examining my witnesses in the beginning, and I was able to successfully object to cumulative evidence.

The point of this is that if your opponent has arguments that may be stronger, and this threatens to sidetrack your main issues, concede them early. Always take responsibility for what you or your client may have done wrong. There is nothing more conciliatory than accepting responsibility and it gives you bargaining strength. By taking responsibility early in the process, you make it a thing of the past, nullifying much of its power against you.

My law partner was preparing for a tough divorce negotiation. He seemed to be struggling as he was preparing his case. He was concerned about the bad behavior of his client and he was fearful that her behavior, which resulted from attempting to gain the strength to leave her abusive husband, might cause the judge to rule against her and favor the husband. I suggested this strategy of taking responsibility for her behavior at the very beginning of the trial. He followed that suggestion and later reported to me that the trial ended early, the judge ignored the bad behavior of our client, and ruled in her favor. You obtain great strength from accepting responsibility, and doing so early in discussions.

The Seven Golden Keys To Negotiation

To negotiate from strength also requires that you have your end results clearly in mind. You know where you are going in your conversation and how to get there. You must be confident that your objectives meet their needs. In almost all negotiations there exist some common ground, and finding that common ground must be your goal.

Strength means that you have a clear understanding of your opponent's objectives. You have strength from finding the common ground you both share. You have strength from identifying to your opponent your knowledge of their needs and concerns. Their sense of appreciation for your concern for their needs gives you great bargaining power.

One of the most important sources of strength is when you are not out to win and cause your opponent to lose. Your strength is heightened when you are seeking a *win-win* result. Most sales people are out only to make the sale. The truly great salespeople seek this *win-win* result. It is the mindset that if I get the benefit of the sale and you have only lost the money that was paid, then I have failed. In order for me to win, I must know that you value what you have received in the deal every bit as much as I value what you paid. That is truly a *win-win* result. You obtain a great amount of negotiating strength from this attitude and objective.

You obtain negotiating strength from many sources. You may think that the greatest source of strength is possessed only if you have something to hold over your opponents, that you can hurt them in some way if they do not respond favorably to you. Many people think that *holding them over a barrel* is the greatest source of strength. They are wrong!

Yes, most negotiators seek a *win-lose* result by searching for some power or negative impact to leverage over their opponents. A lot of people go through life always looking for that ability to hold someone over a barrel. They think that without this sledge hammer in hand, they have no negotiating strength. Again, they are wrong!

Some of my greatest *wins* in negotiating have come about by not even disclosing that I possessed any leverage. I usually disregard the sledge hammer if possible and recognize that my opponent's knowledge of their behavior may help motivate them to enter into discussions, but I find it a great strength to ignore that leverage. Is it ever possible to have this kind of leverage and appropriate to use it? Yes, of course. That leverage is appropriately utilized to back someone in the corner if they raise a barrier to conciliation, but I always let them back out of the corner after *balancing the table*.

Balancing the table is maintaining both of you as equals. If you must use leverage to back your opponent into the corner, you are usurping power. This is appropriate if your purpose is to stop them from inappropriately usurping power against you and trying to bully their way to a result. If you are able to balance the power between you without using what you hold over them, you gain great bargaining strength.

Bargaining from strength also comes from understanding that you have a mission, and that mission is to serve *your opponent's needs*, not your own. Do not underestimate the strength in this. What does this mean? The words you choose should draw from your opponent their underlying concerns and needs. It is important to affirm their needs, speak to those concerns and needs, identify them, and help your opponent to understand that

The Seven Golden Keys To Negotiation

you are looking out for their best interests, even if they appear at first to be adverse to yours. You are seeking a *win-win* result, so your focus is on ways to make the result for your opponent a win as well. This will be explored in depth shortly.

Next, the strength-building process involves cultivating the negotiating relationship. If you cannot find a way early on to break the ice and have a friendly chat, then you have little strength. Find effective ways, with your type of personality, to break the ice and if at all possible, get them laughing, even a little, or at least have them enjoying their time with you, even if it is only on the phone. *Breaking the ice* is then transformed into *bridge-building*, creating a collaborative, rather than adversarial relationship. Practice this. Practice this with every business call. Really refine this skill.

Associated with bridge-building is developing the skill of *active listening*. Most of the time when someone says something to us about themselves, we respond with an answer about us. Active listening is discovering more about them. The following dialog illustrates this well.

> "I just got back to work from vacation today."
> "Really? Where did you go?"
> "Nowhere, I just stayed home. I needed to rest my back."
> "Oh? Did you injure your back?"
> "No, my office chair causes me a lot of backaches."
> "Oh, I am sorry that you are hurting."
> "Thanks, I appreciate your concern, but it will be ok."
> "Would any of those back rests help you any?"
> "Maybe. Maybe I should stop at the store and find one that will work."

"Well, I'm sorry you had to use your vacation for recovery. I hope you find something that works for you."

This dialog demonstrated active listening. It is about discovering *more* details about your opponent than wanting them to know about you. This is how the conversation often is like.

"I just got back to work from vacation today."
"Really? Where did you go?"
"Nowhere, I just stayed home. I needed to rest my back."
"Oh? Did you injure your back?"
"No, my office chair causes me a lot of backaches."
"I understand, sometimes my back hurts from sitting at work all day. Would any of those back rests help you any?"
"Maybe. Maybe I should stop at the store and find one that will work."
"Yes,, I'm thinking about doing the same."

The idea of active listening is to discover the underlying *interests* that your opponent is protecting. You are then showing your own interest in your opponent. There is great strength in that. The first conversation above demonstrated that interest in the opponent. The second conversation missed that opportunity.

Sharing information about you in response is not automatically wrong, but make sure it is far outweighed by your concern for your opponent. Stay away from asking sensitive, private information though and just stick to usual and culturally appropriate conversation topics.

When negotiating, delineate and negotiate the issues, one at a time, from smallest to largest. As you find common

The Seven Golden Keys To Negotiation

ground on the easier topics, momentum develops and your opponent is more inclined to continue that momentum to find common ground on the more difficult or energy-charged topics. Delineating means telling them in advance the issues that need to be addressed, keeping those issues to as few as possible. Other, less meaningful, issues can be reserved for later. *"Say, Bill, there are three things we need to talk about, the time we should meet, where we should meet, and what we should bring. Let's first find an agreeable time, shall we?"* delineating and then negotiating the issues from easiest to more difficult provides the opportunity to develop rapport, reveals their interests and weaknesses, helps you gain control over the process, thereby building momentum that adds strength to your negotiating.

Further, negotiating from a position of strength is accomplished by gaining control of the actual negotiation process. Whenever possible you should set up negotiating opportunities so that your opponent is seeking the resolution. The *seeker is the weaker* holds a lot of truth. When someone seeks me out to ask me for something, I have much more strength in bargaining. When I talk to another attorney or a bank negotiator and that person says they will call me with a response to a query within two days, I wait for him to call me. Even if it takes three or four days. If I call him, then I am the seeker and in the weaker bargaining position. However, if I wait longer, I may actually gain bargaining position by calling because my opponent at some point may feel guilty over breaking the promise to call me quickly. Do not underestimate the power you gain, the strength you gain, from getting others to do the seeking.

Another method of gaining control of the negotiating process is the same as you use to prevent bullying and balance the table when your opponent initially has a barrier to conciliation. It is backing your opponent into the corner as we discussed, but then using a little humor to let him out of the corner. Sometimes you must make your opponent face reality and disclose what you may hold over them when suddenly they stop collaborating on the solution and raise a sudden emotional barrier. You then use what you hold over them to reveal their position is being absurd and how it prevents reaching agreement. This is backing them into the corner. So not only might you balance the table initially with your sledgehammer information, you might need to use this leverage to take back control whenever your opponent attempts to usurp power. However, when you back someone in the corner with your leverage, the *fight vs. flight* reflex kicks in at some point and causes them to react emotionally, thereby blocking progress. It is vital to stop backing them into the corner when you sense this happening and let them out of the corner with either a little humor or affirmation, such as *"I know you are just fulfilling your responsibility. You're a great guy and I appreciate the way we're able to work together"*.

Recently, I had to again contact the customer service department of a company that kept repeating an error in my billing statement. I know that when I am calling in to complain, my strong personality can become quite overbearing to some introverted person who is just trying to do a difficult job. After making my complaint, I said, *"There is something else I need to tell you."* After a pause, a quiet voice said, *"What?"* I then said *"Listen, I know you are just working there and I am not mad at you. So don't take this personally ok? I am just mad at the company, not you. You are actually the nicest customer service rep I've talked to.* She said ok and said she really appreciated me saying that. She

The Seven Golden Keys To Negotiation

went on to describe how she sometimes goes home and cries after hearing everybody's complaints all day. I had made a connection. I usurped power to get my point across, but I built a bridge with that customer service representative who fixed the problem correctly for me. I was able to bring a smile into her life and even laughing a bit. I gained a lot of strength in negotiating this recurring problem that recurred no more.

Let me be clear. This rep had likely been trained to not follow up as others had done before her. This company has a history of not taking care of their customers. My technique for gaining control resulted in successfully balancing the table and getting her to take effective action to solve the problem.

Gaining control of the process can be performed through alternating choices. *Would you rather meet on Tuesday evening, or on Saturday morning?* I made it a practice to take my office staff to lunch occasionally. When I would ask where they would like to go, they always said *"I don't care."* So I would choose, and eventually I started hearing complaints that we always went to my favorite restaurants. The next time, I changed my query and asked, *"Would you rather go to Ryan's or Chili's?"* They made a choice and everyone was happy. I gained great strength in bargaining and a lot of good will.

Negotiating short sales and loan modifications with servicing lenders basically consists of not making the negotiator mad at you so they will not tank the proposal's acceptance by the SMI, which happens often. However, it should be more about establishing such a good relationship with that person and the call center representatives so they may do little things that might actually help it along. They are in control of what goes to the lender. The better my relationship with that negotiator and call center representatives, the more likely the persuasive parts of the proposal will be submitted to the SMI.

There are, though, times where you may actually negotiate with the servicing lender. That is when their contract with a secondary market investment firm provides them with this authority to approve or reject a proposal. This happens usually with either relatively small investment groups made up primarily of wealthy professionals such as doctors, major contractors, and the like. If the servicing lender has this authority, then you will utilize your skills with them. It is rare though, and you may never encounter this situation.

Another time to negotiate with the servicing lender is when they want to reduce broker commissions. Remember, though, that it is not negotiable if required by the SMI or MI carrier. It is only when the servicing lender themselves want to bite the hand that is feeding them.

A common tactic is for them is to say that they are taking a big loss on the short sale so it only makes sense that the agents give a little too. The fallacy in the argument is that the agents did not make the bad financial deal with the borrowers, and it is the agents who are rescuing them and mitigating their losses.

Pointing out the logic of this, though, is seldom effective. A more effective approach is to ask questions about their written policies. If they are attempting to require something of you or your client, then it must be a written policy and consistently applied. After all, most of the time at least someone involved is in a legally protected class, either by gender, race, age, national origin, or religion. If they *ever* give a full commission to someone else, then by asking them if they understand that one of the parties is a *minority* (meaning protected class status), you

The Seven Golden Keys To Negotiation

are causing them to tread more carefully. You are not stating that one of the people involved actually is; you are only asking if they are aware that one is. They should understand that if they treat a protected class differently from everyone else, that is discrimination. You may need to help them understand that if they violate discrimination laws, they will be held liable. You do this in ways that communicate that you are trying to be *helpful* to them. The question could be asked like this, "*I have an agent who is concerned about being discriminated against as a minority, are you certain that your policy of reducing the broker commission is in writing and a full commission is never approved? This agent seems to believe that it has happened, and I would hate to see your company get sued again.*" Here, you are *partnering* with your opponent, taking a neutral position and showing concern for them, rather than taking an adversarial position.

There is another tactic to gaining bargaining strength. I call it the *persistent student* approach. You will from time to time negotiate with someone who sees themselves as your intellectual superior. They may actually have a lot of knowledge and experience, as well as the success to back up that claim. This person may dominate the conversation, attempting to bully their way through the negotiations. Normally we would conclude that this person has a barrier to conciliation. There is, though, a way to effectively balance this usurping of power and bring them back down to earth.

The *persistent student* is best described by illustration. I was attempting to negotiate a property dispute lawsuit in which I represented the plaintiff, and a well-known and successful trial lawyer represented the defendant. The defendant had built his garage so that it extended across the property line onto my client's land, and had deliberately removed the boundary marker in the process.

When we met to negotiate a settlement, the opposing attorney knew that I was in my first year of practicing law, and he refused to be seated. He then looked me in the eye, pointed his finger at me and said his client is not going to settle, they are going to win in court, but that his client would settle for $1,000 and that is all. He then tried to stare me down. Although I had a lot of experience in law enforcement and was not intimidated, I wanted to find a way to resolve the case.

I recognized that the court would only award some monetary for the value of the property that was taken, because the cost of removing the garage would be deemed unconscionable by the court. However, I also knew that the award was going to be a lot more than that measly offer.

Rather than stand and try to force bargaining strength, I played the *persistent student*. I asked to talk to the attorney in private. I then told him that I knew he is one of the best trial lawyers in town and I was brand new. I then told him that my client is very difficult to work with, and that I knew that the client will complain to the judge that the lawyer refused to even try to settle, and asked him to tell me how to convince my client not to make that issue with the judge. Judges do not like it when attorneys refuse to attempt settlement.

The attorney then explored several ridiculous ideas before stating that maybe they should see if there was a possibility of settlement. We continued to negotiate in private, and my tactic was to continually ask the attorney to teach me how to explain to my client the logic behind his positions and various arguments. In other words, instead of arguing back and forth with the other attorney, I played the naïve student who needed help to make my client understand the logic of their arguments. I was the *persistent student*.

The result was that this arrogant and domineering attorney spent considerable time trying to find explanations for me that would make logical sense my client. As he explored the issues and solutions, and with me continually asking him the *"But what if my client says..."* questions, the defendant's attorney eventually came around to suggest a settlement that was just and fair. The case was settled for more money than my client was actually willing to accept.

I use the *persistent student* often with servicing lender negotiators and call center representatives. I ask the reps a lot of questions about how their process works, why it takes so long, and what steps the proposal must go through. I know the answers already, but being the *persistent student* creates within them the desire to teach, to serve, and to take care of me.

A lot of people think they must always convey to the other person how much they know, and they want to make certain the opponent knows it. The *persistent student*, however, is manipulative in a good way, because it builds bridges to form positive relationships as you seek common ground. It can also manufacture common ground where there may have been none before.

All of these are methods of gaining bargaining strength. If you practice incorporating these concepts into your everyday life, including your communications with family, at work, in stores, and in social gatherings, you will refine these skills and be able to apply them to your more serious negotiations.

Key 2: Managing and Balancing Power

Before you work on developing this next skill, be certain to have internalized the techniques in Key 1 and practiced them until you are fairly comfortable with all of them. Then you are ready to *add* to the skills. If you are comfortable with bargaining from a position of strength, and you have learned to apply that skill in day to day living, then it is time to learn to manage the power that exists between you and your opposing negotiating partner and balance that power.

We discussed balancing power to some extent in Key 1, and it is an important skill. Now, let's expand this discussion. An extreme example is a domestic call that I received as a police officer. The police dispatcher assigned me to respond to a particular address. The neighbors had called in a complaint that they heard a lot of screaming and yelling. Upon arrival, I found the front door open and heard a lot of yelling. I decided to not await my back up, and entered the house very cautiously. As I entered the living room I saw a very large male subject standing in front of a very small woman who was seated in a chair, cowering before him. The man was bent over with his finger shaking in her face and was yelling loudly his opinions of her and threatening her. Who possessed the power? He did. His size, his posture, his body language, his proximity to her, his tone of voice, and volume all usurped a massive amount of

The Seven Golden Keys To Negotiation

power that he held over her. That power shifted when I entered the room with my police uniform a sign of authority and he immediately assumed a fighting stance directed at me. He was a lot bigger than me, so I needed to find a way to balance that power with him or I would have to fight him and arrest him in order to protect both of us, and likely we would both get hurt. There are techniques for balancing this power without having to fight. More on this in a moment.

That is an extreme example of a common situation. Men *tend* to have more power than women in negotiations, but is often overcome through experience and confidence. Extrovert personalities have greater power than corresponding introvert personalities. The size of the person is often used to affect power between negotiators. People talk over each other when arguing in order to usurp power so the table will not be balanced. People naturally try to usurp power so they will have greater power than their adversary. They naturally want a *win-lose* result because they fear their opponent will otherwise win and they will lose. They do not realize that when the power is equal both sides can win.

In mediation sessions when the parties are in the same room, the best furniture arrangement for balancing power is to have a round table. With common rectangular tables, the *head of the table* in traditional homes is where the father would sit, and the affect has been passed down to the current generation as a sense of power when someone sits in that position, and a sense of powerlessness where the others are seated. Of course, there are two seats of power with a rectangular table, both ends. When I must use rectangular tables in mediation, I often move the table so I am sitting at the head of the table but the other *head* is against a wall making it impossible for anyone else to be seated there. This helps both parties feel a sense of equal power. It helps to *balance* the table.

In order to have a negotiating session in which there is the highest likelihood of success in creating a *win-win*, all of the people involved must have a sense that power is balanced. If the opposing partner senses too much power, it is very difficult to find a *win-win* solution. If that person senses too little power, the same may be true. It is only when there is a balanced sense of power between the negotiators is there the highest likelihood of resolution.

Opposing negotiators will usurp power in different ways. We discussed some situations, let's look some more. One is through a strong adamant demand. They are saying *"this is the way it will be and that's that!"* There is no bargaining with this statement, their mind is made up and there is not going to be any negotiating. This method is quite common. In order to counter this tactic, you have to *balance the table* so to speak. There are several ways to do this. One is to say *"you seem to be really angry"*, whether or not they really do. They will usually respond with something like, *"no I'm not, but this is where we stand on this issue."* This could be followed up with *"yes, I can understand this issue is really important to you. I'd like to hear how you arrived at this decision."* The opponent will then state the reason behind the position and I could then ask more questions to discover the real underlying concern or interest that is being protected. My initial statements countered the usurping of power and *balanced the table*. By responding appropriately to their usurping of power, rather than reacting as a victim,

The Seven Golden Keys To Negotiation

you may be able to successfully return to a balanced bargaining discussion based upon reason.

Another way power is usurped is through the use of strong emotion, such as anger or tears. Both the seemingly angry person and the *po-pitiful* are attempting to make themselves appear as victims, designed to cause you to move their direction in bargaining either by being intimidated, feeling guilty, or feeling sorry for them. They may or may not be actually aware they are using a tactic; rather they may have learned this method of manipulation from early childhood as part of their adjusting to and learning to manipulate their environment. You can balance the table through a number of methods. One is to just remain silent for a while, with an uncomfortable pause where they will likely break the pause and expose their vulnerability. Another is to address their victimization and ask them directly if they are feeling personally attacked or hurt in some way. You might find out that they have experienced other people who took advantage of them. They may continue this appearance of victimization to which you could then ask them if they think they should take advantage of you just because someone else took advantage of them in the past.

Some people usurp power by raising their voice and talking faster. This is common in law enforcement contacts, but I have experienced it with negotiators from service lenders and even other agents as well. To counter this, there is a technique called *Matching, Pacing, Leading* in which you first *match* their volume and talking speed (*pace*); then *lead* them by slowly reducing your volume and talking speed as you lead them down to a normal volume and pace. You will discover there will be the tendency to follow you down, draining their emotional energy as you both descend. This is commonly used in law enforcement with drunks, criminals, and even ordinary angry motorists. It works wonders to help balance the table of power.

If you are standing while negotiating, your opponent's stance can be used to usurp power, but you can also use stance to balance that power. In law enforcement, the normal stance for an angry or threatening subject is to stand squarely facing the officer, and the officer's trained stance is to stand at about a 45 degree angle with the gun side away from the subject. There are a number of subtle signs of violence, including the clenching of fists just prior to an assault. The normal response when an officer observes these signs is to pre-empt and take physical action to control the subject before he attacks the officer. However, I experimented with the following stance response with a high level of success. When I observed the clenching of hands, I immediately moved by just taking a step so that I was beside the subject and facing the same direction. I was standing beside him instead of facing him. It is a symbolic gesture of *partnering up* with him. Verbal techniques are then used to drain the energy of emotion. Often this changing of stance alone provided an immediate environment of cooperation rather than being adversarial. In those rare occasions it did not work, I was still in a strong defensive position to take physical action. This method though has a strong positive effect in difficult negotiations one on one. The timing of this move can add to the effect of balancing power. It is especially effective with opponents who are much larger than you and prevents them from easily using size to usurp power. In my domestic call example, I used this technique and managed to avoid

The Seven Golden Keys To Negotiation

violence until backup officers arrived. The presence of the backup officers usurped additional power to our side to cause the man to submit. When I changed my stance into the *partnering up* stance, and stated that I could see that he seemed very angry and requested that he tell me the reason he was so angry, he immediately relaxed his fists somewhat, still remaining tense, but as he responded to me the anger energy continued to drain and he became less threatening.

Balancing power when seated is accomplished by ensuring that you use chairs of equal height. In mediation we always use the same height chairs all around. In mediations involving domestic violence, I have deliberately used a lower chair for an abuser who enters the room inappropriately usurping power with his attitude, and it effectively communicated to him that as mediator, I would not tolerate that behavior. It was unspoken but clear. If I cannot avoid the possibility of uneven seating heights, I will usually choose to be seated in the lowest one because there are many ways that I can usurp a little needed extra power to balance the table.

Some people will usurp power by talking rapidly, cutting you off, making statements, and then trying to change the subject. You see this demonstrated often in news shows where they talk over each other as they argue. You balance this power by slowing down and talking softer (except when you use the technique of *matching, pacing, leading*). When they cut you off, you immediately stop, when they stop talking, you ignore what your opponent just said. Instead, you give your previous answer again. If they cut you off again, you merely say, *"Is it ok if I finish my sentence, what I have to say is important and I really want to work this out between us."* Make certain, though, that you do not use sarcasm in your voice, but sincerity.

People often usurp power by throwing *flaming arrows*. These are little barbs of criticism or attack. They are comments intended to provoke you into a negative reaction. They are intended as *red herrings* to distract you. *"you're just a dumb lawyer"* is a flaming arrow. So is *"what do you care?!"*, *"you are feeding off our losses"*, etc. What is the appropriate response? Do not react to these flaming arrows; rather, just let them go by and respond as though they were not said at all. Do not let these flaming arrows usurp the power. Your ignoring them balances the power so that conciliation can progress.

Another method opponents may use to usurp power is a long tirade. How do you balance that? Silence. Just let them continue. When they stop, continue an uncomfortable silence until they break the silence with either continuing the tirade or they ask if you are still on the phone. In person, you maintain that silence, even when it become uncomfortable and they eventually either continue the tirade or they ask you a question. Then use body language to show you are thinking, followed by a quiet appropriate response.

Learning to balance power in various situations is a critical skill to effective negotiations. These methods of usurping power and balancing power are very common in intense negotiations and I have observed them all repeatedly, not only in law enforcement, but in law, mediation, in sales, in real estate, in church, and they occur in the majority of negotiation or conflict settings.

I recommend that if you will practice identifying when an opponent is usurping power and respond appropriately to balance that power, you will develop and refine them into skills. If you apply them to all of life's little situations, regardless of the setting, who the parties are, what the issues may be, and apply power balancing in all of normal life experiences, you will add a high level of professionalism and success to your negotiations as well.

Key 3: Reframing Techniques

The first key to unlocking an impasse is to prepare and plan your negotiations so you are negotiating from a position of strength. We outlined the various methods you can employ to gain this strength in negotiating and provided examples of how to apply them.

Then we discussed the second key, balancing power. Opponents in conflict or negotiation will often attempt to usurp power and dominate for their own purposes. A truly *win-win* result comes when neither side has the greater power; rather a result that benefits both sides comes about most often when power is balanced.

The third key to negotiating is the application of *reframing*. Reframing includes both *reframing* statements and *restating* statements. You *restate* feelings and perceptions, you *reframe* positions, issues, and needs.

At this point in a law enforcement training class, one police officer raised his hand and said, *"I don't need all this touchy-feely stuff, I will just slap the cuffs on him"*. A lot of people feel this way about learning these techniques. Why? Because these techniques are difficult to understand and learn to apply. We only resist learning what seems uncomfortable. That officer ended up one of the best students in the class. His emotional resistance was overcome when he started practicing the concepts in the field. Some people prefer to be *concrete thinkers* and do not enjoy learning *concepts*. They often state, *"Just give me a rule!"* However, these concepts are powerful, the keys are effective. These keys, when understood, internalized, practiced and turned into skills will create within you a powerful and effective negotiator. It is better than the mind control special power of the TV character in *Heroes*.

It is important to understand the difference between *thoughts* and *feelings*, and learn to respond appropriately to each. People will often say *"I feel that you don't care about me"*. You can't feel a thought. The correct statement is to say *"I think you don't care about me"*. You don't need to correct the person, but you should understand that it is a *thought*, not a *feeling*. In conversation, when someone states a feeling, like anger, disappointment, frustration, depression, happiness, stress, and other emotions, the technique is to restate that feeling back to him. *"So, you feel disappointed?"*, *"So, you feel stressed over these issues?"*.

Likewise, you *restate* perceptions. When someone says, *"I feel that you are just trying to rip me off"*, your response would be *"So, you think I am just trying to rip you off?"* Whether they state their perceptions as a *feeling* or a *thought*, find opportunities throughout the conversation to restate perceptions and feelings. Do not carry this to excess and merely keep repeating everything they say if they are providing multiple feelings and perceptions. You might wait, actively listening, until they are finished with several thought and feeling comments, and them restate them as sort of a summary.

The Seven Golden Keys To Negotiation

At times you may believe the other person is lying about certain facts. However, it is better to assume that the person is not lying, but may have a different perspective than you, and their *perceptions* may be merely different than yours. *Restate* these perceptions, *"So it is your belief that I said..."* You can correct them by stating *"I can see why you may have thought that I said that, but what I was attempting to say to you..."* Never call the person a liar or correct the facts. Assume that people process information they hear differently than you intended and allow for mistakes in prior communication. Own the misperception, by taking responsibility for the mistake in communication and you will help to reduce barriers and resistance.

When you restate feelings and thoughts from time to time, you show sincerity. You demonstrate that you are actually listening to what they have to say, and you place yourself in a position of control over the negotiations. As a result, you reduce the need for your opponent to dominate and are often granted permission to explore freely the *interests* of both of you.

That brings us to *reframing*. Reframing is merely restating what was just said but in other words. You reframe from positions to interests, from the past to the future, and from the problem to the solution.

You reframe from the past to the future whenever your opponent refers to the past. A lot of people bring up not only recent wounds, but old wounds as well. A gentle reframing often includes some *affirmation* of feelings, such as *"yes, I know you must feel frustrated about what happened, and we are now looking ahead to reach an agreement of what we should do for the future"*. Sometimes we merely reframe to the future, *"we cannot change the past; we can now look forward to a new way of working together"*. This reframing from the past to the future is important whenever an emotional barrier threatens to bottleneck the negotiations. Bear in mind, however, that it may be important early on in the conversation to permit quietly your opponent's discussion of the problem and the past in order to drain a high level of negative energy caused by their feelings. In mediation, after the initial ground rules and gaining the trust of the parties, mediators often intentionally request the parties to each verbalize and share what happened that brought them to this point. Once the problem has been identified, however, and some emotional energy drained, the mediator then reframes the discussions to the future.

You reframe from the problem to the solution again when your opponent occasionally returns to focus on the problem. You are there to find solutions and your job is to guide the conversations toward those solutions. An example of a reframing statement might be *"yes, it is true that we did not listen to you and I can see now that it offended you. Let's find a solution to our communication problems of the past. Would it solve this problem by Mr. Jones calling you each Friday?"*.

Reframing from positions to underlying concerns and interests is a critical part of the process. When your opponent makes a *position statement* (*I want..., you will..., from now on...*, etc.), you then summarize the underlying concern or *interest* in a one sentence summary of that interest. For example, the dialog of a police officer issuing a speeding ticket might go like this:

Driver: *"Why don't you do something useful, like going after rapists and murderers, instead of picking on decent citizens like me!"*

The Seven Golden Keys To Negotiation

Officer: *"You seem quite angry, tell me the reason that you don't think you should receive a speeding ticket."*

Driver: *"Because I didn't mean to go that fast and this is going to cost me a lot of money!"*

Officer: *"So the reason you are upset is you are concerned about how the cost of the ticket is going to affect your finances?"*

In this example, the officer reframed from the obvious position statement of *no ticket* to the underlying *interest* or concern of the affect the cost of the ticket will have on this driver's finances. Notice also the driver started out throwing a *flaming arrow* in the comment about rapists and murderers and the officer picking on him.

Whenever you encounter resistance, a position may seem like a final position. For example, a lender's negotiator may say over the phone, *"The total agent commissions have to be reduced to 4%"*. That sounds like a final answer. However, a reframing question might be *"tell me the reason that your company wants to bite the hand that is feeding them? What is the reason for this reduction?"* Following the answer, a follow-up reframing question might be, *"Is this a policy of your company, or is this a restriction by the MI carrier or investor?"* By digging with reframing questions, you can arrive at the final underlying interest and reframe it: *"I want to make sure that I understand exactly what you are saying. The MI carrier is restricting the commissions to 5% and you are merely trying to save your company another 1% from agent commissions, even though the agents are the ones who are helping you mitigate your losses through this short sale?"*

The concept is that every *position* protects an *interest* or underlying concern. If you find another way to protect the *interest*, their position will likely change to correspond with yours.

That is always true except when it is not. As we have previously stated, some people have barriers to conciliation, and no matter how well you protect the interest and come up with a logical result, some people are so selfish, ego-centric, hateful, superficial, or other descriptor to use good sense to see that the result is a *win-win*. I recently had a case with a second mortgage holder who would not approve the short sale, even though it was not in full satisfaction of their debt, there was no equity to secure the debt, and this lender would be receiving some cash in the deal. A good example of a barrier to conciliation, this negotiator let it slip that no matter what, they were not going to allow the short sale because they did not want the borrower to receive any benefit like protecting their credit. They only wanted to hurt the borrower! This negotiator was so focused on hurting him that even though her position looked totally foolish, she was not going to give in and allow the borrower the simple benefit of getting out from under the mortgage, even though the result of foreclosure was the discharge of the mortgage lien, no cash, the borrower was judgment-proof and they would get nothing.

Barriers to conciliation can also emanate from emotional disturbances and mental disorders. Further, anytime a person has a deep mistrust for the other party, or the representative of that party, they may hold a barrier to conciliation. In my law practice, there were many occasions when an unrepresented divorce party would not trust anything that I would tell them, especially if they were the opposite gender. Always remain alert for the possibilities of gender differences, emotional disturbances, and mental illnesses affecting the ability to reach agreement.

This key requires a lot of thoughtful consideration to truly understand. Again, as in the other keys, it takes practice to transform this from an abstract and possibly confusing idea into a skill that you can add to your toolbox of skills that will transform you into an effective negotiator.

Key 4: Leading to Paradigm Shifts

You now have a toolbox of some skills to practice and refine. Each of these keys when developed will move you to a level of skill on par with some of the greatest negotiators.

This key is related to the previous key in several ways. A paradigm (pronounced para-dime) shift is a shift from level of thinking to another. It is a shift off the problem and onto the solution, off the past onto the future. It is a shift off you and onto the process. This skill is your ability to get your opponent to focus on the new level of thinking and discussion. You utilize the other skills to help convince them to shift *their* thinking onto the solutions, the future, and the process.

Key 3 was what you do. Key 4 is the result you achieve. It is your objective to use the other skills to get your opponent to focus on a new level of thinking: the solution, the future, an agreement.

How do you know when you have succeeded? You know when the conversation and discussion has moved almost entirely onto that process, the solutions, the future and you are headed toward an agreement. All of your other skills lead you here. You know you are using this skill when you are talking about a solution, the future, exploring various options to see if an agreement can be reached.

When you practice reframing and restating, practice also using those skills to identify that you are now discussing options, solutions, the future, and are seeking out a possible resolution.

Key 5: Bargaining *from* Interests

The greatest source of negotiating strength comes from bargaining from *interests*. Say what?

The modern mediation and negotiation training programs that are most effective are called *interest-based* mediation or negotiation. Developed by the Harvard Negotiation Project, this method of mediation is practiced widely in many areas for resolving court cases, as well as in a number of federal agencies where mediation is the preferred method of conflict resolution. It is the preferred method by the U.S. State Department when negotiating with foreign companies or mediating between warring factions and countries. However, many mediators after receiving the training and using it for a while, revert back to the old *shuttle mediation* approach of pressuring for a compromise. Why? Because pressuring people to compromise takes a lot less time and requires a lot less thinking. *Interest-based*, or *collaborative* mediation and negotiation takes a lot more time, but results in more cases remaining settled.

The Seven Golden Keys To Negotiation

Likewise, interest-based negotiation is most effective, but after training, a lot of negotiators return to the old style *win-lose* approach. The old style impresses your team as they watch you, but interest-based negotiations take more time. However, it reaches a *win-win* more often.

Most negotiators think they need greater power to force the opponent's hand. Effective interest-based negotiators balance the power and convey that both sides are equal. By balancing the power, an interest-based approach to negotiation actually provides greater strength in bargaining.

Let's discuss how interest-based negotiation works. In a conflict, each of us holds a *position* that is important to us. A *position* is the demand that is determinedly asserted. Examples include in various contexts

> *I don't want that speeding ticket*
> *I want you to hire me*
> *I want half the children's pictures in the divorce*
> *I want the SMI to approve my short sale proposal*
> *You cannot sell that to me*
> *Don't call me or show up at my door*

Get the picture? It is the barrier, standard, or boundary you establish. It is what you want or do not want. Positions always show themselves either as assertive demands with an exclamation (!) point, or as subtle assertions that might even be missed. Sometimes a position is very easy to identify, but other times it may leave you uncertain of your opponent's position.

Every position, though, is asserted because of an underlying concern. It is the *real reason* for that position. It is the underlying reason for the statement that I don't want the ticket. It is the real reason that you may not want to hire me. It is the reason that the servicing lender may not want to obtain lienholder approval for your case. Every position has this underlying concern. This underlying concern, or reason for the position, is called the *interest* that the person is trying to *protect*. We all have interests that we protect by our positions.

I once had a cell phone that was a pre-paid account. I was getting such a good deal on it, that I decided to keep it for a while. Well, it did not last long, for the service was really poor. However, before I replaced it with a standard plan, I was almost at the end of my pre-paid minutes and only had a few minutes left when someone at court asked to borrow it for a call. A simple request. There would have been no problem in admitting that it was pre-paid and there were only a few minutes left, but at the time for some reason I did not want to disclose that. I merely said, "Oh, I'm sorry, but I have to be upstairs in court!" I then left immediately and went upstairs. I suddenly recognized the absurdity in this behavior, but I never did admit the lie. My position was "no, you cannot use my phone". The *interest* I was trying to *protect* was to save those last few minutes in case I needed to make an emergency call.

In every conflict or resistance, asserted *positions protect interests*. In my example, I asserted a false interest. That happens quite often in life, and in negotiating it is important to be aware of possible *false interests*.

When I was a police officer, I encountered a lot of people I had stopped for various traffic violations. Their position: *I don't want a ticket!* Gee, you think? Everyone has that position! Nobody wants to get a ticket. The position is the same

The Seven Golden Keys To Negotiation

with everybody I stopped over all those years. But, the actual interests they were trying to protect varied. The underlying interest for some was their already-difficult financial situation. For others it was a likely rise in insurance rates, particularly if they had teenage drivers. For still others, the primary concern was the added points on their driving record and their fear of losing their license. Same position, different interests. Most police officers do not speak to those interests and just leave it with the motorist as *their problem, not mine.*

In one of my law enforcement training classes for dealing with hostile contacts, a police officer who was a student in the class, challenged me by saying, *"let's see you do it for real"*. He did not believe that our role playing in class represented its application to the real world. I was actually working part time for that department at the time just to keep my foot in law enforcement, so I took on the challenge. The police cruisers were equipped with police dash cams and we would wear a remote wireless microphone. I went to an area well-known for speeders and started making traffic stops. I was able to demonstrate on videotape quite a few irate motorists adamant about their position (here, no ticket), I was able to demonstrate that if you understand and address the underlying interest they are trying to protect, you not only drain the energy of the hostility, but you also have much greater strength in negotiating. In these cases, when they made angry comments, I requested them to tell me the reason they were so angry. When I discovered the underlying interest, I addressed that concern. We will discuss this in more detail shortly.

Always negotiate from strength. It requires planning, practice, and setting up the situation in a way that provides you with strength. Asking questions to get behind the stated position to determine the underlying concern or interest they are attempting to protect will provide you with a great amount of strength from which to bargain. Practice asking questions to determine the underlying interests any time you hear someone assert a position. Questions of clarification help you to find out the details of those interests. This is not the time to assert your own position or to argue; rather, this is the time to discover the details of the underlying interests and how they fear that if that interest is not protected, they will suffer some negative impact.

The objective here: if you find another way to protect their interest, they will modify their position to correspond with your interests. Then, you have real bargaining power!

After you have prepared for negotiation and understand that real bargaining strength comes from clarifying your opponent's interests, the next step is to gather intelligence, or information, from all available sources. This is doing your homework. In short sales, this is about knowing everything about your case, the value of the home, the situation of the sellers, the situation of the buyers, so that you can address any and every objection raised by your opponent. With kids it's about asking questions to discover what they are *not* telling you. Kids can be such deceptive little creatures, but so are many adults, particularly in negotiations. Learn to ask questions in ways that are *nonthreatening*. Don't ask questions that start with "Why…" Rather, ask it this way: "Tell me the reason…" The word *Why* makes people defensive. *Tell me the reason* with the right voice tone and body language is more cooperative and shows acceptance and concern for your opponent.

The Seven Golden Keys To Negotiation

You utilized the first three keys to transform the discussion into productive negotiating. With evidence of a paradigm shift happening, it is important, even critical, to not falter or let down your guard. You are now exploring underlying interests to find solutions that will protect those interests. You should continue to verbalize whether each considered solution will protect or not protect the interest being protected. Your opponent should hear you verbalizing an ongoing search to find a solution that will protect their interests as well as yours. It is ok to verbalize it's effect on your own interest you are trying to protect, but the prevailing discussion should focus on their interest to protect that you know will work for you. You are finding a new position that protects both of your interests.

This key takes a lot of practice. As you develop this skill in normal conversation at home and elsewhere, you will eventually refine it for effective use in negotiations in business as well.

Key 6: Bargaining to needs

The earlier keys utilize communication (verbal, tone, body language) to create an environment that will permit you to focus on the solutions and get beyond the resistance. Bargaining from interests allows you to find new ways to protect these interests. If you can protect their underlying concern or interest in a new way, they will automatically be willing to move away from their position to a more acceptable one.

As stated, *positions* protect *interests*. There is, though, another deeper level. Sometimes the stated interest cannot be protected, or it is not the *real* interest, but a fake one. In these cases, the conflict may be on a deeper level. As *positions* protect *interests*, these *interests* fill *needs*. In my example where the position is not to get a ticket, the interest being protected was the financial difficulty the cost of the ticket would have on their finances. If you are still running into resistance, it is time to obtain more information. Using restating and reframing questions, you can find out the true *need* that is remaining unfilled. In this case, questioning yields the information that the driver's wife just got out of the hospital and was recovering from surgery, and they were losing wage income from her illness. There is an unfulfilling of basic survival needs going on here.

The psychological researcher Abraham Maslow writing in 1943 in his paper entitled *A Theory of Human Motivation* developed his *Hierarchy of Needs* in which he postulated that people are motivated to fill their needs in the following hierarchy or importance: Physiological (shelter, food, water, sex, sleep, etc.), Safety (protection, employment, morality, health, etc.), Love/belonging (friendship, family, intimacy), Esteem (confidence, achievement, respect), and self-actualization (morality, creativity, problem-solving, etc.).

As an advanced skill, this key, when internalized, practiced, and refined as a skill, will enable you to go behind the scenes to motivators that rise to the surface as barriers or resistance to conciliation.

So if it is an advanced skill, why is it part of the seven? Because even though it may take you a long time to develop, now is the time to start being aware when it may exist as the reason behind resistance you discover through reframing and bargaining from interests. You can discover these unfilled needs by asking more questions, digging deeper behind the positions and interests. When you find the real reason for the resistance, you have a good opportunity to find a new way to protect that interest or fill the need.

Obviously you cannot meet all of their needs, nor is it your responsibility. It is more about identifying and merely speaking to those unfilled needs preventing the finding of common ground. Providing *affirmation* of their circumstances will help you find another way to fill the need with a more appropriate interest that can be protected by an acceptable new position. In our example, the officer could resolve this unfilled need by encouraging the motorist to plead *not guilty*. The case would be set for trial and the officer could agree to work with the prosecutor to give the motorist more time to pay the ticket, or to continue the case for about six months and dismiss it if the motorist does not get any more tickets. This fills the needs and protects the interest, and the motorist will accept the ticket with less resistance. I utilized this approach many times in law enforcement.

This was a simple example of how this key can be applied, and with practice, this skill can be developed for application for all negotiation situations. Practice, practice, practice!

Key 7: Lead to Agree

The ultimate goal of negotiating is to reach an agreement. This becomes much easier when you are using all of the key skills for this negotiation process. When you are exploring options, you are testing each option by whether it will protect their interest or underlying concern. Each time you discover an option that will protect an interest, you are accumulating the solution components for an agreement. As you reach these points where you find acceptable solutions, write them down consecutively. When you are done, you simply state the list of solutions and ask if this will work for them. If so, then you have the list of components for the agreement. If not, then you continue the process to discover what other interests (or needs) might need to be addressed.

The agreement then, is a written summary of new positions agreed upon that protect each of your respective interests (and perhaps fills needs). Once you have your agreement, you should write the formal agreement then and there if in person. You should at the very least confirm the agreement with a follow-up email or letter.

Summary

There are seven golden, or valuable, keys or skill sets to effective negotiating. They are the skills of negotiating from strength, managing and balancing power, reframing techniques, leading to paradigm shifts, bargaining from interests, bargaining to needs, and leading to agree. These skills require understanding, internalizing, and practicing in a variety of life settings at home, in business, and elsewhere.

Developing these skills will create within you a skillful and effective negotiator. Merely reading them will not. They are skills that must be practiced, developed, and refined purposely over time.

In the next chapter, we will focus on communicating and negotiating with lienholders.

CHAPTER 11

Communicating and Negotiating With Lienholders

For years I have heard agents complain about communicating and negotiating with lenders, mostly concerning the amount of time they spend on the phone and how difficult it is to contact the right person. These complaints do not match my own experience with lenders, so I have requested a number of agents to provide me with more specificity about the circumstances so frustrating to them. Responses included that the agents did not having the right telephone number, being referred to so many different numbers to reach the right people, the case not being assigned to someone to review for weeks at a time, the inability to reach supervisors, the on-hold time, the telephone systems with too many menus, representatives lying about the case, and arguments with representatives.

First, some of these responses indicate a lack of understanding of certain realities and an inappropriate expectation. In a technological society, telephone menu systems are the reality that we must accept, and being frustrated over it is not helpful. One mediation instructor taught that *all of our negative emotions come from the determination to control what we do not have the responsibility to control*. That means that the only reason I get frustrated is when I can't have my circumstances be the way I want them to be. If I am more willing to accept my circumstances, then I will not feel nearly as frustrated. Indeed, both frustration and feelings of stress are emotions that come from not getting what we want or our circumstances not being the way we wish them to be, or the *fear* that we will not have them the way we wish them to be.

Using this theory then, if I am able to convince myself to accept my circumstances, I cannot become frustrated, depressed, or discouraged because I am accepting the circumstances, not needing for them to be different. My age decade of the 50's has been the best time in my life. One of the reasons for this is that many of the circumstances that used to frustrate, annoy, discourage, or stress me no long seem to bother me at all. The result is a greater amount of peace. When I work my way through telephone voice menus, I accept this as a reality, and I consider the first time as a walk through the woods, carefully taking notes of the path to my destination, so that next time, I don't have to wait for all the voice prompts, I already have the notes of which options to select.

Supervisors? You do not need to talk to supervisors, and actually I prefer not talking to them. I attended a short sale training seminar taught by a former employee of one of our largest SMIs. She is a well-known instructor and so-called expert in short sales. In the class, she spent a lot of time teaching different techniques to get by the call center people and reach supervisors. In fact, as I will explain shortly, this is a mistake in tactics when working with lenders. This tactic may be useful when dealing with a small local or regional bank when the supervisor has authority to make decisions that the normal contact person cannot make, however, this is rare and I find that generally the call center representatives will actually do more to assist than will supervisors.

Communicating and Negotiating With Lienholders

It is important to remember that the *holder in due course* of the mortgage loan note is not the servicing lender, but the SMI. It is also important to remember that the MI carrier must also approve any short sale proposal, and if they have paid a claim, they may even now hold that note. So since the SMI is the owner of the note and the one from whom we are seeking approval, the servicing lender is merely the go-between contact entity with little authority beyond processing and ordering an appraisal. So, there is no need to talk to a supervisor.

Most servicing lenders have call centers staffed with trained people whose sole responsibility is to communicate with agents, negotiators, and mediators who have submitted short sale proposals or loan modifications. Most of the time, they are merely information managers who provide information to you and to log information you provide into the borrower's database file.

These servicing lenders may have a *tiered system* of review. In this system, one person reviews the proposal upon submission for certain documents. It is then passed to the next person for review of some other information, and so forth. Other lenders have an *analyst* or *negotiator* review the entire file for the required documents, making notes and ensuring that all of the technical requirements have been met. That analyst or negotiator has the authority to order an appraisal if that is required by the SMI. When the appraisal is returned, the analyst or negotiator *may* have the authority to calculate the *net receipt to lender percentage of the fair market value*, if the SMI will use a threshold percentage analysis as we have previously discussed. The analyst or negotiator though, may not even have the authority to perform that calculation. In a comparison analysis of the short sale proposal versus the value of the property if seized and sold as a bank-owned or REO property, the negotiator may have some basic guidelines, and may negotiate for a higher price or lower commissions, but they usually do not have the authority to approve the deal. Even some of the call center representatives may occasionally have authority to try to mitigate the losses to a small extent, but it is the SMI that must approve the deal.

Understand that when communicating with the servicing lender, usually your sole objectives are for the negotiator or analyst to order the appraisal as soon as possible, and forward your proposal to the SMI or MI also as soon as possible. This is true except when it is not, but it is true for most lenders. Your most common telephone calls will primarily be status calls to find out if it has been assigned yet to a negotiator or analyst, if the appraisal has returned, or whether the MI carrier or SMI has responded.

Many agents who have been through training classes like I've attended, make the mistake of trying to actually *negotiate* with this analyst or negotiator. I do not. When a negotiator talks to me about commissions, for example, and I know that the proposal has not been submitted to the lender, I merely tell the negotiator *"Let's wait for the MI carrier's and investor's response to my proposal. The only commissions that will be reduced is if there is an investor or MI carrier policy that limits commissions. After all, it is discrimination to pay minority agents less than what other agents receive"*. In this example, I have told the negotiator two things: that it is the investor who will set the commission maximum, and you the lender should be careful to not violate these agents' rights against discrimination. If the negotiator is an idiot, he will argue that they, the servicing lender, are losing a lot of money, so it is only fair that the agents share in that loss a little

Communicating and Negotiating With Lienholders

bit. If he is open and honest, he still may likely tell you that the commission is always limited to a set percentage. Your response: *"Maybe that's true, but let's see what the SMI and MI carrier say."*

A review is appropriate here. All financial institutions doing business in the United States must treat everyone equally and are not allowed to *discriminate*. Discrimination occurs when someone from a *protected class* is not treated equally, even if the institution did not know about it. A protected class is anyone who is not treated equally on the basis of race, national origin, religion, age, and gender. Some states also include sexual orientation as a protected class. Financial institutions are required by law to make certain these classes are protected. Thus they must have company-wide policies, in writing, that prohibit behavior that could create exposure to discrimination, which can arise even if they do not know if the person is in a protected class. The personnel should be well-trained to avoid statements and actions that could be construed as discriminatory.

If an agent or the agent's client is in a protected class and the agent is granted a lower commission than an agent or whose client is not in a protected class, then discrimination has occurred. The company may not ask if the agents are of color, women, etc., so they must create this equality in their dealings with the public through policy. Most short sale proposals contain at least one person of a protected class. You have leverage to back the servicing lender into a corner for trying to reduce commissions. In our chapter on developing negotiating skills, I pointed out that you use leverage out of necessity to back your opponent into a corner, but you must let them out of the corner before the fight/flight reflex is triggered.

So, going back to our discussion, another approach might be to ask, *"Did you know that your company cannot push for a lower commission for a person of color than any other white person receives?"* Another way is *"John, do you know that another agent was paid a higher commission recently? Did you know that if you pay a lower commission to a female agent, you might get in a lot of trouble? Why don't we just wait until the we see what the MI carrier or investor will approve, shall we?"* Then you need to let them out of the corner with friendly chatter. *"John, I really appreciate working with you, you are smart and professional, yet very personable. I like that in a negotiator"* might be a good way to do this.

There is a good chance that the negotiator will call your bluff, so do not lie or bluff. When you ask the question, *"Do you know that another agent was paid a higher commission recently?"*, you are not saying that it happened; you are only asking the negotiator if they *know* it happened. You are communicating an honest message, that it is illegal to discriminate against protected classes. If the negotiator requests details, your response could include statements like *"My client is watching to see if anyone discriminates in this case."*, or *"I cannot provide the details right now, I am merely conveying that we have people watching us to make sure we are not discriminating against protected groups of people."*

We are discussing limitations placed on the proposal by the *servicing lender*. Most of the time, they will not have the authority to negotiate these cases, even though their title may be *negotiator*. The title of *analyst* is more accurate. If they do have that authority, they would often be placing their company at risk of discrimination lawsuits unless they have a written policy of a set commission in all cases. The servicing lender

Communicating and Negotiating With Lienholders

cannot legally require a different commission if the SMI retains approval rights of short sales.

Most of the time, you will be dealing with call center people who are really decent and courteous. However, I usually am able to bring out the best side of even the jerks among them though a little humor and personal chatter. I always make it my objective to get chuckles out of them, no matter how business-like they try to be. When you make that personal connection, they will do anything for you and will usually not lie to you.

However, some people will lie. There are times when a negotiator will tell me that the total commission is lower, or there is a cap on seller concessions. I will always ask, *"has this gone yet to the investor for approval?"* If the answer is no, then they are likely lying to you and only trying to beat you down and possibly disregarding their exposure to discrimination. There is a large SMI who has corporate offices in Florida and India who have employees who will often lie and attempt this maneuver. If they do this, ask if the person is in India. If so, ask to be transferred back into the Que so that you can talk to someone from the Florida office. When you talk to someone here in our country, tell them immediately that you have called about your short sale proposal and one of the representatives has made statements that may be discriminating against a minority class. This will usually get them really serious about what they say to you.

One agent I know when he calls a call center, always starts out the conversation with *"This call is being recorded for quality assurance, my name is Ken, what did you say your name is?"* Of course, I used my own name in this example, but it lets them know they are being recorded and you can still break the ice and have an enjoyable conversation. I do not personally use this approach, but I am fairly good at getting them be truthful with me and I can usually tell when they are lying. I work as a mediator, though, and my relationship with them is different. I am a *neutral* and not their adversary, so there is a tendency for them to relax and be open.

It is always important to be nice, courteous, and above all, try to build bridges to get them to be friendly and even laughing if possible. Humor helps to build friendships, and quickly. Building instant friendships creates a desire in the other person to help you. I have had many experiences when a call center representative put me on hold and walked to other parts of the building just to help cut some time off the process for me.

Let's now start at the beginning and work our way through the process of communicating with the lender. When you set up your casebook, you will have the needed information on your cheat sheet, and you are open to an Activity Log and ready to make your entries and take notes.

There is an online service that provides an information database containing financial institutions doing business in the United States. That service is www.laneguide.com, and the fee is reasonable. I highly recommend this service. It will save you a lot of time and frustration getting to the right call center department. There are many institutions with similar names, and this service will allow you to locate the specific institution and provide addresses, phone numbers and fax numbers. My experience is that it is not very up-to-date when it comes to the phone and fax numbers, however, those numbers will get you to people who can provide the updated numbers

Communicating and Negotiating With Lienholders

to you. You will be looking for the *Loss Mitigation* department with most of them. Some companies use other names for the same department, such as the *Home Retention Department*, *Short Sale Department*, etc. You do not want the *Customer Service Department* because that is the collection department and they are often aggressive collectors who may lie to you and tell you that the company does not allow short sales. Likewise it is not a good idea to call the number found on the mortgage statement sent to the borrowers. I never call the contact number on the mortgage statement, because it is merely the Customer Service department and all they care about is *collections*. In fact, they will often not steer you to the *Loss Mitigation* because they do not want the file taken from them.

On one occasion I could not access the Lane Guides. So I found the corporate website and located the main corporate number. I called and talked to the corporate office operator who provided me with the phone number for the short sale department. It was not the correct number, but a few transfers later brought me to the right people. I was able to bypass *Customer Service* who might have taken up a lot of my time needlessly and still not provide me with the correct number.

Now that you have the right telephone number to call, and your proposal is ready in draft (not final) form, it is time to make the call. Start your Activity Log notes as you make the call. Take notes on a *post-it note* as you work your way through the telephone menu until you get someone on the line from loss mitigation or the short sale department. This will be a call center person in a big room full of tiny cubicles, wearing a headset with a computer monitor in front of them. They spend all day every day just talking to people, most of whom are not so friendly, are whiners, complainers, desperate, or angry. Your call is going to really make their day. You are going to break from the ordinary, provide a friendly voice, caring words of encouragement, a bit of self-deprecating humor perhaps, and something positive for them to tell their friends at coffee break or lunch.

When you make the call, you will work your way through the telephone menu system. I suggest that you have on your computer screen something to do to occupy your time while on hold but not requiring deep thought, like *Solitaire* or *Freecell*. Also, make certain you are not holding a phone received, but wearing a headset. This will alleviate the temptation to stress out over the process and make it easier to maintain that attitude of not needing to become frustrated. When the representative answers, your mind is alert, fresh, and you can have a great visit with them on the phone.

The menu system will likely require you to enter the loan number and perhaps other information such as the property zip code or primary borrower's social security number. If the menu asks you if you are calling to check on the *status* of your loan, the answer is *no*. Sometimes it may be difficult to figure out which option to select to find loss mitigation because the choices may be worded in a confusing manner. If nothing seems to fit, try option *0* and see where it takes you.

An important point should be made here. I have mentioned several times that lender representatives may lie to you. Some companies are so well run that they only hire and promote people to representative positions who are honest and faithful to the company. However, other companies especially companies whose history and roots may have been the financing of

Communicating and Negotiating With Lienholders

consumer loans in store fronts or financing high interest mobile home loans, may allow their representatives to use questionable tactics. Collections people in the *Customer Service Department*, in their eagerness to collect and who may be rewarded for the results of their collection activities, may lie in order to keep the case in collection out a misguided belief they are doing the right thing.

It happens quite often that your seller provides the name of someone at the lender who is wanting to talk to you about the short sale, and may even indicate they are from loss mitigation when, in fact, it is a collector. I do not return those calls; rather, I contact the loss mitigation office through the numbers I obtain from the Lane Guides. If that person truly is the negotiator assigned to the case, the call center will be able to tell me from the computer notes.

When you reach the loss mitigation call center, after the initial friendly discourse and you get down to business, tell them that you are going to be submitting a short sale proposal to them, and you need the fax number for submitting the *Authorization & Release*, and that you also need a list of their specific documents. The representative will provide you with the fax number for the authorization, and may or may not be willing to provide you with the list of short sale documents required to be included. The reason? They may require the *Authorization & Release* to be submitted before disclosing the document list because the document list could be construed to be disclosing confidential information. Is that likely? Of course not, but the *potential* is the concern.

Ask the representative for the fax number where you should fax the short sale proposal. This is often a different fax number than where you need to fax the authorization. Finally, ask what number you should call after the authorization is faxed. It may or may not be the same number you just called.

The representative may ask you if there is anything else they can do for you, say *"yes, there is."* By now, I would know at least the state in which he or she is located, so when asked *"what?"*, I respond, *"I hope you have a great Kentucky day!"*, or whichever state is correct.

Immediately following the phone call, make certain that your Activity Log is complete, and then fax the *Authorization & Release*. On the fax cover sheet, make certain that you have the loan number, the name of the borrower, and the property address. In the *Subject* field, state *Please see the attached Authorization & Release*. Then record it in the Activity Log.

Again, this is true except when it is not. There is one large company that almost always loses the first submitted documents, and I have to re-submit the proposal. I have learned that it is best to have *no fax cover sheet* for this company. When reps talk to you about submitting documents, I always ask if there are any little secrets to getting documents through without them getting lost by their fax department. If I talk to different reps in other phone calls, I ask the same of them.

You should wait three business days after faxing the authorization. Many of these lenders have fax departments that may require this length of time to receive the faxed pages and image them into their computer network systems.

Once you have obtained the list of documents, you can prepare the finished draft of the proposal and either convert it into a format suitable for online faxing, or print it out for faxing by fax machine. If there are additional documents

Communicating and Negotiating With Lienholders

needed, or specific forms provided by the servicing lender to be completed, then you should immediately obtain those documents and include them in the finished draft. Tips and suggestions for the mechanics of drafting this proposal are contained in the *Short Sale Business Manual*.

If you do not have the list of documents, you need to call after the three day period and tell them who you are. The representative will need some time to locate your name as being authorized on the account. When it is found, you will be asked to confirm certain information of the borrower. They may request such information as the borrower's name, social security number (usually the last 4 digits), and the property address (or alternatively the borrower's mailing address). That information will be right in front of you on the cheat sheet. After they have confirmed that you are the authorized person, then you should ask for the list of documents and confirm the telephone number to which your proposal should be faxed.

Most servicing lenders now require all documents to be faxed. With some smaller local or regional banks or mortgage companies, the representative may show a sign of confusion or say, *"If you want to"*. Take this as an opportunity to ship it and confirm that you will send it by Priority Mail, FedEx, or UPS. This is better, because they are likely to send your professionally drafted proposal in great form to the SMI. It is not necessary to pay a lot for overnight; two or three days is best.

The proposal will be submitted in two or three fax groups. Some companies cannot receive faxes in groups larger than ten pages, so adjust accordingly. On each fax cover sheet make certain that you provide the loan number, borrowers' names, and the property address. In the *Subject* field, insert *This is the 2nd*

fax of 3 faxes, or whichever number it is. Also be certain that the loan number, property address, and borrowers' names are on *each* and *every* page of the proposal. The instructions in the *Short Sale Business Manual* makes this easy and prevents mistakes and loss of documents, except when the lender loses them anyway.

Wait at least three business days after submitting the proposal and then call. Tell the representative that you submitted a proposal and you are calling to make certain that all of the documents have been received. The rep will review to see if all the documents they need are imaged in.

When the rep confirms that they have the proposal, the next step will be likely for it to be assigned to a negotiator or analyst. In some companies it may need to be referred to the *Short Sale Department*. Another company sends them to a *Review Team* to check the documents. Whichever way the rep tells you that it needs to go, your purpose is to find out what happens next and to periodically check on the status.

Your next call will be several days later. I have some basic guidelines that I utilize to guide my calling the lender. Basically I need to call as often as necessary to make sure it is still in line to be processed, but not so often that they see me as a time-wasting pest. If the rep tells you that it will be about 15 days until it is assigned to a negotiator, then calling every couple of days will only make too many entries on their computer log and they will immediately take a negative attitude toward your call. Once a week is usually sufficient until you are getting close for it to be assigned.

Ask the representative who the investor is. They may or may not tell you. They are not required to disclose this information, and many private investors prohibit release of this

Communicating and Negotiating With Lienholders

information. I sometimes can find out at some point when I have a call that is particularly fun and upbeat. They usually eventually tell me unless it is a private investor. The reason this is helpful to you is that Fannie Mae, Freddie Mac, and others have web sites on which you can find their guidelines and rules for short sale approval, broker commissions, and the like. Knowledge is power and gives you bargaining strength. It also helps you to know if the rep is lying to you.

Once it has been assigned, if you are still only able to talk to a call center rep, then ask if the rep has the authority to order the appraisal or BPO (Broker Price Opinion). Sometimes they do at this point. If not, then keep checking back about once or twice weekly. Seldom make your regular calls on Monday, because this is the highest volume call day and they are often very stressed.

When you talk to the negotiator, the discussion is going to be mainly a review of the information and the documents. You should be prepared if the negotiator asks you the net amount to be received by the lender, and you can volunteer the percentage of the fmv if it is a high percentage. You should probably say nothing about it if it is not 82% fmv or better. Do not hide it, but do not volunteer a discussion of an iffy case. Your objective in this call is for the negotiator to order the appraisal. If asked who the point of contact is for the appraiser, always state that you are.

It is often the case that the appraiser or broker will call you that very day to gain access. Make certain that this person knows that it is for purposes of a short sale, and that the high end of the market price range is not helpful to anyone. That is a hint to value the property low. Make certain that this person finds you friendly and that the call is an enjoyable one for him or her.

If the appraiser was hired through a brokerage (appraiser brokerage), the arrangements were made by the lender to an appraisal company who acts as an intermediary who then hires a local appraisal. In this case, it may take 5–15 days for the appraisal to get back to the lender and imaged into the system. You should call and check weekly. If the lender contacted the local appraiser directly, they will likely get it back the same day as the appraisal, but it may not be entered into the system for a few days.

When the appraisal has returned, ask the negotiator what the appraisal amount is. They may or may not be able to tell you. They are not required to tell you, but you can respond by telling them that your data says the market value is $xxx,xxx, and ask if the appraisal is consistent. They will usually tell you if it is or not. If there is a significant difference, and the appraisal is much higher, you should tell the negotiator that you have completed a marketing analysis of the property and that you believe that the appraisal may be in error. Tell them you would like the opportunity to *appeal* the appraisal and ask their procedure for this. You may meet with some resistance, and if so, tell them that you are doing your very best to reduce the losses to their company, and that this detail can make the difference between approval and not.

Appealing the appraisal usually amounts to providing documentation to the appraiser via the negotiator and asking them to correct their result. I usually obtain the latest data from the listing agent, so if you are the listing agent, then send your data with a cover letter to the lender, and copy it to the appraiser

Communicating and Negotiating With Lienholders

directly. Try to find additional comps that pended or sold after the original appraisal. It is best if in your appeal letter you are able to find a no-fault reason for the error, such as the possibility that it may have been based upon data that may not have been available to the appraiser. If you are a real estate investor, you may wish to call the appraiser directly. Remember, be nice and find ways to break the ice and establish a great relationship.

The next step in the process is the negotiator to forward the proposal to the MI carrier if there is private mortgage insurance on the loan. Always ask, because the negotiator might not tell you unless you do. After approval by the MI carrier, the proposal is forwarded to the SMI for approval.

Summary

A lot of people find working with lenders to be a stressful, frustrating, and distasteful experience. I find contacting these lenders to be quite enjoyable. The difference? The difference could include the attitude that I choose toward this part of the process, being able to locate the right phone numbers and the correct people. Having a bit of a distraction helps alleviate the time working through the telephone menu and waiting on hold. A headset makes it much more comfortable. Taking notes of the telephone menu will make the process of calling them much easier.

The process of communicating and negotiating with the lender begins with submitting the authorization to permit them to disclose information about the borrower to you. Next is obtaining the list of documents they require plus any specific forms that must be completed by the borrowers. The proposal is then submitted to them. Of course, it is important to know if there is a different fax number to where you must fax the proposal. It is best if they prefer the proposal shipped to them, but that is rare.

Following submission of the proposal, there may be a different number to call. Your first inquiry will be to substantiate that the proposal was received. Then you will be waiting for the proposal to be assigned to a negotiator or analyst, which could take several weeks. Check to see if the order could be sent out early for the appraisal. You should call for status checks often enough to stay on top of the case, but not so often as to annoy them. Calling about once a week is often the most appropriate, but sometimes it may be appropriate to call a little sooner.

When the case is assigned to a negotiator or analyst, that person is really only making certain all of the required information and documentation is available to submit to the MI carrier if one is involved, and then to the SMI. That assigned representative is not really *negotiating* anything usually, merely processing. A good relationship with negotiators and call center people is far more effective than trying to reach supervisors, and these people will often go out of their way to help the person who gave them the nicest telephone experience of their day. Supervisors will often be annoyed at your call, stick more to the rules, and help you less often.

The appraisal will be ordered immediately when the negotiator starts working on the file, but sometimes the call center people may be able to start that process. The appraiser needs to understand that in determining a market range, that it is not helpful to value the property in the upper part of market value range. If excessive, the appraisal can be appealed back to the appraiser and presented with additional data and, if they are cooperative, may alter their appraisal.

You will encounter a number of lender representatives who will lie to you to keep you from truly understanding the inner workings of the process. In this book, I provided you with detailed information about this process, and you will hopefully be in a better position to deal with these people. Their dislike for agents can be transformed by you and others like you if you show them respect, establish good relationships, and demonstrate that you are knowledgeable and savvy.

In Chapter 12 we will show you how to manage multiple cases and prepare for closing.

CHAPTER 12

Managing Multiple Cases and Preparing For Closing

Running a short sale business, if you are going to be successful, must of necessity require that you are well-organized, manage your time wisely, and efficiently perform many tasks. For the real estate agent or investor who has other responsibilities or employment, handling multiple cases can be a real challenge.

Time Management

In the chapter on negotiation skills, it was emphasized that effective negotiation consists a number of skills that must be developed and finely tuned. The same is true with time management. Most people say they *know how* to manage their time, but when testing this so-called *knowledge*, I find it seldom is true.

My first career after college was in the full-time pastoral ministry. The term *full-time* is actually quite an understatement. There are constant demands by church members for time, attention, counsel, and visits, and they want the pastor to be all things to all people. They want the pastor to be an administrator, teacher, preacher, counselor, therapist, organizer, worker, and a host of other activities. They do not understand the length of time it takes to prepare a sermon or lesson.

The pastor visits the sick, intervenes in crises, conducts funerals and weddings, and the pastor finds little time for self, family, or professional development. I hold a very high level of respect for my friends who function well in the ministry.

The denomination for which I worked provided a time management seminar and required that I attend for three days. With all of the work I had to accomplish in my district, I quietly resented and resisted being sent away for three entire days for such a stupid course like *time management*. Like everyone else, I thought that time management was intuitive and I was using good common sense in the management of my time. I discovered otherwise.

The time management seminar was a *lights-on* experience, as well as a lot of great training. It turned my professional life around and I was able to better manage my time for family and professional development as well. When I left the pastoral ministry and went to law school, time management techniques helped me with attending law school full time while continuing to work as a state trooper full time as well. When I left law enforcement for the practice of law, I further developed my time management skills through additional training seminars, and utilizing the FranklinCovey materials and books.

I am not going to attempt to teach you everything you should learn about time management in this little book, because that training is abundantly available to you in the form of books and courses. It is, however, quite important for a business person to obtain that training and expertise using methods and materials that are simply beyond the scope of this book.

I am, however, going to simply describe some basic methods for managing time for short sale activities. Think of time

Managing Multiple Cases and Preparing For Closing

in blocks for specific activities. There are *absolute time blocks* for time that are set aside for specific activities and which you allow virtually nothing to invade. My Monday through Friday morning 45 minute time blocks are set aside for getting ready for the day. I then have an *absolute time block* of 20 minutes for organizing my day and adjusting my schedule.

There are also *flexible time blocks* that are generally set aside for activities or projects, but are flexible enough that I can prioritize those blocks of time for various activities. It is difficult but necessary to understand what should be protected versus what should be prioritized and flexible.

I do not normally contact lenders on Mondays. I set aside a two hour block of time on Tuesdays, Thursdays, and Friday mornings for contacting lenders, and sending out updates. My Tuesday and Thursday contact blocks were absolutes. My Friday time blocks were flexible. That means that on Fridays, I might perform these activities in the mornings or afternoons depending upon other requirements. It is important to have this *flex* time, because if you try to make your entire week absolute time blocks, your system will fail.

I have a number of other professional activities as well, so I have certain absolute time blocks and flexible time blocks for them. Performing a legal and marketing analysis, and drafting and faxing the proposal is quite time-consuming, especially at first. I developed *systems* to make this go much faster, and I have flexible time blocks for *professional projects* in which I perform these activities.

I recommend that you set aside both absolute time blocks and flexible time blocks for every project that you have. Time blocks can be weekly, daily, bi-weekly, and tri-weekly. I have monthly time blocks and weekend time blocks. I have regular *wasting time* blocks, which are to do just that: waste some time either relaxing or having fun.

I have time blocks when I will allow myself to be interrupted by the phone, and time blocks when I just let it go to voice mail. Whenever drafting and submitting the proposal, I never allow myself to be interrupted. I am very poor at multi-tasking. I accept that about myself, so when I need to concentrate I do not allow myself to be distracted. However, receiving phone calls is vital to my business, so I am really cautious about setting aside uninterrupted time blocks, and keep them limited to when they are most important.

Getting distracted is a problem for me. Since I do not multi-task well, I use a lot of pre-printed check lists that I force myself to use in case I do get distracted for a moment and then forget what I was doing. I keep a spiral bound notebook for taking notes, voice mail messages, notes from callers, *place-setting* notes when I must be interrupted, and I check those notes off when they are no longer needed. That way, I can go back through the pages to make certain that nothing has been left needing a response. Why spiral-bound? So I am in no danger of losing something that could be important or if I need to go back and review an item.

Managing multiple cases and activities with short sales requires you to manage many hundreds of pages of documents. Keeping every email, phone call, and fax logged on the Activity Sheets enables you at a glance to see if you received or sent a document, and allows you to keep track of all activities and information. Keeping them in the case files with a post-it indicating the date it was received will also help you to stay organized.

As previously mentioned, I do have a database that is capable of effectively managing all of this, but I find the manual system to be faster and keeps me better organized. Additionally, I cannot sit for very long, and my system is easily portable from the office to other areas depending upon where I feel like working at any given time.

There are some excellent books on time management, and I suggest that you find one that either looks appealing to you or is recommended by someone you trust. Personally, I prefer the FranklinCovey systems but other systems have their benefits as well. I also suggest that you develop simple systems for processing everything so you do not get bogged down with tedious time-consuming activities. Adding efficient time management discipline to a systems approach to processing will enable you to accomplish all of your objectives while leaving you time for personal and professional development and time for your family.

Multiple Purchase Contracts

Some of your short sale cases will receive only one acceptable offer, however others may have multiple offers that must all be submitted to the lender. The reason that multiple offers should be submitted to the lender is that the SMI sees only what they receive from the servicing lender, and multiple offers substantiate the legitimacy of the best offer. You would only submit an estimated HUD-1 for the highest offer, but each purchase contract with pre-approval letter would be submitted.

When you receive a purchase contract post-submission (after the initial proposal is submitted) that is now the highest offer, obtain an estimated HUD-1 from the title company that provided the first HUD-1. Submit the offer and HUD-1 to the lender with a fax letter stating what is included. Be sure you have the loan number, borrowers' names, and property address on each page. I merge them into a Word document that automatically includes this information. I describe how to do this in the *Short Sale Business Manual*.

If the additional offer is not the highest offer, then I do not submit it with a HUD-1. Again, be certain you include the loan number, borrowers' names, and property address on each page. Then, notify the other agent(s) that there are now multiple offers, but make no comments indicating its' relative position to the other offers, whether better or worse.

Previously, we discussed sending at least weekly updates to the parties. You should use these updates to educate them *generally* about the short sale process, what is happening with their case, and major events as they happen. You can prepare the general information in the form of articles that you can then copy and paste into the email. Some articles for this purpose are provided in the *Short Sale Business Manual*. When you receive new offers, you can provide some *catch-up* emails with this general information to the newly-joined agents and their clients.

When you do send update emails, do not include your sellers' email address visible to other recipients of the updates. Rather, use the *Bcc* feature of Outlook to include them as blind copies, not visible to the others. Your update emails then

Managing Multiple Cases and Preparing For Closing

show only the other agents' email addresses. Those agents can forward them to their respective clients.

When you have multiple buyers' contracts, it is sometimes difficult keeping them engaged in the process. The emails are critical to keeping them on board. Usually the buyers' primary motivation is the return on investment and if they get the deal approved, they will obtain a great return. This is often not enough, though, and the updates greatly help to keep them in the deal.

Preparing For Closing

The day finally comes that the negotiator calls you and says that the short sale was approved, or not approved. If approved, you will be either faxed or emailed the terms in the form of a bank release. There are several issues of concern for which you must watch carefully.

The bank release will state the net to be received by the lender. Check the HUD-1 to make certain there are no surprises. Also check to see if the release limits total closing costs. You will need to forward this release to the title company and request them to update the HUD-1 to see if this offer will work.

The release may limit broker commissions. If it does, then you need to call the other agent and make sure you agree on the amount each of you will receive.

The release document will state that upon closing and the forwarding of the proceeds to the lender, they will release the lien, cancel any pending foreclosure sale, and dismiss any pending litigation. If you are in a judicial foreclosure state make certain that if a Judgment of Foreclosure has been obtained, even though the house has not been sold in a foreclosure sale, that the Judgment of Foreclosure is set aside and the case dismissed. If not, then the judgment will show up on the credit report for the borrowers.

The release should provide for the sale to be in full satisfaction of the borrowers' debt. If not, and this is happening with increasing frequency, read the language carefully. They are often worded with this unclear. Some signs to watch for is if there is wording that says to the effect *"report to credit reporting agencies that the account is satisfied for less than the full amount of the account"*. This is a hint that it is in full satisfaction. Second mortgage will often not be in full satisfaction, especially if the debt is substantial.

If the conditions require the borrowers to sign a note agreeing to make payments on a reduced deficiency balance, this is usually not a bad deal. Remember, they still owe a huge deficiency so signing a note for a lesser amount is not an issue. They are already obligated; this only obligates the lender to accepting reduced payments, usually without interest. Even if they do not make one payment under the new note, they are in no worse condition than they were previously.

This issue of a deficiency balance by the first mortgage lienholder can often be negotiated away. Ask who is making this condition. It is likely the SMI or MI carrier. If it is the MI carrier, ask for the name and contact number for the point of contact with the MI carrier. The negotiator may give it to you. If so, then call and explain your borrowers' situation and that they cannot make that payment. Tell them that you have worked hard to mitigate the losses here and that we need to leave the borrowers in a financial condition that permits rehabilitation.

Managing Multiple Cases and Preparing For Closing

This may move them out of this position. You have limited ability to negotiate this item if it is a requirement of the SMI. If you know that your seller cannot pay the terms of the note they are demanding, then ask if the SMI will accept a slightly higher purchase price from the buyer instead of the note. You are not really asking the negotiator to give you approval, you are merely asking if, in their experience, the SMI will negotiate this.

If it is the servicing lender making this condition, then tell them you are concerned that the borrowers may not be able to afford this, and that you are also concerned that they may find that they are facing some discrimination because there are other borrowers who have not been so required. Use a paradigm shift that the issue of discrimination is not you, but the borrowers having that concern. Do not lie, but do remember that if it turns out that there is a protected class here and if there is discrimination, the borrowers may have a legal cause of action.

If the condition is being required by the investor (SMI), ask who the investor is if you do not know already. If you can find out, find the web site for that entity, call them and ask to talk to someone about an unreasonable short sale condition that has been provided to you from the servicing lender. Tell them that their borrowers are facing concerns of discrimination. Use the same process of negotiating from a position of strength. Make certain that you let them out of the corner and present yourself as more of a *neutral* to this case, concerned about both the borrowers and the investor.

If you cannot get the condition set aside, then see if your borrowers are willing to accept this condition. They should remember that right now they are obligated for the full amount, and you only need the *agreement*, not actual performance. Once the closing has happened, the borrowers are free to deal with this creditor as they are with their other creditors. Additionally, if they have trouble paying, the lender will likely work with them graciously concerning the payments.

Another issue may be the closing date. Some lenders only give a couple weeks to close, and I had one that only provided 3 days to close. If there is financing that will likely be impossible. Most, however, will provide at least 30 days or more to close the deal.

If the response from the negotiator is that the deal is rejected, it is important to ask questions to find out who it is that rejected the proposal. Was it the MI carrier or the investor? If the servicing lender is also the investor, you will be told that management rejected it. However, sometimes the negotiator will not be truthful and may say it was rejected by management. You need to ascertain through good questioning whether it was the investor or servicing lender. For lower price homes, if they would not tell you who the investor is, ask them directly if the investor is Fannie Mae or Freddie Mac. These investors likely have minimum threshold percentages of the fair market value that must be netted to them, depending upon the loan product. If you are certain that you have this minimum, then ask more questions about that, whether the minimum was just not achieved. If the answer is in the affirmative, then ask how close your market valuation is to the what their appraiser stated.

When you ask follow-up questions, make certain the negotiator does not get defensive toward you. The way to accomplish this may be something like *"John, you are really great to work with and I know it may be hard for you to bring bad news. I know that you have no control over what the investor does, and I need*

Managing Multiple Cases and Preparing For Closing

your help understanding what I need to do in order to make a deal acceptable to them." Another thing you might add is *"one of the people in the deal may be thinking that the investor is discriminating against them because they are a minority, so I need help understanding the real reason this deal was not successful."* Again, leverage can be used to back them into the corner, but you must let them out through friendly discourse. Leverage in this situation can be used to help you create the paradigm shift from off the negotiator and onto the actual decision-makers.

If you are able to discover the reason for the rejection, then you may be in a position to go back to the drawing board and see if there is an alternative solution. The solution could come in the form of a need for a better offer. When you are talking to the negotiator it is important to ask directly what the minimum is that must net to the lender. You should get an answer what that may be, although some investors provide no feedback if the minimum is not received. If you discover the minimum net receipt to lender, then you can call each agent and tell them the minimum under the threshold approach for approval by the investor, and see if any of them will decide to amend their offers.

If you get an amendment matching the minimum threshold net receipt to lender, then have the amendment accepted and signed by the seller. Submit the amended offer with a matching HUD-1 from the title company.

If you are not an agent, but a real estate investor negotiating this deal, you may discover that the negotiator is not so forthcoming with you in providing you with details. It is important, though, to respond to their reluctance to provide details with kind and courteous treatment and utilize the negotiating tactics outline above and in the chapter on negotiating.

Utilizing the possible discrimination leverage, you could say, *"Is the reason that the proposal was not approved because of my being a minority?"* This does not say that you are, and do not lie, but it is merely asking if that is the reason. Of course the response will be that it is not, but the tactic should open the door to some details. Remember to let them out of the corner with statements that your concern is not with the negotiator who is merely doing his or her job, but with the investor.

Once you have the bank release document, it is now time to get ready for closing like you would in any other real estate deal. The bank release document must be forwarded immediately to the title company. Please use the title company that prepared the estimated HUD-1 as your closing agent.

For real estate investors, the title company should be able to prepare all of your documents for closing as well. You will need to be sure that you meet all of the requirements of law for your state, and the requirements of the purchase contract. You can help the seller with documents that need to be completed and signed, if any. Maintain good communication with the title company closing agent, who will walk you through everything needed for closing. If you are financing the property, you will need to provide the contact information for your mortgage broker to the closing agent. At the same time you deliver the bank release documents, provide them also to your mortgage broker and the seller.

Summary

It is of utmost importance to learn, develop, and refine good time management skills. It is also important to prepare

Managing Multiple Cases and Preparing For Closing

functioning systems to help you process everything efficiently and effectively without getting bogged down. Maintain good records, especially your casebook, including Activity Logs in which you record all of the activity that takes place during the short sale process.

Managing multiple cases and multiple contracts requires good management of activities, documents, and contacts. Maintain good communication with the other parties, protect the confidentiality of your clients' contact information, and keep everyone engaged in the process through periodic and interesting update emails.

Upon approval, you will receive a bank release document. You should check carefully the terms of the release and make certain the agreement is workable. Small deficiency balances for which the borrower is asked to sign a note is preferable over a foreclosure. This condition of requiring the borrowers to sign a note may be required by the servicing lender, the MI carrier, or the investor. This may be negotiated away, especially if it is required by the servicing lender, or an alternative might be considered, such as raising the sale price.

The closing should be completed using the title company who provided the free HUD-1 documents. The closing agent is a good resource to help you with the process if you are a real estate investor. Alternatively this could be accomplished at the office of an attorney.

Helpful samples and forms are provided to you in the *Short Sale Business Manual*, available separately.

CHAPTER 13

Alternatives To Foreclosure, Part B

In Chapter 3, we reviewed the various alternatives to foreclosure. The alternative that was not discussed is *loan modification*. The reason? If you first learn how a short sale works, along with the corollary training in negotiation and processing, you will have most of the training needed for loan modifications as well.

Loan Modification

A loan modification proposal is very similar to the processing of a short sale. You must still calculate the homeowner's budget, property value, obtain disclosure signatures, complete a legal and marketing analysis, collect financial documents and information from the borrowers, draft a professionally constructed proposal, and negotiate with the SMI via the servicing lender.

The time to modify is best between 2 payments missed and 5 payments missed. Well, except when it is not, since lenders vary in their foreclosure procedures and whether your state is a judicial foreclosure state or a non-judicial state. This time period is the norm.

Another requirement is that the Notice of Default (NOD) must not have yet been filed with the borrowers' county. Even then it may possible to complete a loan modification, but it is

Short Sales & Loan Modifications

less likely. Many banks at the issuance and filing of the NOD have resigned themselves to the foreclosure and are less likely to be cooperative. An important consideration is that there remain time available for a short sale if the modification is rejected.

There are three primary modifications that you may be seeking. First is the interest rate. The rate in the early stages of the amortization period is the bulk of the payment. Sometimes merely getting the rate reduced may resolve the problem.

Second is the term of the loan. Most loan terms are 20, 25, and 30 years. By stretching out the term of the loan, the payment could be further reduced. Some lenders will permit the term to be modified to extend 40 years, and very rarely to 50. Extending the term may help with interest rates that are low, but they become less helpful as the rate becomes higher. Extending the term for a 5% rate is much more helpful than extending the term for a 9% rate.

The third modification is the principal balance of the loan. This is the most difficult to obtain and it requires that home values be substantially reduced below the principal balance of the loan and that the home value reduction is not likely to be regained for many years. At the time of this writing, that is the very situation in many places.

Modifying these three note terms has one primary objective: to get the payment down to an amount the borrowers will be able to pay from that point forward, without fail. The lender has to believe that the borrowers will not default again. There is only one bite at this apple, for once the loan has been modified, the loan cannot be modified again in the future.

If you are an agent, you are likely willing to process the loan modification because it can mean additional income, and

Alternatives To Foreclosure, Part B

then, if rejected, you can process the short sale. Additionally, you could utilize services such as *TheLawsonGroup Mediation Services* to process and mediate cases.

If you are a real estate investor, you may not have an interest in helping the borrowers with a loan modification, however, it is important that you understand the process adequately to help them understand this alternative to foreclosure. If they then choose to attempt this or one of the other alternatives and are not successful for some reason, you still get the property back as a short sale.

Loan Modification Procedure

First, meet with the borrowers and review with them the alternatives to foreclosure along with the positive benefits and negative consequences. There are many lenders who require them to be explored before considering a short sale. In addition, if their loan is an FHA or VA loan, they are required to meet with a HUD-certified financial counselor before processing a short sale.

Loan modification is one of the alternatives that often must be considered. If the sellers are able to make a smaller payment, loan modification may be required by the lender to be explored before consideration of a short sale.

The first step in loan modification is to assist the borrowers with preparing a budget. We discussed this in Chapter 6, and the budget is even more critical with loan modifications. The budget must be accurate, show *all* income and expenses. The budget must be reasonably practical, with the borrower able actually live within it.

Some people, even with a reasonable budget, will never live by it. Some people merely pay expenses as they come up, never paying any attention to monies that are allocated for certain items. For example, if the budget shows that a family needs $1200 each year for clothes and shoes, that is $100 per month, and after two months there will be $200 in that allocated account. Instead of waiting until enough money is saved up to pay for clothing, these people will ignore the allocation and buy a coat for $350. When Christmas comes, they ignore the budget and buy whatever gifts they think they need, and to hell with the consequences.

It is vital, when you meet with borrowers, that you get a sense of whether the borrowers *will* live within a budget. There must be reasonableness in the budget, including a category for incidentals, such as Christmas gifts, birthday gifts, travel for vacation or funerals, and other items. Those incidentals should not exceed about 15-16%.

The budget should provide for their net income after taxes, and include the newly proposed payment along with property taxes and insurance. Upon completing the budget using the income and expense statement included with the *Short Sale Business Manual*, calculate the disposable income after subtracting the expenses from the net income. The disposable income is then used to determine if the borrowers can afford this house if the loan is modified.

Next, determine the current market value of the property. Use great care to determine the actual value of the home. It is important that your value closely approximate an appraiser's value if the lender orders an appraisal, which is likely.

Then, calculate a target loan payment. Using either your amortizing calculator or the online calculator found at

Alternatives To Foreclosure, Part B

http://www.mortgagecalculator.org, use the value of the property as the principal, then pick a reasonable rate (lower than the current rate of the loan), and amortization term. If the loan has 27 years left, for example, you may want use 30 years as the term. Use established terms such as 20, 25, 30, 40 years, not odd numbers of years like 31 years. The resultant payment is the ideal new target payment for the proposal. The budget must show accurately that the borrowers can afford this payment. Make certain there is no doubt, *not merely hoping it will work*, and that they will not need another modification in the future. If they obtain approval and default again, there is no second chance for a loan modification or short sale likely.

Before you go any further, you should strongly encourage the borrowers to take all of their original loan documents, plus all letters they may have received concerning the sale of the note to investors or a change in servicing lender, to a good real estate attorney for a forensic analysis to determine if there are any RESPA or TILA violations. I have seen reports estimating that between 2001 and 2006, about 80% of loans contained those violations. If there are violations, that information can be utilized as leverage to obtain the modification, especially if attempting to modify the principal balance. My mediation firm mandates this review by an attorney before we will accept a loan modification case for processing and mediation.

Now that you know the desired goal for modification, it is time to collect documents. They will need to produce at least the most recent two months of paystubs and bank statements, and a copy of their mortgage statement. They will need the last two federal tax returns. You will need a signed *Authorization & Release* for each lender. There are some disclosures and agreements in the *Short Sale Business Manual* for you to utilize to cover yourself from potential liability.

A *Hardship Letter* is required for loan modification, and it should demonstrate the hardship, but it should also show the reason that they are able to make the new payment. A sample is provided in the *Short Sale Business Manual*. Each borrower must sign the letter. If the borrowers are not living together, a separate hardship letter is required for each borrower.

You should complete a legal and marketing analysis of the case as you would for a short sale. Making certain that all data is accurate and complete is critical to the case. It should be your goal that the lender does not have to remind you to provide additional documentation.

Again, as in short sales, you should submit only a complete proposal. Sending documents to them piecemeal without a professional looking proposal is a recipe for a rejection of the proposal. Remember, the proposal is drafted to meet the needs of the people you cannot contact, the SMI.

The proposal should include a cover letter with the proposed payment and terms. Include a *Table of Contents* and a *Summary* section. Then all of the supporting documentation to follow. They are

> Authorization & Release
> Hardship Letter
> Income & Expense Worksheet
> Most recent two months pay stubs
> Most recent two months bank statements
> Last two years of income tax forms

Alternatives To Foreclosure, Part B

CMA
CMA if Bank-owned

The procedure from this point forward is virtually the same as for a short sale, except that you are seeking approval from the SMI via the servicing lender for a modification of the loan terms. At the end of the process, if approved, you will receive an agreement form for the borrowers to sign. Once signed and returned to the lender, the deal is complete.

As I said before, the process of working with the negotiator or analyst is the same, including how you should relate to the representatives. Be nice, utilize the negotiation skills taught in this book, and build a positive relationship in which you really make the contact's day.

One additional item of great importance. Some states may have laws that require specialized training, qualifications, or certification in order to process loan modifications. Having a real estate license may or may not be enough in those states. It is up to you to ensure that you are qualified and properly licensed if needed to process these cases.

Summary

The alternatives to foreclosure described in Chapter 3 include loan modifications. Since loan modifications are processed in a very similar manner to short sales, this discussion was reserved until now. Loan modifications are focused around the budget, which must be prepared very carefully and accurately, and the market value of the property.

The procedure is straightforward and similar to short sales. First, you meet with the borrowers, determine their ability to live within a reasonable budget, and help them with the forms. You determine the current market value of the property and calculate a reasonable payment they can afford.

The borrowers should be required to take all of their original loan documents plus any notices of a change in financial institution to a real estate attorney for a forensic review for RESPA or TILA violations.

The disclosure documents and the required supporting documentation are collected, after which a legal and marketing analysis is completed and a proposal drafted in a professional format. The proposal is then submitted to the lender.

Initial contact with the lender is coupled with submitting the *Authorization & Release*. The proposal is then submitted, the servicing lender will assign the case to a negotiator or analyst who reviews the proposal for the required elements, and the proposal is forwarded to the SMI for approval. An agent or investor who assists a homeowner with a loan modification should check local state laws to ensure they are qualified and properly licensed, if required, to carry out these activities.

CHAPTER 14

Summary

In chapter 1, we discussed and defined a short sale and outlining the short sale and loan modification opportunities that you should avoid. I also described the short sale and loan modification opportunities available to you that you should accept. I helped you to understand the responsibilities of the servicing lender, the secondary market investors (SMI), and the MI carriers, and how your short sale is approved. We explored structuring a business entity for setting up your short sale business. I explained about systems, and the equipment and software that you may wish to purchase. It is important to be certain your business entity is operated in a manner that will protect itself and you from liability. Finally, we discussed the critical expertise to seek out in the areas of finance, management, and marketing.

There are two forms of marketing, primary and secondary, and three types of marketing, brand, direct, and media. Direct marketing to real estate agents may be effective, especially if you can create some form of viral marketing to obtain referrals. Marketing to homeowners is relatively easy because you can check the NOD listings at your county clerk's office. You can also subscribe to an online service that provides the names and addresses of homeowners who have missed a payment, or two or three. Homeowners have a tendency to be emotionally frozen, so you may need specialized methods of reaching them.

Short Sales & Loan Modifications

Using common sales techniques on them often are not effective and may backfire on you. Some emotionally frozen people are reached in similar methods as may be effective for strong difficult personalities. There are some rules for effectively working with emotionally frozen people, and it is usually more effective to put away your salesman hat and just be a problem-solver for them. Using a *red light, green light* approach, you should test different methods of marketing, including letters that must stand out from those sent to them by the crowd of agents and investors marketing to these same defaulting homeowners.

I discussed and described the alternatives to foreclosure and the importance of your being a knowledgeable resource for the homeowner. I intentionally omitted loan modifications and short sales from this discussion and left loan modifications for later. These alternatives include doing nothing, paying off or refinancing the loan, reinstatement, forbearance, partial claims, a deed-in-lieu, bankruptcy Chapter 7, and bankruptcy Chapter 13. These alternatives are all viable options for differing situations. By being knowledgeable of the alternatives, you can provide the homeowner with a number of options that best fit their situation. Of course, which alternative is the right one for them should be their own informed decision. It is important that you not advise them which alternative to select, but if you are an agent, you may tell them that you may be able to help them with either a loan modification or short sale. If you are an investor, you can tell them that you can help them by purchasing their home in a short sale.

When preparing for a listing presentation, a good script is very helpful. Being able to properly articulate the answers to questions and objections is vital to being able to help them

Summary

form a correct picture of how the alternatives apply or do not apply to their specific fact situation. Even though I provided some script material, there are many excellent agents who are far more gifted in articulating to homeowners than am I. For those of you who have these skills, feel free to work your magic on the basic framework that I provided.

Do not underestimate the importance of disclosures, and although I cannot guarantee that the disclosures that I provide to you in the *Short Sale Business Manual* will protect you from all possible liability, and although I am not providing you with legal advice or representing that the documents will meet all of the requirements for your state, I have endeavored to provide as much educational material and support as possible. I strongly recommend that you check with your local attorney about the adequacy of those disclosures and documents as applicable under your state laws.

Every agent should have errors and omissions (E&O) insurance, and you should read your policy carefully. You should discuss the policy with your insurance agent to be certain that it will cover the particular risks involved in short sales. Then it is important to understand that you may be liable not only for intentional torts involving gross negligence, but negligence torts as well.

Even with the disclosures and insurance, you still face potential liability if you do not exercise due diligence to determine if a foreclosure sale date is imminent. You should advise your clients to consider other alternatives if the sale date is approaching and you do not yet have approval from the lender. Additionally, if the sale date is very close and the lender will not reschedule the date, you should advise your clients to seek legal counsel to discuss the possibility of using a bankruptcy Chapter 13 Plan to stop the foreclosure sale and permit the short sale as part of a plan to mitigate damages for the lender and at the same time the losses to the client.

It is recommended that every agent ensure that all buyer contracts are written so as to be binding before they are accepted, or that you obtain a signed waiver from the clients prior to their accepting a nonbinding contract. Then with a binding contract, the clients should be referred to an attorney if the buyers want out of the contract.

When the seller decides to list the property with you as a possible short sale, there are a number of documents to review with them. Some are legal disclosures, terms and conditions in the form of addendums, and various required information and documents for the borrowers to produce for submission to the lender.

Of special importance is the hardship letter and financial statements which most people do not accurately provide and this accounts for many rejections of short sales, but agents seldom discover the real reasons their proposal was rejected. Budget items must be calculated carefully and weekly, bi-weekly, semi-monthly, and annual expenses properly calculated to determine the monthly amount.

You should calculate the list price strategy carefully, beginning with a percentage of the fair market value and leveling off about 8 weeks later with a net to lender amount that will still have a chance of being approved by the majority of investors, somewhere around 80–82% of the fair market value. There is no practical way in advance, of determining who the investor is and what their threshold requirement will be.

Summary

When the amount of the debt far exceeds the value of the property, adding some weeks where you list the property at a price point between the fair market value and the amount of the debt will help the lenders see you are attempting to mitigate their losses.

As lengthy a process as short sales tend to be, they still close faster than many normal sales. One advantage is that you merely have to list the property in the MLS or on property websites. You do not normally need to spend money marketing them such as flyers, advertisements, or open houses.

The information entered into the MLS listing should include special disclosures to prevent misunderstanding and complaints from cooperating agents who may not otherwise realize that their commission could be reduced as a condition for approval by the lenders. You should make certain that you and the BA will agree on how you are going to handle any reduction in the commission if it is required by the SMI or MI carrier. An equal split of the reduction is fair if the published BAC is one-half of the total commission. However, if there is originally an unequal split, then the reduction should be split pro rata and so indicated on the *Commission Modification Agreement*.

Real estate investors will not need to allow for commissions, so your purchase contracts will have an advantage and be more attractive to the lienholders. Be sure you do not take advantage of real estate agents and title companies when asking for documents, CMAs and the like, making certain that you always reward them in some acceptable way for the valuable information and/or documents that they provide to you. They will in the future open many doors of opportunity to you if you do not damage your reputation with them.

The *Short Sale Business Manual* will provide and identify documents and forms needed by agents and those needed by real estate investors.

I emphasized the value of establishing systems that can cut your time and allow you to accomplish more work in less time. Some systems work best utilizing high tech software, but other systems are more efficient and effective with old fashioned manual methods. Microsoft Outlook and Microsoft Office, including Word and Excel are software systems that allow for efficient management of your data. However, the proper use of binders and file folders still have their place even in this world of high technology. Sometimes modern technology is better and more efficient; sometimes it is not. Sometimes the old ways are the tried, true and best ways. Sometimes they are not. You decide.

It is important to draft a professional looking proposal, not just submitting the required documents to the lender. The reason is that although you are submitting this proposal to the servicing lender, it is really for the benefit of the SMI and MI carrier, who are the entities that will approve or reject the proposal. You will not be able to speak with these decision-makers, so your only opportunity to impress and persuade them is through a professionally-drafted proposal.

I utilize a format with a number of features, a sample of which is included in the *Short Sale Business Manual*, obtained separately. The proposal contains a *table of contents*, a *summary*, the *Authorization & Release*, and all of the documents required by the lender (which have been dictated by the MI carrier and SMI). The proposal also includes a CMA (comparable market

Summary

analysis) or BPO (broker price opinion), which is virtually the same as an appraisal except performed by agents.

It is highly recommended that you perform a complete legal and market analysis. The legal analysis is a thorough check of each document ensuring that everything is complete and accurate with nothing missing. It also includes obtaining a preliminary title report and checking for other liens and borrowers. It is vital that you include all borrowers, whether or not they have an ownership interest in the property, and that you include all the required information and documentation from each borrower.

A marketing analysis is critical to determine if the appraisal obtained by the lender is accurate or not. If it is not accurate, the amount required by the SMI determined by the net percentage of the fair market value that must be received by the lender will be affected. There are multiple methods that agents use to calculate the fair market value, and it is important to check their work, or your work, utilizing an alternate method for calculating value.

There are seven golden, or valuable, keys or skill sets to effective negotiations. They are the skills of negotiating from strength, managing and balancing power, reframing techniques, leading to paradigm shifts, bargaining from interests, bargaining to needs, and leading to agree. These skills require understanding, internalizing, and practice in a variety of life settings at home, in business, and elsewhere.

Developing these skills will create within you a skillful and effective negotiator. Merely reading them will not. They are skills that must be practiced, developed, and refined purposely over time.

Short Sales & Loan Modifications

A lot of people find working with lenders to be a stressful, frustrating, and distasteful process. I find contacting lenders to be rather enjoyable. The difference? The difference could be the attitude that I choose toward this part of the process, being able to locate the right phone numbers and the correct people. Having a bit of a distraction can help alleviate the time working through telephone menu and waiting on hold. A headset makes it much more comfortable. Taking notes of the telephone menu will make the process of calling them much easier the next time.

The process of communicating and negotiating with the lender begins with getting the authorization to allow them to disclose information about the case to you. Next you obtain the list of documents they require plus any specific forms to be completed by the borrowers. When ready, you submit the proposal to them. Of course it is important to know if there is a different fax number to where you fax the proposal. It is best if they prefer the proposal shipped to them.

Following submission of the proposal, there may be a different number to call. Your first inquiry will be to substantiate they received the proposal. If they have, you will be waiting for the proposal to be assigned to a negotiator or analyst. You make occasional status checks and you should ask if the order can be sent out early for the appraisal. You should call for status checks often enough to stay on top of the case, but not so often as to annoy them. Calling about once a week is often the most appropriate, but sometimes it is appropriate to call a little earlier.

Summary

When the case has been assigned to a negotiator or analyst, that person is really only making certain all of the data is there for submitting to the MI carrier if one is involved, and then to the SMI. That assigned representative is not really *negotiating* anything, merely processing. A good relationship with negotiators and even call center people is far more effective than trying to reach supervisors, and these people will often go out of their way to help the person who gave them the nicest telephone experience of their day. Supervisors will often be annoyed at your call, stick more to the rules, and help you less often.

The appraisal will be ordered immediately when the negotiator starts working on the file, but sometimes the call center people may be able to start that process. The appraiser needs to understand that in determining a market range, it is not helpful to value the property in the upper part of market value range. If excessive, the appraisal can be appealed back to the appraiser and presented with additional data and, if they are cooperative, may alter their appraisal.

You will encounter a number of lender representatives who may lie to you to keep you from truly understanding the inner workings of the process. This book provided you with a detailed information about this process and hopefully you will be in a better position to deal with them in the future. Their dislike for agents can be transformed by you and others like you who will show them respect, establish good relationships, and demonstrate that you are knowledgeable and savvy.

It is of utmost importance to learn, develop, and refine good time management skills. It is also important to prepare functioning systems to help you process everything efficiently and effectively without getting bogged down. Maintain good records, especially your casebook including Activity Logs which maintain a record of every activity occurring during the short sale process.

Managing multiple cases and multiple contracts requires good management of activities, documents, and contacts. Maintain good communication with other parties, protect the confidentiality of contact information for your clients, and keep everyone engaged in the process through periodic and interesting update emails.

Upon approval, you will receive a bank release document. You should check carefully the terms of the release and make certain it is workable. Small deficiency balances for which the borrower is asked to sign a note is preferable to the foreclosure. This condition of a note to be signed by the borrowers may be required by the servicing lender, the MI carrier, or the investor. This may be negotiated away or an alternative considered, such as raising the sale price.

The closing should be completed utilizing the title company who provided the free HUD-1 documents. The closing agent is a good resource to help you with the process if you are a real estate investor. Alternatively this could be accomplished at the office of an attorney.

As mentioned earlier, the alternatives to foreclosure include loan modifications. Since loan modifications are processed in a very similar manner as are short sales, this discussion was reserved until later. Loan modifications are focused around the budget which must be prepared very carefully and accurately and the market value of the property.

Summary

The procedure is straightforward and similar to short sales. First, you meet with the borrowers, determine their ability to live within a reasonable budget, and help them with the forms. You then determine the current market value of the property and calculate a reasonable payment they can afford.

The borrowers should be required to take all of their original loan documents plus any notices of a change in financial institution to an attorney for a forensic review for RESPA or TILA violations. The disclosure documents and the required supporting documentation are collected after which a legal and marketing analysis is completed and a proposal drafted in a professional format. The proposal is then submitted to the lender.

Initial contact with the lender is coupled with submitting the *Authorization & Release*. The proposal is then submitted, the servicing lender assigns the case to a negotiator or analyst who reviews the proposal for the required elements, and the proposal is forwarded to the SMI for approval.

An agent or investor who assists a homeowner with a loan modification should check local state laws to ensure they are qualified and properly licensed, if required, to carry out these activities.

Please be advised that nothing in this book was intended to provide any legal, accounting, or tax advice. This book was written for educational purposes only and the reader is advised to seek the advice of a competent licensed attorney in your own state. There is no guarantee that third party lenders will approve a short sale or loan modification, and the author makes no warranty, expressed or implied, concerning any of the instruction or statements made herein.

Short Sales & Loan Modifications

To obtain information concerning the *Short Sale Business Manual* or to order additional copies of this book, go to the internet website of www.LawsonGroupMediation.com and follow the link to *Books & Manuals*.

To learn more about the services of TheLawsonGroup Mediation Services, go to the internet website of www.LawsonGroupMediation.com.

ABOUT THE AUTHOR

Kenneth R. Lawson, J.D. has been an attorney for about 20 years, beginning his practice in a creditors' rights and creditors' rights in bankruptcy firm. Later, he formed his own successful law firm in Tennessee. Mr. Lawson developed mediation skills and added a mediation practice to the law firm.

Mr. Lawson developed mediation and negotiation training programs and has been an instructor in police contact management training and religious institution conciliation and mediation training. He continues to provide training and mediation to churches and other religious institutions.

Mr. Lawson also has a strong background in law enforcement, having worked as a Wisconsin State Trooper and Special Agent for Maine Drug Enforcement Agency, as well as for city and town police departments.

For a time, Mr. Lawson sold real estate and discovered a great amount of mistakes being made in the processing and negotiating of short sales and loan modifications. Of particular concern was the amount of errors in short sale training provided to real estate agents and brokers.

Mr. Lawson formed TheLawsonGroup Mediation Services, a mediation firm serving as neutrals to process and mediate short sale cases submitted by real estate agents. This firm continues to provide mediation not only for short sales and loan modifications, but for federal and state court cases where the parties reside in differing jurisdictions.

To contact TheLawsonGroup Mediation Services for training seminars, additional books and materials, mediation, speaking engagements, or other services, go online to the website of www.LawsonGroupMediation.com.

Made in the USA